Bootstrapping Democracy

Bootstrapping Democracy

TRANSFORMING LOCAL GOVERNANCE

AND CIVIL SOCIETY IN BRAZIL

Gianpaolo Baiocchi, Patrick Heller, and Marcelo K. Silva

Stanford University Press
Stanford, California

Stanford University Press
Stanford, California

Printed in the United States of America on acid-free, archival-quality paper.

Library of Congress Cataloging-in-Publication Data

Baiocchi, Gianpaolo, 1971-
  Bootstrapping democracy : transforming local governance and civil society in Brazil / Gianpaolo Baiocchi, Patrick Heller, and Marcelo K. Silva.
    pages cm
  Includes bibliographical references and index.
  ISBN 978-0-8047-6055-3 (cloth : alk. paper) -- ISBN 978-0-8047-6056-0 (pbk. : alk. paper)
  1. Municipal government--Brazil--Citizen participation. 2. Municipal budgets--Brazil--Citizen participation. 3. Political participation--Brazil. 4. Democracy--Brazil. 5. Civil society--Brazil. I. Heller, Patrick, author. II. Silva, Marcelo Kunrath, author. III. Title.
  JS2417.A2B35 2011
  320.80981--dc22

                        2011002878

Typeset by Bruce Lundquist in 10/14 Minion

To our children: Aisha, Carol, Dylan, João Pedro, Nadia and Safina.

TABLE OF CONTENTS

ILLUSTRATIONS

PREFACE

We did not set out to write a book on *bootstrapping* democracy. We set out, rather, to explore a well-known example of participatory democracy—Participatory Budgeting (PB)—and to really put it to the test. More than anything else that test was about looking at cases of PB in places where it was less likely—given what the literature predicted—to be successful. PB is the idea, started in the late 1980s in Brazil, that citizens can and should play a direct role in shaping the budgets of the towns and cities in which they live. If the idea is simple enough, the devil is in the details of actually getting the process to work. What we found were a range of outcomes, and this book tries to put some order to those outcomes and use the findings to say something concrete about the possibilities and challenges of building local institutions of participatory democracy. Of all of our findings, the most striking, but in retrospect one that should have been anything but surprising, was the degree to which local actors proved to be extremely inventive, indeed ingenious, in designing local variants of PB. In those cases in which we found that some form of genuine participatory budgeting was built, local activists and state actors (administrators, politicians, and technocrats) proved to be extremely adept at taking a widely diffused national "blueprint" and adapting it to local realities. In trying to describe this phenomenon, as is all too often the case, a colloquialism provided the most evocative description. *Bootstrapping* is an English expression that refers to the leveraging of a few initial resources into something larger and more significant. In computer science, it means using a small program to load ("to boot") an operating system.[1] In business, it refers to creative entrepreneurship using a small amount of start-up funds. In development theory it has been used by Charles Sabel (2004) as a metaphor that suggests a process of building institutions that are capable of constant adjustment, "where each move suggests the next" and that benefit from social learning (7). Sabel's interest is in institutions that are growth favoring, and he argues that such bootstrapped institutions "are as much the outcome as the starting points of development" (7).

We borrow the spirit of these various usages, and in particular the notion of bootstrapping as a dynamic form of social learning. PB, it turns out, is not a model or a blueprint, but rather an assemblage of various participatory practices and ideas developed by social movements and a previous generation of local government experimenters, and it has been adapted as an *instituted process* to local conditions. As we have encountered it, *bootstrapping democracy* takes on an expanded meaning that assumes a double-edged agency: on the one hand, following conventional usage it refers to problem-solving and is specifically an *instrumental* response to the challenge of coordinating the functions of local state with the inputs of local civil society; on the other hand, and departing from conventional usage, it is an *ethico-political* project of empowering citizens.

With its specifically Anglo American etymology, bootstrapping unfortunately may not travel well. Our first reaction when we thought of the term was that it has no obvious translation in Portuguese, the language of the bootstrappers in this book. To them we sincerely apologize. We considered more familiar Latinates such as "inventing," "designing," and "creating," but we decided that in the English language these more readily bring to mind detached observers in laboratories, ivory towers, offices, or workshops, rather than the contested field of local politics in Brazilian *municípios*. The Brazilian expression "dar um jeito" (to find a way) rightly brings to mind improvisation, but it is pejorative and also implies informality. We wanted something that evoked the inventiveness but also the messiness, conflicts, strategic calculations, and principled pragmatism that building democratic institutions necessarily calls for. In our usage, we intend not only to emphasize the novel means and designs that were developed to make PB work, but also the new alliances, and in particular the delicate blurring of the boundaries between state and civil society that genuine participation entails. Indeed, what we discovered was that the most central preoccupation of architects of PB was precisely finding the right balance between "bringing civil society in" and preserving the autonomous logic and energy of civic engagement.

The question of contexts conducive to bottom-up democratic deepening is an extremely important one, of relevance well beyond the countries of the Latin American "pink tide." It is for this reason that we wanted a title that emphasized *agency* in the face of obstacles. There is something defeatist, in our view, in the social scientific diagnosis that asserts that there are necessary preconditions for democratic empowerment and that these preconditions invariably end up being those read back from the developmental trajectory of

Western democracies. In fact, one could just as well make the argument that most democratic innovations of the past two decades have taken place in the context of "less developed democracies." And while the stories in this book are not an argument for a participatory blueprint or imposed change from the outside (quite the contrary), they invite us to have a broader imagination of the possible, including one that might travel from south to north. Meaningful social change is, after all, in the words of the social theorist and former Brazilian minister Roberto Unger, change that is "context-smashing."[2]

This project began with reasons and a design, but its execution, including the interpretation of the findings has been a process of discovery, one in which so many contributed in large and small ways that it is impossible to give full credit where it is due. Institutionally, we received support from Brown University, the Federal University of Rio Grande do Sul, the Watson Institute of International Studies, the Brazilian National Council on Scientific Research (CNPQ), as well as generous funding from the World Bank. All of the research was made possible by our partner NGOs in Brazil: CIDADE in Porto Alegre; POLIS in São Paulo; and ETAPAS in Recife. The individual municipal administrations gracefully made themselves available, as did our respondents, who sometimes spent many hours being interviewed. The Brazil research team—Ana Neri dos Santos, Clarice Barreto Linhares, Cristiane Vianna Amaral, Daniela Oliveira Tolfo, Georgia Christ Sarris, Isabela Valença Vaz, Roberto Rocha Coelho Pires, Tatiana de Amorim Maranhão—carried out their tasks with consummate professionalism and dogged determination.

We owe many intellectual debts. Our principal debt is to Shubham Chaudhuri who helped develop this project and collaborated with us in its early stages before being pulled away by professional responsibilities. His idea of matched-pair municipalities has by now spawned a small cottage industry in Brazil, and we wish we had been able to count on his abilities for the later stages of the project. We also especially thank Peter Evans, who engaged us at every step of the project, and Kate Wahl, our editor at Stanford, for her support and insightful commentary. We also received extremely useful feedback on the entire manuscript from Phil Oxhorn. Michael Walton, Ruth Alsop, and André Herzog gave us feedback on the early stages of the research, and we are especially indebted to Michael Walton for his commitment to this project. Along the way we also received insightful comments and suggestions from a number of our colleagues: Dietrich Rueschemeyer, Richard Snyder, Sonia Alvarez, Jeff Rubin, Millie Thayer, Agustin Lao Montes, Vijayendra Rao, Adrian Gurza

Lavalle, Brian Wampler, Einaar Braten, Judith Tendler, Christian Stokke, Olle Tornqüist, Jonathan Fox, Leonardo Avritzer, Erik Olin Wright, Archon Fung, Frances Moore Lappe, Sergio Baierle, Regina Pozzobon, Marcus Melo, Roberto Pires, Peter Spink, André Herzog, Peter Houtzager, Michael Kennedy, and John Markoff. We were extremely fortunate to have some wonderful graduate students at Brown to work with and are especially thankful to Diana Graizbord, Esther Herández-Medina, and Jennifer Costanza. The writing stage of the project would not have been possible without a postdoctoral fellowship from CNPQ for Marcelo and the support of the Watson Institute in giving him an intellectual home for the year.

An early version of the argument developed in Chapter 5 appeared in Social Forces (2008). Some of the findings reported in Chapter 4 appeared in an article in an edited book by Stokke, Tornqüist, and Webster (2009).

ACRONYMS AND TERMS

ANAMPOS   Associação Nacional de Movimentos Populares e Sindicatos, or National Association of Popular Movements and Trade Unions

ANC   African National Congress

CDF   Community Development Forums

CEB   Comunidades Eclesiais de Base, or Ecclesiastic Base Communities

CSO   Civil Society Organization

CUT   Central Única dos Trabalhadores, or Central Workers Union (CUT)

FAMOCA   Federation of Neighborhood Associations of Camaragibe

IBGE   Instituto Brasileiro de Geografia e Estatística, or Brazilian Institute of Geography and Statistics

ICMS   Imposto sobre Circulação de Mercadorias e Serviços, or Tax on the Circulation of Merchandise and Services

IDP   Integrated Development Plan

IPTU   Imposto Predial e Territorial Urbano, or Tax on Buildings and Urban Lands

ISSQN   Imposto sobre Serviços de Qualquer Natureza, or Services Tax

KSSP   Kerala Sastra Sahitya Parishad, or Kerala's peoples science movement

MSC   Movimento dos Sem Casa

PA   Participatory Administration

PB   Participatory Budget

PC do B   Partido Comunista do Brasil, or Communist Party of Brazil

PCB   Partido Comunista Brasileiro, or Brazilian Communist Party

PDS   Partido Democrático Social, or Democratic Social Party (the PDS became the PPR in 1993)

PDT   Partido Democrático Trabalhista, or Democratic Labor Party

PFL   Partido da Frente Liberal, or Liberal Front Party

PI   Plano de Investimento, or Yearly Investment Plan

PMDB   Partido do Movimento Democrático Brasileiro, or Brazilian
        Democratic Movement Party

Prefeito/Prefeitura   the mayor, and city hall

PSB   Partido Socialista Brasileiro, or Brazilian Socialist Party

PT   Partido dos Trabalhadores, or Workers' Party

PTB   Partido Trabalhista Brasileiro, or Brazilian Labor Party

RDP   Reconstruction and Development Program

SABS   the *sociedades de amigos de bairro*, or Societies of Friends of the
        Neighborhood

SANCO   South African National Civics Organisation

STMJM   Sindicato de Trabalhadores Metalúrgicos de João Monlevade, or
        Metalworkers' Union of João Monlevade

Vereador(a)   a member of the municipal legislature, equivalent to a city
        councilor in the United States

Bootstrapping Democracy

INTRODUCTION
Evaluating Participatory Democracy

In the modern world, there is hardly an idea more fundamentally contested than the idea of democracy. Indeed, if there is anything that we can agree on it is that democracy is always being redefined. In recent times, ideas of participatory democracy have gained renewed interest. The lineage of this idea goes back to the most classic conceptions of democracy with roots in the thought of Aristotle, but the idea has also periodically been revitalized in the works of Rousseau, Carole Pateman, and most recently Habermas among many others. The poles of the debate have hardened between those who define democracy as a set of representative institutions and those who define democracy as a set of qualitative practices that approximate normative ideals of democratic opinion-and-will formation. This divide has been usefully summarized by Shapiro (2003) as pitting aggregative theories of democracy versus deliberative theories. Shapiro observes that while aggregative theories, which focus on how individual preferences are added up, are strong on evidence and well grounded empirically in a range of studies on formal democracy (and have taken center stage in the mainstream political science literature), ideas of participatory democracy are strong on theory and moral-philosophical grounding, but rather weak on evidence and empirical testing. If the case for participatory democracy has received voluminous attention,[1] it rests on what are rather fragmented and thin empirical grounds. The literature is full of rich, contextualized, and extremely informative accounts of successful cases of participatory democracy.[2] But in almost all of these cases the empirical findings generally suffer from two limitations. First, it has been difficult to actually isolate the impact of participation and to determine how and why participation makes a difference. Second, because much of the literature is still preoccupied with making a normative argument and with contesting the dominant focus on representative institutions, it has largely failed to examine the relationship between participatory practices and state institutions.

1

Renewed interest in participatory democracy has been driven by a range of real-world struggles that run the gamut from daily engagements to make state actors more accountable to broad-based mobilizations to wrest control of nominally democratic systems from elites. Arguably, such struggles are a continuous, necessary, and vital dimension of any democratic society, constantly being played out in countless institutions and through diverse modes of contention. If scholars have increasingly turned their attention to the specific notion of participatory democracy it is because we can now identify an increasing number of cases, particularly in the global South, where political and social actors have made concerted efforts to translate these democratic churnings into institutionalized processes of citizen engagement. These experiments in participatory governance have taken many forms, emerging at different scales and with varied scopes. Some have been driven by highly organized demands, others by more inchoate forces. This variation in part explains why scholarly research has yet to produce the quality of empirical research associated with studies of electoral systems, political parties, and more the formalized and familiar expressions of representative democracy. The case of Brazil's *Orçamento Participativo*, or Participatory Budgeting (henceforth PB), presents as such a unique opportunity.

THE "CHAMPION OF POPULAR PARTICIPATION"

The city of Gravataí (pop. 232,000), in the state of Rio Grande do Sul, is a nondescript, medium-sized industrial city at the edge of the Metropolitan Region of Porto Alegre. Often seen as little more than a bedroom community, most of the city consists of large expanses of unplanned settlements, poorly served by urban infrastructure. Long in the grip of a few influential charismatic politicians tied to the small, local elite, the town was all but bypassed by the social movements so present in larger cities in the country since the 1980s. Things began to change in the mid-1990s, however, when word of the celebrated "Participatory Budget" reached Gravataí. The apparent success of that institution in drawing thousands of ordinary citizens to participate in governance and promote redistribution captured the imagination of the small number of local activists. The rightist administration of Edir de Oliveira was coming to a disastrous end, leaving behind unfinished public works projects, serious problems in the Health and Education Department, and months of nonpayment of municipal employees, so the 1996 elections were seen as a moment of opportunity.

One of the candidates was former mayor (1989–92) Marianno Motta, of the Democratic Labor Party (PDT), who ran with the support of neighborhood associations and who emphasized health and education for the poor. The other was a local community activist and high school history teacher, Daniel Bordignon, from the Workers' Party (PT). Bordignon was backed by teachers' unions and ran on a platform centered on the immediate implementation of Participatory Budgeting.

Bordignon won by a slim margin and almost immediately after assuming office delivered on his promise of Participatory Budgeting. Veterans of the Porto Alegre administration came to offer technical assistance, and by March of 1997 the first meetings of the Participatory Budget were held. As in Porto Alegre, ordinary citizens were called upon to decide on the municipal budget in a series of meetings organized in a yearly cycle. Also as in Porto Alegre, these meetings were organized throughout the city to define local priorities and projects; delegates from the various districts would then formulate a budget of projects. But unlike Porto Alegre, the idea of Participatory Budgeting did not come from the city's social movements, and there were no social movements to contest the format or the rules of the process. In fact, the few neighborhood associations in Gravataí, which were tied into the clietelistic networks of the traditional political oligarchs, boycotted the process only to be discredited entirely as the process took hold.

At first, the process bore more than passing resemblance to Porto Alegre's model. Its rules, yearly cycle, and format were for that first year copies of the original but changed quite starkly for the second year as a pragmatic adaptation to the perceived lack of capacity of civil society. The willingness to experiment with a blueprint and to transform it based on local context is a hallmark of the Gravataí story, and indeed of all of our cases of PB in this book.

The resulting institutional process was simplified to focus on tangible infrastructure projects and was significantly decentralized so that it included a round of eighty-five assemblies in the various neighborhoods. Government employees would now also play a much more active role in drawing participants and coordinating demands, a function carried out by civil society in Porto Alegre. As a result of these changes, the process drew massive numbers of participants. In Gravataí, almost twelve thousand adults participated in the city's PB in 2000—-that is, roughly 10 percent of the adult population. Proportionally, this was four times greater participation than in Porto Alegre. These high numbers were bandied about with pride by administrators, and the slogan "The Champion of Popular Participation" became part of the advertisement for subsequent yearly cycles of PB in 1999.

Municipalities (municípios) like Gravataí are good places to examine and evaluate the impact of participatory reforms. Unlike the much celebrated and much studied marquee cities of Porto Alegre, Belo Horizonte, and São Paulo, the eight municípios we study in this book are far more representative of Brazil's more than five thousand municípios. Using a sampling logic that was designed to allow us to isolate the impact of PB, we ended up pairing four PB municípios with four non-PB municípios that were all midsized. In contrast to the more celebrated cases in the literature, these urban settings lack many of the attributes that one might normally associate with innovative democratic experiments. None of our eight is a capital city or critical regional center. All are either on the periphery of more dominant urban centers such as Porto Alegre and Sao Paulo, or in regional hinterlands such as the Brazilian northeast. Medium-sized cities are often poorer and have smaller middle classes of professionals; they tend not to have universities, and thus the student activists and professors that have led so many of Brazil's civil society organizations; with one exception they were largely bypassed by the organized actions of the pro-democracy movement in the 1980s and are largely disconnected from national networks of political and social elites. These cities also face distinct challenges in a federal arrangement that privileges large metropolises: their fiscal capacity is smaller; they are more dependent on government transfers for the provision of services; and they are often caught in the institutional vacuum of metropolitan governance.

Yet, increasingly, these second-tier cities have become more representative of the developmental and democratization challenges of contemporary urban Brazil. First, population growth in these cities has outpaced larger ones as metropolises have tended to deconcentrate toward metropolitan regions in the 1990s. Second, in fact it is in these cities that experiments with democratic participation expanded in the late 1990s. Of the 104 municípios with Participatory Budgeting in 1997–2000, 94 were in cities with fewer than five hundred thousand residents. Most of the new expansion has been precisely in places like Gravataí—medium-sized cities, without much prior experience of social movement mobilization, and faced with significant fiscal challenges.

As such these cities represent particularly important test cases for the impact of participatory reforms. In pairing cities that adopted PB with cities that did not, our most immediate objective was to develop a methodologically rigorous test of the impact of PB. But our broader goal in this book is to use PB as a window into understanding processes of democratic transformation and to do so in settings that provide significant challenges to making participatory governance work. The lessons we hope to draw from these cases have broader significance. As a set of reforms, PB implies a significant shift in distributional power from the local state and elected representatives to ordinary citizens. Understanding when and how such a power shift actually occurs can directly inform a wide range of debates on participatory democracy and urban transformation.

LOCAL GOVERNMENT AND DEMOCRATIC TRANSFORMATION

Local government is a critical domain of democratic life. A long line of democratic theorists running from John Stuart Mill to Robert Dahl have argued that it is in local settings that citizens learn democracy. Just as assuredly, it is through local government that most of the services and resources that constitute development and that people care most about—basic infrastructure, primary health care, education, economic support, policing—are either provided for or actually delivered. Yet the debate about democracy and development has for most of the post-WWII period focused on national and global units of analysis. The metric of development has invariably been highly aggregated measures such as Gross Domestic Product (GPD) or the Human Development Index (HDI), or broad institutional measures such as developmental states, the rule of law, or good governance. Three important developments in recent years have drawn our attention to local government.

The first has been the increasing recognition by scholars that within-country variations in levels of development and democratic practice are sometimes more pronounced than between-country variations. In a country as big and diverse as Brazil, variations in social and economic indicators are dramatic, and scholars of democratic politics have shown that democratic norms and practices, and in particular the degree to which public legality is actually established, can vary dramatically within the same national territory (O'Donnell 1999; Heller 2001). These observations have spawned a whole new literature focusing on subnational units of analysis (Snyder 2001).

Second, accelerated rates of urbanization have made towns and cities increasingly important, both as centers of economic activity but also as complex sociopolitical units that pose particularly acute challenges of governance. If cities and urban issues long lived in the shadow of the traditional development literature focus on rural areas, the study of urban settings, and with it of the related fields of urban politics, planning and urban sociology, have assumed a new prominence in the development literature.

Third, in the 1990s scholars looking to the global South found what often appeared to be contradictory effects of globalization: the deregulation and liberalization of national economies; the decentralization of national states; and tentative steps toward democratic consolidation. Particularly contested in the literature, and on the ground, was the understanding and experience of decentralization that occurred nearly universally in the developing world. For some, decentralization was the necessary vehicle for dismantling bloated, rent-seeking national-level bureaucracies by making government more responsive to local demands. For others, it was little more than a neoliberal Trojan horse for hollowing out the developmental state through the devolution of unfunded mandates. A more productive vantage point, we argue, is to focus on the way that globalization has altered the "socio-spatial scales" of the functioning of states.[3] As the nature of traditional nation-state sovereignty has been transformed in the current period of globalization the state has not simply "withered away," but rather has seen its functions and authority displaced into new or reconfigured subnational institutions, creating new arenas of political contestation. In many settings the local urban state has emerged as an especially important site because it is more malleable than national states and is situated "in the confluence of globalization dynamics and increased local political action based in civil society" (Keil 1998, 618). Local governments have thus assumed increased importance as the perceived new site for democratic deepening and as the new arena in which public authority and socially transformative projects are being reconstituted in the era of globalization (Heller and Evans 2010).

Within this larger dynamic of transformation, some of the most exciting developments in the last two decades are myriad new instances of participatory democracy implemented by municipal governments in both consolidated and new democracies. These instances of urban participatory democracy, which we define as direct citizen participation in municipal government's decision-making, range from broad-based forms of participatory planning to citizen councils to direct health policy, to various other forms of citizen participation and input into the management of local government. These cases have attracted a great deal of academic and policy attention, and they have provided fodder for creative thinking on some of the fundamental questions about democracy, the state, and civil society.

Brazil's postauthoritarian history represents a particularly marked example of these trends. During the past four decades, Brazil has gone from being a predominantly rural society to an overwhelmingly urban one. In 1960, the urban population represented 44.7 percent of the population, but by 2000 urban residents accounted for 81.2 percent of the population. Driven by an agrarian transition that has not only been exceptionally rapid but also dominated by capital intensive and labor-displacing modernization, rural-urban migration has exploded and Brazil's cities have had to accommodate one hundred million new residents since 1960. This has produced a rapid and largely unregulated growth of precarious peripheral areas, exacerbating what were already pronounced problems of urban poverty and informality.[4] At the same time, Brazilian cities have also become increasingly important developmental actors in their own rights. Brazil's 1988 constitution gave municípios a critical role in delivering services and promoting development and also set the legal groundwork for some of the most innovative democratic reforms ever undertaken in a young democracy. Indeed, as we argue at length in Chapter 1, the degree of democratic responsibility and authority (and to a lesser extent, resources) that Brazilian municípios currently enjoy is, with the possible exception of South Africa, unsurpassed in the developing world. These developments are all the more remarkable because if anything, local government in Brazil's predemocratic period was in many ways the social base of elite power and authoritarian control. Local politics in Brazil have traditionally been dominated by powerful families or narrow cliques, and the business of governing has essentially been one of elite collusion. These local patterns of elite domination have been reproduced at the state and national level where under both democratic and authoritarian regimes politics have been dominated by particularistic interests and organized rent-seeking. Political scientists have, in fact, made Brazil into something of a paragon of a dysfunctional electoral democracy marked by pervasive patronage in politics, a weak and incoherent party system (Mainwaring 1999), an "excess of veto players" in a democratic system that is systematically biased toward pork-barrel politics over institutional changes (Ames 2001), and the pervasive fragmentation of the bureaucracy (Weyland 1996).

This is precisely what makes Brazil such an interesting setting for understanding the possibilities for democratic transformation. Despite these significant authoritarian legacies and institutional distortions, over the past three decades elite domination has been fundamentally challenged by democratization and by the mobilization of civil society. Across a wide range of sectors and involving a wide range of groups, Brazilian civil society has developed sophisticated forms of collective agency and political engagement. In areas as far ranging as HIV-AIDS treatment, the environment, and urban reforms, Brazil-

ian civil society has not only exerted a significant voice but has specifically mobilized to demand changes in the practice of democracy and to strengthen the
participatory character of local governance (Avritzer 2002).

Many commentators have noted the scale, sophistication, and range of these
efforts. This apparent paradox of *democratization within a dysfunctional polity*
raises some very important questions that are central to the debate on development and democracy and that are at the heart of this book. First, how exactly
has "civil society" contributed to helping create the political and institutional
conditions for democratizing democracy in Brazil? Second, how have these dynamics—and specifically the interaction of civil society and the state—effected
real changes in governance, and in particular changes in the character of local
democracy? Third, when such change does indeed occur, how do we explain it,
and how do we explain variation across localities? Fourth, when democratic reforms are introduced, what impact do they have on the quality of democratic
practices, and in particular how do they impact the capacity of the civil society
to exert effective pressure on democratic institutions?

The past decade has provided an interesting opportunity to address these
questions and in particular to explore local state-civil society relations. As democracy consolidated in Brazil in the 1990s, municípios began experimenting
with institutional reforms designed to promote civil society participation. In
Chapter 1, we review the wide range of reforms that were undertaken. Among
the most visible and innovative reforms was Participatory Budgeting. First introduced by the Partido dos Trabalhadores, or Workers' Party (PT), in the city
of Porto Alegre in 1990, PB has been widely acclaimed as a novel means of increasing accountability and participation in the formation of municipal budgets. By 1997, more than 104 municípios, including large metropolises such as
Belo Horizonte and São Paulo, had adopted PB.

Though there is marked variation in the actual design and implementation
of PB, the baseline institutional feature is the creation of submunicipal assemblies of ordinary citizens that discuss and then prioritize budget demands
for their areas. These demands are then integrated into the city budget. The
most notable feature of PB is that it represents a form of citizen-controlled
demand-making that takes place *parallel* to the existing system of party-based
representation and as such marks a dramatic break with the patronage-driven
politics that have long dominated municipal budgeting in Brazil. The basic
idea and design of PB came out of Brazil's urban social movements in the
1980s. While PB, and especially the case of Porto Alegre, is probably the most

celebrated case of participatory democracy in the global South, it does bear important similarities to a wide range of other cases including democratic decentralization in the Indian state of Kerala, the Reconstruction and Development Program in post-apartheid South Africa (Heller 2001; Van Donk et al. 2008), other instances of democratic decentralization in Latin America (Chavez and Goldfrank 2004; Van Cott 2008), as well as a proliferation of other movements and reforms that have explicitly sought to open up democratic spaces (Fung and Wright 2003; Cornwall and Coelho 2007). In all of these instances, the case for democratic decentralization has been made on both instrumental and normative grounds. Devolving decision-making authority downward and into the hands of local actors increases transparency, taps into local sources of information, improves accountability of elected officials, and encourages innovation. But expanding the actual spaces in which citizens can directly impact authoritative resource allocation, it is argued, also incentivizes citizen engagement and strengthens the political capacity of civil society. To the extent that it does so, PB (and these other reforms) would then represent an institutional solution to a recurrent, and some would say intractable problem in many democracies, that is bringing the modes of claim-making that characterize civil society into alignment with the logic of aggregation that defines political society. In this respect, the goal of this book is straightforward: we propose to evaluate the extent to which PB can supplement the structures of representative democracy in a highly inegalitarian society with more direct and participatory forms of democracy.

There is now a large body of literature on PB, particularly on Brazilian and Latin American cases, though there is also a growing literature on various efforts in Europe to make local budgeting processes more participatory. After a first wave of studies that helped establish the impact of PB in particular cases (Abers 2000; Avritzer 2002; Baiocchi 2005; Nylen 2003; Silva 2003), a number of recent notable works evaluated PB using a comparative design, a move made possible by the broad diffusion of the experience (Avritzer 2009; Wampler 2009; Van Cott 2008; Goldfrank forthcoming). This body of scholarship leaves little doubt that PB can indeed provide new opportunities for civil society actors to engage and impact the local state.

The literature has come to a near-consensus that the right combination of a capacitated civil society and a committed executive branch is the most auspicious context to institute Participatory Budgeting. Avritzer (2009) argues that "bottom-up institutions" like Participatory Budgeting work best with a "highly empowered civil society" and a "pro-participation political society." In a similar vein, Wampler (2009) shows that PB experiences are most successful when there is a "high" willingness of civil society to be contentious, and "high" mayoral support for delegating authority to citizens. In absence of these conditions, experiences can be failures, producing increased cynicism in the context of "conceded citizenship rights."

But as rich as this literature is, we depart from it in a number of ways. While we join the call for comparative research, we shift the logic of inquiry. Instead of comparing cases of PB to try to understand the causes of success and failure (that is, holding the institution *somewhat* constant to assess the consequence of contextual factors), our design holds the *context* constant by pairing cities that adopted PB with similar cities that did not. This matched-pair analysis allows us to answer a question that the existing body of comparative research cannot address: *Does PB make a difference at all?* Only then do we turn to an analysis of how context impacts outcomes.

We also take a more nuanced view of the idea of success and failure. The general point that PB works best with a strong civil society and politically sympathetic administrations is important, but not surprising. In our thinking, failures and successes are relative to their contexts. A town with no history of participation may eventually develop a participatory process that pales in comparison to one with "vibrant social movements," but in comparison to its earlier history represents a significant advance.

Another point of departure from this comparative literature is that we are attentive to the *choices* of administrators in crafting participatory institutions—thus, our attention to "bootstrapping." In fact, while PB institutions are broadly similar in many places in Brazil, the literature tends to underplay the agency (and reflexivity) of administrators in strategically drawing on and modifying the repertoire of previous experiences. Finally, our research is different in its attention to the practices of civil society itself as an outcome.

In order to address these questions, we developed a research design (discussed in Chapter 3) that would answer three questions. First, does the introduction of PB change the manner in which citizens engage with the local state and transform governance, and if so what are the various ways in which this happens? Second, how do changes in the ways in which the local state interfaces with local society shape the democratic capabilities of civil society? Third, how are the observed outcomes (new institutional interfaces and transformed civil society capacities) explained by antecedent political and social conditions?

For reasons that we elaborate in Chapter 3, we chose to address these questions by carefully selecting and examining eight municípios. Exploring the questions we have posed requires a deep and highly contextualized understanding of the political, social, and institutional conditions in which the reforms are introduced. Identifying mechanisms at work and being able to isolate the factors or configurations that explain outcomes requires careful and controlled comparison. Accordingly, using a natural experiment design, we selected each município as part of a pair that shared characteristics of size, region, and political configuration (specifically the vote share of the PT), but with only one city having adopted PB in each pair. For each município we conducted field visits, collected primary source data, and administered carefully structured interviews with key respondents. In Chapters 3, 4, and 5, we assess each pair, evaluate the impact of Participatory Budgeting on governance and on civil society capacity, and flesh out a typology of local state-civil society configurations and corresponding democratic regimes.

PARTICIPATION AND DEMOCRATIC DEEPENING

In recent years the literature on participatory democracy has grown exponentially. Driven in part by important theoretical developments in normative democratic theory (Habermas 1996; Cohen and Arato 1992; Sen 1999) the interest in participatory democracy has grown apace with the increasing recognition of the deficits of representative democracy, especially in the developing world. The case for participatory democracy can be made in both Weberian and Tocquevillian terms. In Weberian terms—and through the contributions of Guillermo O'Donnell (1999) in particular—the claim is that many new democracies suffer from poor institutionalization and in particular weak channels of vertical integration between states and citizens. State-society relations tend to be dominated by patronage and populism, with citizens having either no effective means of holding government accountable (other than periodic elections) or being reduced to dependent clients. The chain of sovereignty, in other words, has many broken links.[5] For de Tocqueville the problem focuses on the quality of associational life, a concern also shared by scholars like Gramsci. In much of Latin America formal democracy has endowed citizens with formal rights, but pervasive inequalities within society limit the capacity of citizens to act on their rights effectively, producing what Dagnino (1998) has dubbed the problem of "social authoritarianism." Taken together, the vertical problem of state-society relations and the horizontal problem of perverse social inequalities undermine the associational autonomy of citizens, the sine qua non of any effective democracy (Fox 1994).

These two problems also bring us back to the core problematics that the aggregative and deliberative view of democracy respectively focus on. The Weberian problematic raises the question of the *chain of sovereignty*, that is, the degree to which the system of representation effectively translates inputs into outputs. The focus here is on the efficacy with which specific institutional processes and mechanisms can translate the popular will into actual programs and expenditures. This is what the literature on representative democracy is generally focused on, albeit with a heavy emphasis on the electoral mechanisms. The Tocquevillian problematic can be slightly reinterpreted to in effect overlap with the concerns of deliberative democratic theory. Here the issue is not how the popular will is transmitted to the state, but rather with how the popular will is actually formed. That is, rather than taking preferences for granted and simply assuming that the work of democracy is to aggregate and transmit those preferences, a more sociologically grounded view of democratic practices insists on understanding how power, social structures, and institutions shape processes of preference formation. We argue that a serious engagement with the problem of democratic deepening requires drawing from both these perspectives and focusing on what we call the twin dynamic of preference formation and preserving the chain of sovereignty.

In its design, Participatory Budgeting, as it evolved in its Porto Alegre prototype, is in effect an effort to nurture and secure this twin dynamic. On the one hand, PB levels the associational playing field by creating decision-making structures that are biased toward inclusivity. More specifically, the process is designed, as it were, to reduce the transaction costs of participation for the poor while increasing the transaction costs of traditional elites.[6] On the other hand, PB secures the chain of sovereignty through a complex set of nested fora through which popular inputs are transmitted to the local state. It address these twin challenges through four mechanisms:

1. Giving citizens a direct role in city governance by creating a range of public fora (microregional councils, district councils, sectoral committees, plenary meetings, delegate councils) in which citizens and/or delegates can publicly articulate and debate their needs;

2. Linking participatory inputs to the actual budgeting process through rule-bound procedures;

3. Improving transparency in the budgeting process by increasing the range of actors involved and publicizing the process and by the same token reducing the possibility or extent of elite-capture; and

4. Incentivizing agency by providing tangible returns, in the form of urban investment projects chosen by participants, to grass-roots participation.

The logic of PB closely corresponds to core assumptions in the participatory democracy literature about the nature of political capabilities. The literature works from the fundamental premise that associational life is to a large degree artifactual. The patterns of interaction that define groups are "not merely the result of natural tendencies to association among citizens with like preferences; they reflect structural features of the political economy in which they form, from the distribution of wealth and income to the locus of policy-making in different areas" (Cohen and Rogers 1995, 46). Because states organize and regulate not only relations between the state and citizens but also between citizens (Skcopol 1985), the associational democracy literature argues that the forms and impact of citizen engagement significantly reflects institutional arrangements and can be changed through public policy. Moreover, recent empirical work in this literature has shown how new institutional designs can significantly transform the scale, quality, and impact of citizen participation (Fung and Wright 2003). A critical insight of this literature is the recognition that an affirmative state can compensate for the higher transaction costs of participation faced by subordinate groups and can in fact transform the social composition of participation (Heller, Harilal, and Chaudhuri 2007). The case of Porto Alegre certainly provides strong support for participatory democracy. Abers (2001), Baiocchi (2005), and Avritzer (2002) have all shown that the introduction of PB in Porto Alegre not only created new channels of participation but also helped democratize civil society practices.

Much of the participatory democracy literature draws its insights from cases in advanced, institutionalized democracies, where the associational autonomy of citizens is taken for granted. And Porto Alegre is hardly representative of Brazil, since it is widely seen to have an exceptionally strong and well-organized civil society. In contrast, in settings where the formal associational autonomy of citizens is compromised by weak institutions and pervasive social inequalities, promoting democratic participation is far more difficult. Developing a more empirically contextualized understanding of the prospects for institutional reform in democracies characterized by low-intensity citizenship leads us to draw on the state-society literature (Migdal, Kohli, and Shue 1994; Evans 2002; Fox 1994).

Developed with a view to understanding the formidable challenges that state formation has faced in much of the late-developing world, the state-society literature has highlighted how preexisting forms of social power, including forms of authority that are fundamentally in opposition with public authority, can sidetrack and even highjack the most determined and carefully designed efforts to reform institutions of governance. Across a wide range of case studies that include Brazil (Hagopian 1994), state-society theorists have shown that efforts to expand the reach and the impact of the state rarely have the intended effects. Even when reformers enjoy significant capacity, reform efforts can be compromised by general problems of compliance (the existence of extra-institutional norms and rules), the resistance of elites (a recurrent theme in the decentralization literature), or the absence or disorganization of civil society partners. State-society theorists would thus criticize the associational democracy literature as well as much of the development community that has been arguing in favor of "empowerment" for overstating the extent to which institutional reforms—even when backed by significant resources and sound ideas—can transform power relations and the nature of authority. Viewed from this vantage point it becomes clear that even if PB is explicitly designed to facilitate citizen involvement and is backed by significant political authority, the actual impact of institutional reform is conditioned by the nature of pre-existing civil society, a point established by studies in which PB practices are either facilitated by or come into conflict with existing civic practices (Abers 2001; Avritzer 2002; Baiocchi 2005; Silva 2003).

This book, then, offers three contributions to the literature: first, it provides new evidence on the impact of institutional reforms on the capacity of civil society to effectively influence democratic governance. These findings speak directly to claims made in the associational democracy literature about the artifactuality of associational life. Second, by developing close and carefully controlled analyses of local state-civil society interactions, we provide new insights into the state of *actually existing civil society*. In particular, we show that the democratizing effects of civil society are highly contextual. Third, we use our findings to develop a new typology of state-civil society relations that directly builds on the state-society literature. Our goal here is to demonstrate that specific configurations of civil and political society can have markedly different implications for democratization.

THE STRUCTURE OF THE BOOK

In writing this book, we found ourselves confronted with one particularly challenging problem. On the one hand, we wanted to carefully and systematically
present what we believe is a very rich set of findings. From our research we
have learned a lot about the politics, the social contexts and institutional speci-
ficities of how demands are made, budgets are formed, and projects are implemented in eight medium-sized Brazilian cities. As the consummate politician
Tip O'Neil once so famously said, "All politics are local." So we were determined
to present each of our cases in their full complexity and to give the local its
full due. On the other hand, we quickly came to realize that eight cases, presented in full detail, present much too much to absorb. Our municípios vary
not only in size and region, but all turned out to have their distinctive political
histories and contemporary configurations. Doing justice to this diversity and
complexity, while at the same time teasing out patterns of civil society-state relations, turned out to be a difficult task. We have tried to balance these impera-
tives by organizing the book as an analytic narrative. The chapters are outlined
below, but there are two features of our narrative that need to be highlighted.
Chapters 3–5 focus specifically on the cases. In Chapter 3 we deal with all our
cases and assess the degree of transformation in governance practices across
all our pairs. Having established that governance was more or less "business
as usual" in our four control cases, in Chapters 4 and 5 we narrow the focus to
the four PB adopters. Second, though we forefront our analytic typologies of
state-society relations in Chapter 1, which sets the framework for our analysis,
these typologies are inductively derived from our cases studies and our reading
of the larger empirical literature.

Chapter 1 provides the theoretical frame of the book. We begin by arguing that the democratization literature has been split between institutionalist perspectives that focus on the procedural aspects of democracy and a societal
perspective that focuses on the assumed democratizing effects of civil society,
but that neither can cope with the complexities of democratic deepening in new
democracies in general and with Brazil's democratic transformation in particular. We then develop an analytic framework for exploring local civil societies that
revolves around a theoretical distinction between modes of civil society engagement and capacity of self-organization. Building on insights from the case literature, we make an argument for how a relational and disaggregated analysis of
civil society can be translated into a testable set of conceptual typologies. Drawing extensively on examples from the developed as well as the developing world,

the chapter fleshes out a typology of state-civil society relations that proposes four democratic regimes types: affirmative, mobilized, prostrate, and bifurcated.

In Chapter 2, we review the historically specific context in which local democratic transformation is taking place in Brazil. We begin by exploring Brazil's history of local authoritarian government and the dynamic processes of the democracy movements that created spaces for democratic decentralization. We carefully review the scope of participatory institutions introduced during this period and evaluate the impact of decentralization. The chapter makes the case that despite significant problems of fiscal and political decentralization, new spaces have been opened up, most notably PB. After a discussion of PB, the chapter makes the general point that politics happens at different levels, and that the institutionalist literature has by and large neglected these important areas of reform and change.

Chapter 3 provides an overview of the methods and design of the study, including the criteria for selecting our cases. We then introduce our eight municípios and provide an assessment of the degree to which basic budgeting practices were transformed (or not) in the period of study. We show that in the four cases that adopted PB, the budgeting process was opened up to significant involvement by citizens, whereas as in three of the four control municípios there was little evidence of change.

In Chapters 4 and 5 we focus on the "treatment cases," that is, those that adopted PB, but do so by emphasizing the factors and mechanisms that stand in contrast with their paired cases and assessing each case through the analytic prism of our typology of state-civil society relations. The goal of Chapter 4 is to excavate and explain the range of institutional designs that actual experiments with PB have produced. The chapter carefully traces the nature of the reforms and the way that they have impacted modes of representation and budgeting cycles in each of the municípios. Drawing on close analysis of interviews with city officials as well as civil society participants, and careful process tracing of budgeting cycles, the chapter discusses the impact of the reforms on the business of government in each of the municípios. The analysis is organized around a model of participatory governance that explicitly measures the degree and effectiveness of participatory engagement.

In Chapter 5 we explore the process of democratic deepening in the municípios with Participatory Budgeting by comparing the state of civil society before and after the reforms in the pairs of cities. We show that the reforms do indeed open up spaces for civil society, but that this impact is contingent on the preexisting state of civil society. In particular, whether civil society had the capacity for autonomous organizing *before* the reforms is crucial to the type of democratic regime that emerged. We then discuss the democratic possibilities of a civil society that is highly dependent on the support of the state (affirmative democracy) as well as the paradoxical case of civil society contraction that occurred in one PB município.

The Conclusion sets the findings of the book in a broader, comparative context. It makes the case that PB represents only one form of a varied range of new political practices and institutional reforms that explicitly embrace the ideal of participatory democracy. The Conclusion goes on to argue that in contrast to much of the civil society literature and to the various forms of participatory boosterism, we need to take institutional reform more seriously. At the same time, we caution that any understanding of how institutional reforms might impact participation needs to account for the relational configuration of civil society and state, and that simple, blueprint, or "best practices" replications of Participatory Budgeting models are unlikely to succeed.

1 CIVIL SOCIETY AND THE LOCAL STATE
Toward a Relational Framework

Although the concept of civil society has a long and complicated history in political theory, it is only in recent decades that it has become an object of sustained empirical interest. After a first revival in the late 1980s driven by the waves of democratization in Eastern Europe and Latin America (Kaldor 2004), and subsequent world events like the World Social Forum, the idea of civil society has continued to animate a variety of scholarship on the potentials and pitfalls of associational life. Civil society has been referred to as a "millennial idea" (Comaroff and Comaroff 2001), and its rediscovery marks a turning point in political sociology. Somers has argued that for much of the twentieth century, political sociology worked with the assumption that there were "only two essential towering protagonists of social organization that forged the modern world: the modern administrative state and the market economy" (1995, 230). It has now become commonplace to theorize civil society as a necessary third leg of modernity providing a necessary complement to the market and the state. As Somers argues, "It has been called a 'third' space of popular social movements and collective mobilization, of informal networks and associations, and of community solidarities that sustain a participatory public life symbolized not by the sovereign individualism of the market or by the state" (1995, 230).

Certain scholarly works, such as the 1989 English translation of Habermas's *The Public Sphere* and the publication of Putnam, Leonardi, and Nanetti's *Making Democracy Work,* have been particularly influential in shaping the debate and most notably in reconceptualizing democracy from the vantage point of civil society. Our toolkit for understanding democratization has been expanded to include concepts such as the "public sphere" and "citizenship," concepts that have been specifically developed to highlight how political practices are culturally specific to peoples, places, and issues (Dagnino 1998; Mahajan 1999).

We find the problematic that has emerged around civil society to be as exciting as it is confusing, however. The civil society literature has made a strong case that different patterns of association can substantively improve the quality of democracy, but any such general claim is subject to five important qualifications. First, as many critics have noted, the normative ideal of civil society—rights-bearing citizens who achieve a degree of democratic governance through deliberation—is often substituted for the actual practices in civil society. In this celebratory view of civil society, the democratizing effects of civil society are taken for granted rather than demonstrated. Second, while the literature has had much to say about the mobilizational capacity of civil society, it has had little to say about how civil society can effectively engage the state and influence public policy. While civil society actors may be good at problematizing new issues, mobilizing previously marginalized populations, and in some cases even transforming societal norms, we know little about when and how such efforts are effectively scaled-up into institutional practices that can sustain a new political equilibrium. Third, most of the literature has focused on national civil societies or transnational networks, and far too little research has focused on local civil societies. Fourth, even though it is widely recognized that there is enormous variation in the configuration of actual civil societies, efforts to develop useful typologies have barely gotten beyond highly descriptive terms such as "vibrant," "thick," and "effervescent." Fifth, many recent treatments of civil society have tempered the celebratory view by emphasizing the extent to which many aspects of associational life are artifactual, that is, based on the institutional context in which they are embedded. We find this criticism to be basically sound (indeed, it is confirmed by the findings in this book), but we caution that the emphasis in this artifactual literature (for example, Armony 2004) has often swung to the other extreme of the celebratory literature in its emphasis on how civil society is constrained or hemmed in by social and state power. Between these two extremes, there have been few attempts to examine how institutional designs and reforms might actually encourage and strengthen citizen participation, that is, how civil society itself might become more or less democratic as a result of its interaction with institutions of the state.

TOWARD A RELATIONAL ACCOUNT OF CIVIL SOCIETY

"Follow the actors!"—Bruno Latour

Following the call of scholars like Mamdani (1996) who urge us to look at "actually existing civil societies," in this book we offer what we have come to think of as a "middle-way," or a sociologically realistic account of civil society. Drawing on the relational tradition in sociology, we propose to move beyond what we call the "institutional-associational divide," the divide between those who emphasize formal institutions and those who emphasize society-side factors, or roughly speaking, the divide between political science and sociology. The relational tools we deploy here both illuminate spaces in the interstices of society and state and expose the centrality of relationships across those divides in shaping practices on both sides. But our account is also a "middle-way" account in the sense that it relies on and dialogues with normative political theory while it is also informed by sociologically realistic accounts of inequality and power. We thus develop a de-ontologized account of civil society, one that rejects the confusion of the empirical with the romantic, but nonetheless holds it up to the critical gaze of normative theory. Concretely situated in the sociological literature, this means drawing on authors who are attentive to power dynamics within civil society and relatively cynical of its potential (Bourdieu) as well as authors who are attentive to the emancipatory possibilities of association and communication (Habermas).

The democratic possibilities of civil society have received extensive theoretical attention from scholars in recent years, most influentially in the work of Jürgen Habermas (1984, 1989, 1996), Jeffrey Alexander (2006), Margaret Somers (1993, 1994), and Jean Cohen and Andrew Arato (1992). This view of civil society rests on two critical claims. First, under certain historical and sociopolitical conditions, civil society can emerge as a relatively independent sphere governed by associational and communicative practices that are differentiated from the market, state, and traditional affiliations. Second, in such a sphere, citizens engaged in a plurality of forms of deliberation—from microinstitutions to the national media—effectively supplement interest-group bargaining and simple aggregation (elections) as authoritative sources of decision-making. The primary mechanisms through which deliberation produces effects are through the transformation of preferences when the force of the better argument wins out and the resulting elaboration of new norms. Since the underlying rationale of deliberation is predicated on reason-giving rather than money, power, or status, deliberative processes are in principle inclusionary, that is, the only precondition to participation is membership in the political community. This, then, is the sense in which civil society scholars have emphasized the liberatory potential of associational life. As elaborated by Habermas (1989) and more recently by Alexander, the concept of the "public sphere" attempts to salvage the role of democratic deliberation as a potentially emancipatory activity from the theoretical pessimism of the Marxist tradition in which power trumps voice, and the reductivism of aggregative theories of democracy (the liberal tradition and most notably Schumpeter) that limit democracy to its delegative function. It is in the public sphere that citizens debate common problems in a publicly minded way. In a similar way, for Alexander it is in the civil sphere, a "society of individuals before the state" that solidarity emerges and communicative judgments are pronounced: "Standing firmly inside the civil rather than the state sphere, communicative institutions become free to broadcast interpretations that are not only independent of the state, but can challenge its commands" (2006, 108).

But a relational treatment of the public sphere demands that we carefully contextualize it, and in particular that we recognize the ways in which it is constituted and constantly constrained by power relations. No sociologist has given the question of power more systematic attention than Bourdieu. If civil society theorists have focused on the emancipatory potential of the public sphere, Bourdieu emphasizes the workings of power within those voluntary spheres. All spheres of action—"fields" in Bourdieu's terminology—are constituted by power. Fields such as art, education, academia, and politics are the balance sheet at any given time of past struggles, representing and reproducing an equation of power. The ability to compete effectively in any field is a function of the forms and combinations of capital—cultural, social, and economic—that are valorized in that field. Because of lifelong processes of socialization—the habitus—different actors embody specific dispositions and bring different bundles of capital to any given field, more or less predetermining their trajectory within that field. If Bourdieu's sociology is one of reproduction—that is, a theory of how patterns of inequality are actively reproduced—it differs from other theories of reproduction by its emphasis on the cultural and in particular on the centrality of symbolic domination in the reproduction of modern, institutionally differentiated societies. For Bourdieu, symbolic power, the power to define what is given as natural, and specifically "every power which manages to impose meaning and to impose them as legitimate by concealing the power relations which are the basis of its force" (1977, 4) is the key structuring element of modern societies, especially societies that model themselves on the liberal ideals of reason and merit. Dominant groups, enjoying a surplus of cultural and educational capital, have the power to define the various classification systems through which competencies are distributed and groups hierarchically defined.

The dominated, having internalized, through the habitus—"the internalized form of the class condition of the conditionings it entails" (1984, 101)—the cognitive structures through which their practical knowledge of the social world is gained, learn to "refuse what they are refused" (1984, 471). In this respect, Bourdieu's work stands as a powerful critique of modern civil societies. For Bourdieu, deliberation and participatory democracy reproduce hierarchies. On the one hand, it reproduces class hierarchies, since the outcome of the political struggle, predetermined by the existing distributions of power, is only further misrecognized when represented as freed from power. On the other hand, it reproduces hierarchies of *political competence* of "experts" against non-experts within the field of politics (a hierarchy that is likely to align along, roughly, class lines, but need not be coterminous with it). Bourdieu denounces fictions of "linguistic communism"—that the ability to speak is equally distributed to all, asserting that "not all linguistic utterances are equally acceptable and not all locutors equal."[1] As Bourdieu writes, "The authorized speech of status-generated competence, a powerful speech which helps to create what it says, is answered by the silence of an equally status-linked incompetence, which is experienced as technical incapacity and leaves no choice but delegation—a misrecognized dispossession of the less competent by the more competent, of women by men, of the less educated by the more educated, of those who 'do not know to speak' to those who 'speak well'" (1984, 413–14).

Instead of opting to emphasize power and inequality *or* association and dialogue, our account is attentive to both possibilities. Actually existing civil societies are ones in which association and dialogue exist, but that are also shaped by power and inequalities. In our view the existence of inequalities does not nullify the emancipatory possibilities of association, just as association does not need perfect equality as a precondition. Following Burawoy's (2008) critique of Bourdieu, we locate the limits and constraints to association and liberated speech not in the habitus—the deeply internalized dispositions and practices that makes agents complicit in their own subordination—but rather in the institutions and social arrangements that unevenly distribute associational capabilities and deliberative competencies. Pragmatically, this means coming to terms with the simple observation that organizations operating in the space of civil society are as likely to be schools of democracy as they are to be vehicles of clientelistic control and hierarchy. Or to put it another way, working with Gramsci's original formulation of civil society as a terrain of both contestation and legitimation, we recognize that civil society is the terrain where new claims emerge but also where consent to the dominant order is organized.[2] Examining civil society without romanticism, Laclau (2006) urges us to decompose it into component parts *and* to problematize its democracy-enhancing effects. As Alexander puts it, "Real civil societies are created by social actors at a particular time and in a particular place" (2006, 6). In what follows, we develop the tools to carry out the task of understanding these "real civil societies."

BEYOND THE INSTITUTIONAL-ASSOCIATIONAL DIVIDE

The literature on democracy has become split between an institutionalist view and a societal one. In the institutionalist view, democracy is defined in formal, procedural terms. A consolidated democracy is one in which certain basic institutions—the electoral system and the constitution that guarantees rights of association—function properly. Less-than-democratic is simply defined in terms of underdeveloped or poorly functioning democratic institutions.[3] With their formalist view of democracy, institutionalists are generally more preoccupied with the official venues and events of democracy, and less with the actors and practices of a democratic society. To the extent that they acknowledge the significance of civil society, they do so largely by defining it in terms of the liberal tradition of legally guaranteed individual rights of association and property. The sociological critique of this literature is that it confuses democratic rights with democratic practices (Somers 1993). The problem is that even if the institutions did, in fact, conform perfectly with the principles of democratic practice, they are routinely and readily subverted by nondemocratic norms and extrademocratic powers. Moreover, the institutions themselves have a perverse logic. In the absence of countervailing powers, they are subject to being instrumentalized, that is, transformed into instruments of power (as in Michel's *Iron Law of Oligarchy*) that have distinctly illiberal effects. Thus if we are concerned with how democracies actually work, we need to look beyond institutions to discover civil society.

In response both to the formalism of the institutionalist view and its lack of concern with the normative dimension of democracy—that is, the degree to which democratic practices approximate democratic norms—the recent civil society literature has directed the spotlight to the democracy-enhancing role of civil society. Often drawing inspiration from Rousseauian conceptions of democracy that emphasize the deliberations of citizens as the heart of democratic practice, this literature argues that the real measure of a democracy lies in the actual practices and norms of civil society. The civil society view argues that politics are not confined to formal arenas and takes the institutionalists to task for failing in particular to recognize "the possibility that nongovernmental and extrainstitutional public arenas—constructed principally by (often less-than-loyal) social movements—might be equally essential to the consolidation of meaningful democratic citizenship for subaltern social groups and social classes" (Alvarez 1997, 85). But if the civil society view has helped refocus our attention and has brought to light a range of political practices obscured by the institutionalist view, its engagement with the institutionalist literature suffers from two related shortcomings.

First, in its haste to move beyond formal institutions and discover subaltern publics, the civil society literature has sometimes tended to dismiss formal democratic institutions as little more than instruments of elite domination. In doing so, it gives short shrift to the institutional requirements of any modern democracy and pays scant attention to the complex ways in which specific institutional forms actually shape democratic practices, including those of subordinate groups. Even the most developed and differentiated civil societies are characterized by patterns and logics of association that are a function of institutional rules. If nothing else, the associational freedom of modern civil society is predicated on the rule of law, and the democratizing possibilities of civil society are necessarily a function of its social and institutional context. The second associated problem is that the civil society literature and the many related variants of the participatory democracy literature, including the new voluminous work on social capital, generally take for granted the democratizing effects of participation. The problem, on the one hand, is the failure to recognize that civil society, as a space in which groups organize voluntarily, can have both civil and uncivil manifestations, can be either inclusionary or exclusionary, and can give voice to the underprivileged or reinforce privilege. On the other hand, because much of the civil society literature suffers from the methodological flaw of selecting on the dependent variable—that is, examining only cases in which an increase in civil society activity has been associated with democratization—the literature cannot come to terms with when or exactly how civil society might have such an effect. This problem stems in large part from the fact that scholarship has followed history, focusing on dramatic cases of civil society mobilization and coalescence in the context of regime breakdowns and political transitions. These historic moments of civil society mobilization not only represent conjunctural moments from which it is always difficult to draw lessons, but also draw attention away from the more mundane role of civil society in "ordinary" times. At the end of the day, then, the civil society literature cannot explain cases of democratic deepening because it does not address the fundamental question of how preferences formed by movements and associational practices are aggregated and translated into actual outcomes.[4]

REAL CIVIL SOCIETIES

If the institutionalists have largely ignored civil society, and much of the civil society literature has tended toward boosterism, we are interested in understanding "actually existing civil societies" (Mamdani 1996). We begin with the very general recognition that civil society is fragile and contingent, that it can vary dramatically in its composition and activity level, as well as in its effects.

In recognizing the democratic potential of civil society, we take our first, broad cue from Rueschemeyer, Stephens, and Stephens (1992). In their comparative exploration of the social roots of democratization, they demonstrate that the presence of a robust civil society was a determining factor in the successful democratic trajectories of Europe, South America, Central America, and the Caribbean. But, in contrast to neo-Toquevillian views of civil society that simply equate associationalism with democratization, Rueschemeyer, Stephens, and Stephens argue that it "is not the density of civil society per se, but the empowerment of previously excluded classes aided by this density that improves the chances of democratization" (1992, 50). Developing an argument first formulated by Therborn (1977), they show that the self-organization of the working class is critical to the prospects of democratization. In turn, the existence of a robust civil society is important because it creates the spaces in which subordinate groups can associate and self-organize, increasing the likelihood that these groups will become coherent political actors capable of independently articulating their interests. Rueschemeyer, Stephens, and Stephens emphasize this point specifically in reference to the state (as is the norm in treatments of civil society), arguing that a strong civil society is one in which state repression or direct control of social activity is limited.[5]

We expand this notion of relative autonomy from state control by noting that the existence of public spaces also means that subordinate actors can organize *free of a range of social dependencies*, most notably direct material dependencies (debt bondage, manor-based tenancy, guilds) as well as nondemocratic authority structures (chiefs, castes, caciques, rural bosses). The existence of such a space, though, hardly guarantees an expansion of democratic practices. Closer attention to the actual politics of civil society in historically specific settings reveals that civil society can also become the conduit through which reactionary elites or authoritarian regimes mobilize support, as in the case of the fall of democracy in Weimar Germany (Berman 1997), the building of authoritarian regimes in Italy and Spain (Riley 2005), or even more broadly state corporatism in Latin America. The rise of Hindu nationalism in India (which is by definition antithetical to secular plural democracy) is only the most recent and dramatic example of how associational practices can be breeding grounds for antidemocratic ideologies (Hansen 1999; Jaffrelot 1996; Fernandes and Heller 2006).

To unpack the relativity of the democratizing effects of civil society, we need to explore three separate dimensions of civil society: associational freedom, communicative power, and publicness. We define civil society as the *institutions, practices, and networks of voluntary life that are oriented toward and legitimate themselves in terms of publicness.* Our conceptualization of civil society proceeds through three nested claims, which taken together constitute necessary and sufficient conditions for civil society's democratizing effects. First, by "voluntary" we specifically refer to forms of associational life that are not structured by binding forms of hierarchical authority (be it traditional or rational-legal) or market incentives. By voluntary we mean to specifically refer to "secondary associations" in which people have chosen to associate, and not primary associations such as families or ethnic groups that are ascribed. Associational forms of course exist in the market and state sphere, but the specific character of associational relations is bounded and constrained by the media of power in the state and the media of money in the market. In contrast, within the sphere of civil society, associational life is both constituted by and protective of, social resources and media. As Warren argues:

> The concept of association evokes the possibilities of collective action, but in a way that retains social (as opposed to legal/bureaucratic or market) modes of mediation among people, through language, norms, shared purposes, and agreements. The concept of association thus connects the normative questions that define politics—What should we do? And how should we live?—to the social and linguistic media that enable these questions to be asked, discussed, and decided. (2001, 8)

The logic of associations that are both of and in civil society is thus to preserve and nurture their social resources and modes of social exchange—be they predicated on a cultural identity or a set of shared ideas or purposes—independently of the media of power and money.[7] The more that associations approximate this autonomy and the more that they are genuinely voluntary (individuals can readily exit), the more they will rely on social and communicative resources and the more they will act in accordance with their normative telos.

Second, we argue that the logic of action of civil society is fundamentally one of modern sociability (Walzer 1992) in which the critical binding element is communication, and specifically the production of new norms through deliberation. We do not presume that such practices and resulting norms are necessarily civil or democratizing and can, in fact, often be based on forms of social closure and social exclusion that in turn harden into new logics of power, resource concentration, or privileged identities. However, we do argue that insofar as associations can have broader effects, they do so through communicative power, that is, the power to influence other actors through the arts of persuasion, or in Habermas's famous trope, the force of the better argument. The art of persuasion is as readily used to protect privilege as it is to expand the demos (a point we elaborate below), but the more communicative power is decoupled from state power and market power, the more that communication is liberated from money and coercion, the more its effectiveness lies in normative legitimacy. Such effectiveness makes us attentive to nonliberal traditions where liberal-democratic values are only one possible set of shared beliefs among the "manifold of practices and pragmatic moves aiming at persuading people to broaden the range of their commitments to others" (Mouffe 2000, 66). But the key point is that the power and effects of civil society are more democratizing when transmitted not through the media of power, money, or traditional authority, but through communicative means. Having said this, identities, ideas, and norms can be effectively mobilized for illiberal causes, which brings us to our third democracy-enhancing condition of publicness.

To the extent that civil society, as a space of practices, has been differentiated from primary social structures, the market, and political society, civil society actors who are interested in having political effects *must* legitimize their action with reference to the public interest and universalizing norms (not to be confused with universal norms), and that the legitimation that is sought from and accorded to such an action-orientation is in direct tension with uncivil claims and exclusionary practices. When such tensions are manifest, civil society, as a normative ideal, is unsustainable. This is how we would then propose to distinguish between patently illiberal forms of associations, such as the Klu Klux Klan which is dedicated to enforcing an exclusion, a-political forms of association such as boy scouts which have no obvious effect on democracy, and those whose very legitimacy is predicated on making claims about publicness. It is of course true that a claim of publicness can be predicated on an exclusion, as when men would argue that women are not competent to participate in politics, but the very fact of having to make such a claim in public—including in a democratic-constitutional complex of mass media, courts, parliaments, and multiple other fora—exposes the claim to a counterclaim. Or as Habermas puts it, "Segmented public spheres are constituted with the help of exclusion mechanisms: however, because publics cannot harden into organizations or systems, there is no exclusion rule without a proviso for its abolishment" (1996, 374).

In its ideal-typical democratic incarnation, then, civil society is characterized by voluntary forms of association that are constituted by and protective off communicative power and that seek to exert their influence by specifically engaging with and seeking support in the public sphere. Taken together, these attributes will trend toward the production of the very types of universalizing norms that must necessarily undergird the democratic ideal of collective self-rule. Stated somewhat differently, the idea of civil society, or better yet the telos of civil society (if not the teleology) both analytically and normatively, rests on a core trope of sociology: the *possibility* of solidarity in modern society.[8]

Unpacking Relational Analysis

Even though we stress that civil society must be understood as a space of practices that is distinct from primary social structures, the market, and political society, we do not treat civil society as unitary or independent, but rather view civil society in relational terms (Somers 1993; Emirbayer and Sheller 1999; Alexander 2006). A central insight of relational sociology in general is that traditional sociological categories, like "class" or "social movements," should be disaggregated and reconfigured into "institutional and relational clusters in which people, power, and organizations are positioned and connected. A relational setting is a patterned matrix of institutional relationships among cultural, economic, social, and political practices" (Somers 1993, 595). In relational hands civil society is not a unitary entity separate from the state or the economy, but rather a criss-crossing of groups of people engaged in voluntary activities, or as we have proposed here, the *institutions, practices, and networks of voluntary life.* A relational approach calls for carefully unpacking the sometimes contradictory relationships between the state and voluntary associations and the way in which these shifting relationships both reflect societal power and shape the functioning of the state and civil society.

We take as our first assumption that civil society is to a significant degree artifactual (Cohen and Rogers 1995). In our framework, we emphasize the recursive and embedded relationships between practices, networks, and institutions, as we examine civil society. We propose that civil society will remain mystified so long as it is defined as a "well-defined, clearly bounded and unitary reality" outside of the state. In some historical settings, most notably under authoritarian regimes, civil society is actively suppressed by the state and its existence is indeed only possible *outside* of the state, while in others, the state is more porous and those interfaces between voluntary associations and the state may actually make up most of existing civil society. In some settings, loosely ordered associations of individuals may be more important than formal associations with legal status. In some contexts, voluntary associations may be constituted by proper Toquevillian citizens—endowed with civic virtues and respectful of others' rights—but in others, the goals of voluntary associations may be exclusionist and chauvinist.

Relational sociologies offer a deeply insightful alternative to circumvent tired questions of material versus ideological interests shaping social action. Central to this framework is the way in which these networks, practices, and institutions function and interact with (and within) a broader social context. This takes into account the regime of state-society relationships in creating a context for the functioning of civil society. A relational approach would make explicit all of the ways in which civil society interacts with the state (formal, informal settings, meetings, protests, and so forth) and attempt to understand how it is that these interactions affect the rules and functioning of civil society.

In our effort to translate these relational conceptions into usable categories, we draw on Tilly's recent efforts to develop a relational theory of democratization.[9] Though he does not use the term civil society, Tilly explicitly builds his model of democratization around the relationship between the state and its citizens. Tilly makes this argument in two steps. First, he places the type or nature of a subject's relation to government at the center of his definition: democracy means the "formation of a regime featuring relatively broad, equal, categorical, binding consultation and protection" (2004, 128). He then links this conception of democracy to a definition of citizenship:

> Citizenship consists, in this context, of mutual rights and obligations binding governmental agents to whole categories of people who are subject to the government's authority, those categories being defined chiefly or exclusively by

relations to the government *rather than by reference to particular connections with rulers or to membership in categories based on imputed durable traits such race, ethnicity, gender, or religion.* It institutionalizes regular, categorical relations between subjects and their governments." (2004, 128; italics added)

Tilly then goes on the identify four conditions that elaborate this fundamental relationship—no one is excluded (breadth), subjects have to be equal in terms of these relations with government (equality), the government must answer to regular binding public consultations (binding consultation), and subjects (especially minorities) are protected from arbitrary state action (protection). Democracy, as such, means "formation of a regime featuring relatively broad, equal, categorical, binding consultation and protection" (2004, 128). It is important to underscore that Tilly treats democratization as a dynamic, historically contingent, open-ended, and hence reversible process. He thus notes that no actually existing democracy lives up to his definition and that democratization should be viewed as a move "*toward* greater categorical regularity, breadth, equality, binding consultation, and protection, and de-democratization consists of moves *away* from them" (2004, 128).

In integrating Tilly's relational view of democracy into our analysis, we want to underscore two points that are critical to our focus in this book on participatory experiments. First, the thrust of most participatory experiments is precisely to expand the breadth, regularity, equality, and bindingness of consultation. In the representative, Schumpetarian view of democracy, "participation" is limited to periodic elections. In contrast, the very idea of Participatory Budgeting (PB) is to give citizens who can vote but not really exert influence regular and more binding modes of influence over a wider range of government actions. If PB empowers the binding nature of the state's democratic relation to its citizen, it also increases the actual institutional surface area of influence. Second, Tilly's relational view gives us greater insight into where pressures in the direction of participatory democracy might come from. If there is any theme that ran through all of Tilly's work it was his insistence that contentious politics—that is, the politics of challengers confronting elites—is the engine of social change. And while Tilly recognized that not all social movements are democratic, often making demands in the name of particularized conceptions of "the people," they nonetheless have democratizing effects:

Social movements assert popular sovereignty. . . . The stress on popular consent fundamentally challenges divine right to kingship, traditional inheritance of rule, warlord control and aristocratic predominance. Even in systems of representative government . . . social movements pose a crucial question: do sovereignty and its accumulated wisdom lie in the legislature or in the people it claims to represent? (2004, 13)

Our analyses in this book thus focus on practices—principally what we call *modes of engagement*—as well as the relational positioning of civil society organizations vis-à-vis state bodies and the formal political field—the question *of autonomy.* Both of these terms will be familiar to readers engaged in civil society debates, though here we combine both dimensions in new ways. But our relational approach also directs attention to *mechanisms of mediation,* which turn out to be causally very important for the outcomes in our cases.

MECHANISMS OF MEDIATION

Our analysis thus far has sought to analytically separate dynamics "internal" and "external" to civil society, isolating practices of civil society from its relational positioning vis-à-vis political society and the state. As we will discuss below, there is a range of logical possibilities instantiated in more or less stable "regimes" that combine different modes of engagement with different relational positionings. There is one more concept we must introduce, however, as it allows us purchase on the question of will-formation and chain of sovereignty. This is the concept of *mediation,* which refers to the question of transmission (or translation) of claims and demands as they emerge in some settings and are represented in others.

Civil society itself can contain many such transmission belts, between different kinds of publics, between different sites, and even between civil society and actors in political society or the state. Public sphere theorists have paid attention to the "terms of translation" between more and less privileged publics (Negt and Kluge 1993). Scholars of social movements have focused on the person of the movement broker, who, in McAdam, Tarrow, and Tilly's words, brings together different sites and thus facilitates "communication and coordination among sites, facilitates the combined use of resources located in different sties, and creates new potential collective actors" (2001, 157). In the context of Latin America in particular, scholars have also pointed to the figure of the community "problem solver," who maintains some reputation and honor in the local community by virtue of her privileged access to powerful persons outside the neighborhood (Auyero 1999). As Latour reminds us, mediators always "transform, translate, distort, and modify meaning or elements they are supposed to carry" (2005, 39).

What unites these diverse examples is that there they are conduits along which demands and claims travel in ways that invariably transform the demands, but also shape the collective identities of those making the demands. In other words, mediation has a double side to it: it is the representation of community's demands, wants, or needs, but the process of doing so constructs and cements that community's identity. One who represents another always, as Laclau suggests, "exceeds the simple transmission of a preconstituted interest" and "constructs and transforms that interest . . . transforming the identity of the represented" (Laclau 1996, 98). Thus, understanding mediation gains us purchase on both the dynamics of chain of sovereignty and will-formation. Mische eloquently articulates this process:

> Mediation consists of communicative practices at the intersection of two or more (partially) disconnected groups, involving the (provisional) conciliation of the identities, projects, or practices associated with those different groups. . . . It involves negotiating between multiple possible public representations of who one is acting "as" as well as what one is acting "for." (Mische 2006, 50)

We recognize that mediation may take a number of forms, ranging, on one end, from that carried out by individuals in the context of favor-trading (and thus only partially accountable to those having their interests mediated) to mediation by democratic associations. The least democratic form of mediation is favor-trading, commonly described as clientelism, a familiar feature of urban politics in Brazil and, indeed, throughout much of the democratic world where modes of engagement are not institutionalized. These are often strategic ways of securing scarce goods or services in neighborhoods in exchange for votes, or promise of votes, or political allegiance. This kind of mediation awards status to the person doing the mediating and tends to isolate the particular demand from others, making less likely broad alliances and a sense of public (Gay 1994). At the other end are forms of mediation carried out by democratic associations. Extremely important during Brazil's transition to democracy were collectives described as "umbrella organizations," "articulating groups," or "popular councils." Imagined precisely as alternatives to clientelist forms of mediation, these associations of associations were spaces of discussion and negotiation that articulated joint platforms that were then to be presented to authorities. What is important about these "mediating publics," in addition to the fact that they are beyond the control of any single individual, is that particular demands come to be related to each other, which in turn transforms them. A particular demand becomes "internally split" and "while it remains a particular demand, it also becomes the signifier of a wider universality" (Laclau 2006, 95). This stands in contrast to the clientelist mediation described above, which promotes the absorption of demands "in a differential way (each in isolation from the others)" and works against the formation of an "equivalential relation" between demands, which is the precondition of a sense of public interest (Laclau 2006, 74).

In sum, mediation is the process of transmission of demands from parts of civil society to other parts or to actors in political society or the state. It plays a crucial part in forming the collective identities of civil society actors and their sense of publicness. We thus can speak of forms of mediation that enhance democracy and those that do not. For example, clientelism as a form of mediation promotes inequalities between those that do the mediating and their communities while isolating those communities from other communities. At the other end of the spectrum are forms of mediation that promote horizontal relationships and equivalence between demands, or a sense of publicness. In between are the range of practices that also exist in Brazilian cities and elsewhere: the mediation by individual social movement activists, the mediation of a single association or organization, and so on. From our point of view these enhance democraticness insofar as they promote the equivalence of democratic demands and are done in a manner accountable to those being represented.

While there are distinct kinds of mediation—that is, it is possible to speak of distinctive practices of mediation, we do not treat it as purely internal to civil society, being as it is very much shaped by the wider institutional context. Different institutional arrangements can promote clientelist or more democratic forms of mediation. As we discuss in Chapter 2, urban regimes in Brazil were often favorable to clientelist forms while often making it challenging for more democratic alternatives to thrive.

MODES OF ENGAGEMENT

We want to conclude this chapter by proposing an analytic framework by which we might capture some of the complexity of state-civil society relations. We do so by identifying different configurations of state and civil society and identifying these with different types of political regimes. Although this framework appears to be deductively derived as presented here, it is the framework that emerged inductively from our analysis of the paired cases in the rest of this book. In fact, the framework that is summarized in Table 1.1 in abstract form here reappears later in the Chapter 5 as a way of categorizing the evolution of state-civil society relations in our empirical cases.

The point of departure for this framework is the recognition that some forms of associational life can promote broad-based participation, just as other forms of associational life can promote exclusions and privilege. We tackle this analytical and empirical challenge by borrowing both from institutionalist and societal view of democracy. Following the civil society literature, we recognize that patterns of association and norms and practices are critical dimensions of democratic life, not only in terms of democratization relations within society itself (as when citizens recognize each other as rights-bearing citizens) but also as a critical complement and countervailing force to the formal, institutional processes of democratic representation. On the other hand, we also take the institutionalist view seriously, recognizing that the way in which the state structures relations within civil society and between the state and civil society is essential to striking a productive and democracy-enhancing balance between political and civil society. Important characteristics include not only the organizational character and scope of CSOs, but also their relationship to the larger political field, including political parties and the state. Accordingly, we develop the following typology of civil society-state relations.

Our typology is organized around two axes of analysis: *self-organization* and *demand-making*. Self-organization refers to the degree to which collective actors in civil society are capable of independently organizing, that is, mobilizing their own resources and forming their own choices (self-determination). This is a critical question since engaging the state always carries risks of oligarchicalization, goal displacement, and even outright cooptation. Civil society organizations, or CSOs, may be said to be either *dependent* when they do not have the capacity for self-organization and self-determination without external support, or *autonomous* when they have the capacity for self-organizing and self-determination. Demand-making refers to *how* civil society actors routinely engage the state and goes directly to Tilly's categorical regularity, breadth, equality, bindingness of engagements with the state. We identify two modes: *institutionalized* (rule bound, regularized, and transparent procedures of demand-making consistent with the relational notion of citizen), and *discretionary* (discretionary demand-making contingent on connections to a broker/patron).

In presenting this model, we offer the standard disclaimer that these are ideal-types to be used as heuristic devises recognizing in particular that on the ground the boundaries between our categories are often blurred. Nonetheless, we believe this model brings greater analytical leverage to understanding actually existing civil society and provides a basis for concrete comparisons across local cases.

Table 1.1 Civil Society-State Relations

Degree of Self-Organization	Dependent	Autonomous
Demand-Making		
Institutionalized	Affirmative Democracy	Mobilized Democracy
Discretionary	Prostrate Democracy	Bifurcated Democracy
Exclusion	Totalitarianism	Authoritarianism

The resulting two-by-three table produces six possible cells. We begin at the bottom. In both these cases civil society is excluded, that is, it has few if any points of interface with the state. Neither of these applies to contemporary Brazil, but we describe them in order to show the range of cases that our typology can effectively describe. Dependent exclusion (the bottom-left cell) represents the absence of civil society that defines totalitarian systems. Here, the space between the state and society is collapsed. The state exerts absolute control over political life, and civil society-like organizations exist only if sponsored by the state. Indeed, what singles out totalitarianism from other nondemocratic regimes (despotism, authoritarianism) is the degree to which the state seeks to directly penetrate and control civil society. The cell of autonomous exclusion (bottom-right) characterizes authoritarian regimes. Here, civil society is to some extent organized and enjoys some autonomy. CSOs can in particular define norms and interests independently of the state. It is nonetheless excluded because there are no channels of representation or engagement with the state. In the most common case, this combination of exclusion and autonomy results from fundamental limits to the capacity of the state to fully penetrate and control society. Such cases would include the anti-apartheid movement in South Africa and the democracy movements throughout Eastern Europe where, despite state repression, civil society structures were able to take root in the authoritarian period and become the basis for broad-based democracy movements. In other cases, and in particular throughout Latin America, past experiences of democracy or prolonged social mobilization (for example, in Mexico), allowed for a high degree of civil society self-organization and quite significant capacities for political engagement. The *poblaciones* of Chile in the Pinochet period are a good example (Oxhorn 1995), as are the Zapatistas in Mexico, and this would also characterize the condition of large segments of civil society under military rule in Brazil (the other segment consisted of civil society groups that were incorporated through corporatist or clientist structures). Precisely because these groups were excluded, they developed particularly rich repertoires of organization and even contention, which were quickly activated when there were openings in the political opportunity structure.

All the other cells in our typology describe civil society under formally democratic conditions. Within these four cells a first crucial distinction must be made. The cells labeled *prostrate* and *bifurcated* describe what more or less is the modal condition of representative democracy in most of the developing world, a condition in which civil society is largely unable to influence the state. Our labels of *affirmative* and *mobilized* democracy, in contrast, mark cases in which civil society does influence the state, marking a move from representative democracy to participatory democracy. If PB has the effect that it is intended to have, then its introduction should result in a move from the lower two cells (prostrate or bifurcated) into either of the upper two cells (affirmative or mobilized).

Mobilized democracy (top right) and prostrate (middle left) represent the two ends of the democratic spectrum. The combination of civil society organizations that are autonomous and that engage the state through institutionalized demand-making, that is, as citizens that do not have to sacrifice their political autonomy in order to have influence represent what we label as *mobilized democracy*. Actors in civil society are autonomous and able to determine their goals and interests through communicative means while at the same time being linked to the state in a manner that does not require loyalty (as in the case of clientelism). This typology corresponds to Fox's (1994) influential distinction between clientelism and associational autonomy in describing different democratic regimes, and Avrizter's (2006) concept of participatory publics.

At the other end of the spectrum, a *prostrate democracy* describes a civil society characterized by organizations that have little capacity for self-determination and engage the state through clientelism. In many respects, this has been the norm through much of Latin America, taking a variety of forms including state corporatism. It has been well described in the literature on "the popular sector" in Brazil and Latin America in general (Auyero 2001). This is the least effective form of civil society since it is by definition self-limiting. This is what James

Scott (1998) has in mind when he speaks of a *prostrate* civil society, that is, one that is incapable of mounting any challenge to the state. It should be noted that this is different from dependent *exclusion* since a dependent civil society that is limited to discretionary demand-making (that is, clientelism) does at least involve an exchange relationship between the principals.

The categories that combine autonomy and discretionary demand-making (*bifurcated*), and dependence and institutionalized demand-making (*affirmative democracy*) are the least familiar. Because neither fit the zero-sum view of state and civil society that most analysts work with, they have received little attention in the literature. Autonomy and discretionary demand-making correspond to what we have described as *bifurcated* civil societies.[10] These are characterized by a well-developed civil society, but one in which the condition of engaging the state is highly discretionary (based on a particular connection to a state actor or broker rather than on the category of citizenship). Depending in large part on the opportunity structure, some CSOs engage the state as clients, while others are sufficiently strong and self-determining that they choose not to engage the state and retain their autonomy. Of course, any relatively well-developed civil society will contain a mix of clientelism and autonomy, but we would argue that the legacy of Brazil's social movements is such that bifurcation characterizes much of the popular sector. As we shall see, this category does effectively capture the highly contested logic of civil society in many Brazilian municípios.

Finally, the category of dependence and institutionalized demand-making, or what we have called *affirmative democracy*, is the most specific to our analysis. This results when a state invites participation without demanding allegiance, but is partnered with a civil society that without state encouragement would not have the wherewithal to organize effectively or simply does not exist in an organized form. This can produce two distinct forms of affirmative democracy based on whether there is collective mediation. If there is mediation, the local state recognizes and respects the fundamental democratic right of CSOs to articulate their interests, but the existing CSOs have little actual capacity to engage the state on their own terms. This is the precisely the pattern of state-civil society relations that Tendler describes in her path-breaking study of how state reformers aligned themselves with local-level actors in promoting new developmental interventions in the Brazilian state of Ceará in the 1980s (Tendler 1998). This is also similar to the state-civil society relationship established in one of the districts in Porto Alegre where there was no preexisting associationalism but where PB fora became central to community life, as described by Baiocchi (2005). In the absence of mediation, many of the relationships between civil society and the state take place through individual channels. In these cases, the introduction of participatory channels, one of the possibilities is individualized participation or that based on primary relationships (family, friendship networks).

We label both of these possibilities *affirmative democracy* to emphasize that this does represent a move in the direction of participatory democracy in that new channels of engagement have been opened up, while highlighting at the same time the precarious balance between the leading role of the state and the dependence of civil society. We are agnostic about the long-term democratic effects of this tutelage. On the one hand, it allows access to the state and gives new voice to civil society without producing clientelism. On the other hand, over time there is a substantial risk that the state (or a political party) will instrumentalize the relationship. Many have argued that the Partido dos Trabalhadores (PT)'s status as a social movement party is undermined when it comes to power and uses patronage to assert control over its movement partners. As we shall see, in three of our cases, the introduction of PB did, in fact, produce complaints that civil society organizations lost much of their autonomy. On the other hand, two of our cases clearly witnessed a strengthening of civil society autonomy after the introduction of PB.

Having laid out our analytic framework, we now turn in Chapter 2 to the national historical context for the appearance of local democracy in Brazil, before our analysis of the cases in Chapters 3, 4, and 5. In Chapter 3, we examine the impact of PB. This is followed in Chapter 4 by a detailed examination of PB institutions in terms of processes of mediation and chains of sovereignty. In Chapter 5 we provide an analysis of the impact of PB reforms on the practices of civil society itself.

2 THE EMERGENCE OF LOCAL DEMOCRACY IN BRAZIL

The literature on democratization has generally focused on national-level processes and institutions. Yet as democratic theorists have long argued, democracy is first and foremost a local affair. It is not only in local arenas that citizens are most likely to encounter the state, but it is in local arenas that citizens are most likely to exercise their democratic rights. Brazil looms as a particularly interesting case for understanding these dynamics because over the past two decades it has arguably undergone more profound institutional reforms in the nature of local government than any other developing world democracy. In the span of a single generation Brazil has evolved from having some of the most authoritarian and exclusionary forms of local governance to some of the most resourced, proactive, inclusive, and democratic local governments in the developing world. This chapter traces this transformation, focusing on the conditions that made possible the experiments in local democracy that are the focus of our later chapters.

This book focuses on the transformation of local practices of democratic governance in Brazil. The decentralization of government in Brazil, codified in the 1988 Constitution, opened up institutional spaces for local actors to carry out innovative reforms. As we discuss below, oppositional political actors turned their attention to local arenas beginning in the late 1970s, but the combination of increased political autonomy, greater discretion with regard to the allocation of resources, and a growing number of local actors with ties to often-interconnected social movements willing to contest elections have increased opportunities for democratic innovation. In this chapter we review Brazil's history of local authoritarianism, the impact of democratic decentralization, the social movement dynamics that brought civil society to the forefront of institutional reforms, and the range of innovations in governance that resulted from civil society engagements. We then examine the history of the rise of one of the most important of these reforms—the introduction of Participatory Budgeting (PB).

THE AUTHORITARIAN PAST

In order to describe the quality of local democratic practices in Brazil before the democratic transition, it is useful to draw on two well-developed concepts. The first—*decentralized despotism*—refers to the almost absolute fusion of economic, coercive, and legal power that traditional oligarchs in Brazil enjoyed for much of the nineteenth and twentieth centuries.[1] The second—*social authoritarianism*—coined by the sociologist Evelina Dagnino, refers to what she has defined as

> a cultural matrix that structures the unequal and hierarchical organization of social relations in the public and private realms. Based on differences of class, race, and gender that constitute the principal basis of a social classification that has historically impregnated Brazilian culture, establishing different categories of persons hierarchically disposed to their respective "places" in society, this matrix reproduces the inequality of social relations at all levels, and subjugating social practices and structuring an authoritarian culture. (Dagnino 2005a, 95)

This combination of concentrated power and hierarchical social relations has long been the underlying source of Brazil's acute social inequalities. In many respects, the idea of rights-bearing citizens—constitutive of civil society—has historically been extremely weak. An overview of Brazilian history reveals instead the preeminence of a recurring set of ideas about *graduated* rights and entitlements with roots in the colonial and slaveholding legacies and manifested in the modern period through Brazilian notions of corporatism. Brazilians inherited a precapitalist Iberian tradition of law and government from the Portuguese, and Brazilian political culture was also deeply marked by a lengthy period of slavery, an incomplete transition to a liberal republic in 1889, and the pervasive influence of a landed oligarchy well into the twentieth century (Sales 1994). In the modern era, these tendencies were reinforced under the long dictatorship of Getúlio Vargas, "father of the poor" (1930–45) and by the period of military dictatorship (1964–84). Following Baiocchi (2005), we refer to this particular logic of rights and entitlements, institutionalized during these two periods, as the "corporate code" which stands in contrast to the "code of liberty" that Alexander and Smith (1993) have used to describe the United States.

As has been widely described by scholars, Brazil's political culture has historically valued authoritarian relationships of dependence, tutelage, and clientelism, personified in the figure of the kind slave master, the paternalistic oligarch, and the fatherly dictator. This is a political culture organized around a holistic and hierarchical vision of society that internalizes conflicts, privileges personal relations and the private, and does not readily recognize free-born citizens (J. Carvalho 1987; Santos 1979; Matta 1979, 1991). There is a clear link between oligarchical power and social authoritarianism. As Sales (1994) has shown, political culture in Brazil has always been marked by the concession of privileges from the powerful to the powerless. In both the colonial and postcolonial periods the association of authority with landed power undergirded the idea that rights were granted as privileges and that obedience existed as the complement to the favor. Rather than the rights of individual citizens, it was ties to persons of importance and the performance of a "useful purpose" in society that formed the building blocks of this vision of society. Thus the asymmetries of power and personalized dependencies that are the hallmark of traditional clientelism were deeply encoded in Brazil's social structure and culture.

These social and cultural practices have proven to be very durable, surviving repeated political transitions. The architects of the First Republic (1889–1929) founded the republic with the intention of breaking with the recent slaveholding, monarchic past. The new regime was organized around a vision of a hierarchical collective, creating a republic that was "little touched by the libertarian aspects of liberalism" (J. Carvalho 1987, 161–62). Citizenship, the great promise of the First Republic, never translated into the expansion of civil, social, or political rights. Political citizenship was denied to those who were illiterate, poor, or members of certain religious orders. At the same time, the republic stopped providing certain social entitlements, such as free primary education and forms of public assistance (Santos 1979).

It was during the corporatist Vargas dictatorship (1930–45) that the modern version of Brazil's political culture crystallized. Political and social rights were distributed on a graduated basis tied to a hierarchy of professions. Those who did not belong to state-sanctioned (regulated) professions became a type of precitizen, and the rights of the citizen became the rights of the profession. Citizenship was contingent on recognition and association with the *sindicatos* (unions) and granted in exchange for political loyalty (Gomes 1991). Santos has famously described this as "regulated citizenship," which is defined not by "a code of political values, but in a system of social stratification" (1979, 94).

IMAGINING LOCAL DEMOCRACY

It is against the backdrop of Brazil's regulated citizenship—a system deeply inscribed in both cultural and social practices and governance institutions—that the political transformation that accompanied the transition to democracy must be evaluated. The social movements that fueled the push for democracy of the 1980s quite explicitly crystallized around claims for full citizenship, developing a vibrant and broad-based discourse that was framed not only in the language of social justice but also along liberal rights-based claims against the rights violations of the dictatorship (Dagnino 1998). The demands for the "right to have rights" brought together unions, urban neighborhood associations, the Base Communities of the Catholic Church, the student movement, and a range of issue movements including health, housing, and cost of living. Broadly, these new actors in civil society defended visions of democratic proceduralism, transparency, autonomy from the state, and civil rights (Telles 1987). Even if some of the early literature on Brazil's transition to democracy has focused on the role of elites in managing the transition (O'Donnell, Schmitter, and Whitehead 1986), there is now a wide consensus that the mobilization of civil society played a critical role not only in forcing the authoritarian regime's *abertura*, or political opening, but also in shaping the actual terms of the transition, as has been well described in the literature.[2]

What has sometimes received less attention in the literature is the way in which these movements mobilized locally and focused their attention on claims-making at the local level while connecting to national networks. Most notably, neighborhood associations, which had been an important vehicle of corporatist control, became sites for local contestation and innovation. The case of the Movimento de Associações de Bairro (MAB), or the Movement of Neighborhood Associations, in the Baixada Fluminense in Rio de Janeiro, is illustrative. Started with support from the Catholic Church in 1976, the MAB was an experiment in establishing a permanent forum for the discussion of urban needs, which brought together representatives of several neighborhood associations in the district. At MAB meetings members sought ways to organize these various associations into a common bloc that could make demands on city and state government (Jacobi 1987). In 1979, the MAB was active in defending residents against evictions, and in 1981 it organized a march to city hall to deliver an open letter to the mayor about the poor quality of public services. The MAB continued to organize throughout the 1980s and 1990s, creating a series of Community Health Councils, a "space of social control and popular demand-making."

By the mid-1980s there were thousands of similarly active neighborhood associations throughout the country. Many were new; others were reimagined or reinvented "Friends of the Neighborhood" associations that had previously held close ties to politicians, but which now were acting in novel ways. They represented the work of community organizers in poorer communities and were a direct response to the perceived political opening as the dictatorship was coming to an end. In most communities these associations were tied to the search for "collective solutions to the lack of education, health facilities, sewage control, and transport" (Alves 1985, 78). These neighborhood associations comprised a mix of practices: contestatory claims-making, collective self-improvement and mutual assistance, and consciousness-raising.

As noted earlier, these movements eventually scaled-up and became central actors in the democracy movement. But looking beyond the political changes they helped forge in the national arena, what bears emphasis is the role they played in cultivating a new politics of citizenship and in promoting, through prefigurative actions and direct interventions, new institutions of participation. In demanding the recognition of new subjects, these movements proposed new forms of social relationships mediated by the state, as well as new relationships between civil society and the state, while emphasizing *autonomy* from manipulative government agencies and politicians (Viola and Mainwaring 1987, 154).

What should also be emphasized regarding these movements is that the state figured *centrally* in their political discourse. The MAB and organizations like it were preoccupied with redistributive issues and were very involved in the project of imagining *another* state at the same time as imagining *another* society and set of relationships. In the Brazilian case, these movements were especially concerned with reforming the local state, and Participatory Budgeting would eventually emerge as the prototype reform strategy.

The pragmatism and basic concern with governance issues that motivated urban social movements is underscored by the short-lived and small-scale experiments in participatory governance of the late 1970s and early 1980s that would serve as models for later reforms. The best known was the experience of Lages (population 180,000) in the southern state of Santa Catarina, that in 1977 elected a mayor whose campaign slogan was "The Power of the People." This mayor created a series of spaces for the population to participate in and even decide on the affairs of town governance, with the purpose of creating "participatory democracy, the utilization of local economic resources, and the search of alternatives to the use of petrol products." While much of the participation revolved around an extensive mutual-assistance and rotating credit program, this experience eventually developed into a participatory structure of intervention in the municipal budget, with representatives of different communities voting on budget priorities for the year. According to Souza, Lages was especially attractive to medium-sized administrations because of the city's focus on small initiatives that were "cooperatively implemented by the government and the community," despite modest outcomes (Souza 2001, 162). As the Lages administration gained recognition, it received scores of "professors, politicians, liberal professionals, and students" interested in learning about, and later promoting, the city's participatory model.[3] Some of the observers of the experience noted its progressive potential, calling it a "small socialist republic" in the middle of an authoritarian country,[4] and the book about the experience, *The Power of the People: Participatory Democracy in Lages* was widely circulated among urban activists and reformers of the time. Similar cases have been noted in Piracicaba (São Paulo state) and in Boa Esperança (Espírito Santo) (Souza 2001, 162).

In sum, we want to underscore that the urban social movements of the period leading up to the democratic transition were very much invested in advancing not only democracy, but participatory democracy, and did so by directly engaging with the local state. Evelina Dagnino (1994) refers to this as "the new citizenship" that dominated Brazilian social movements in the 1980s and 1990s. Its premise was "the right to have rights," and it lauded the invention of "new rights that emerge from specific struggles and concrete practices" (76). Social movement's new propositional practices were grounded in the ideologies of movements of the 1970s and 1980s, and while demanding dialogue with the state, they simultaneously challenged the limits of representative democracy by calling for participatory reforms and expanded versions of traditional rights.

THE TRANSITION TO DEMOCRACY

In 1985, as part of the military government's strategy of gradual opening, and in response to pressure from the opposition, for the first time since 1966 (when elections were suspended in state capitals and municipalities of interest) full municipal elections were held. In 1988 a new, democratic constitution was approved, and in 1989 direct elections were held for the presidency.

The literature on the transition to democracy in Brazil points to a severe tension between two different trends: on the one hand, an unresponsive and corrupt political system dominated by patronage-based politicians determined to entrench themselves, especially at local levels; on the other hand, an emergent civil society driven by social movements that beginning in the mid-1980s developed new practices around citizenship and propositional stances vis-à-vis public policies. The ills of Brazilian democracy are by now well known. The continuation of many policies of the authoritarian period and the disjuncture between formal democracy and actual, lived democracy for the majority of its citizens (O'Donnell 1988; Pinheiro 1991) has contributed to Brazil's "social apartheid" (Weffort 1984). The political system is marked by countless institutional distortions of effective representation, ranging from the highest degree of mal-apportionment of any democracy in the world (Samuels and Snyder 2001), a poorly institutionalized party system marked by personalism and pervasive clientelism (Mainwaring 1999; Ames 2001), to the multiplication of veto points exploited by elites to block reforms (Weyland 1996; Stepan 2000).

These descriptions of the institutional characteristics of Brazilian democracy tend to understate and even obscure the dramatic transformations in democratic practices, including changes in the social and cultural structure of citizenship that occurred in the 1980s and 1990s. By focusing on the national picture, they also tend to underplay the importance of local institutional change. The return to democracy marked the return of competitive elections, but it also marked the institutionalization of full citizenship and the passage of a constitution that enshrined many of the participatory demands of a mobilized civil society. In institutional terms, one of the most notable, and in comparative terms unique, aspects of the constitution was the degree to which it sought to decentralize and empower local democratic government.

Decentralization

A critical dimension of Brazil's transition to democracy was decentralization, which was codified in the 1988 postdictatorship constitution. In order to understand how the decentralization reforms were conceived and ultimately how they unfolded it is important to first understand that decentralization reforms were an integral part of the democratization process. As such, the reforms were specifically shaped by three colliding forces. First, resurgent regional elites that had negotiated with the outgoing military dictatorship remained key players during the crafting of the constitution and worked to ensure that it would protect their interests. Second, the transition also provided a political space for social movements that pressured legislators for constitutional provisions that would enhance local autonomy and enshrine popular participation. Third, the reforms were crafted after the debt crisis of the 1980s. International pressure to comply with fiscal austerity measures and to modernize the state apparatus created internal pressure to transfer government responsibilities in areas such as education, social services, and health to municipal government (Alvarez 1993; Nickson 1995). The decentralization reforms were conceived and implemented in ways that reflected these contradictory pressures.

The role of regional elites deserves some commentary since it largely explains why state-society relations are extremely heterogeneous in Brazil. Souza, among others, has argued that Brazil's decentralization in the postdictatorship period should be understood as part of a continuum of "center-state-local power relationships" (2001, 25). Since the founding of the Brazilian republic in 1889, municipalities and states have traditionally been highly autonomous and have served as strongholds of a variety of regional elites with specific interests. The national state has sought to "rein in" states at various points including during the Vargas dictatorship (1930–37) and the military regime (1964–84) by recentralizing government functions. Since the mid-1970s, however, Brazil has moved steadily toward decentralization, such as the incremental increase of transfers to states. Scholars have argued that the move toward decentralization was a result of the national state's search for political legitimacy among regional elites represented by politicians in the two legal parties (Kugelmas and Sola 1999). The first elections for governors in 1982 (before the full transition to democracy) brought a number of opposition governors to power as well as a number of governors tied to regional elites. Since then the dictatorship sought to appease these local powerbrokers who were seen as the key to political legitimacy (Abrucio 1998). Regional elites played a crucial role in assuring a weakened center in the decentralization reforms, which has curtailed the ability of the national administration to implement reforms evenly throughout the country.

The tenacity of local elites notwithstanding, the 1988 Constitution marked a dramatic change in Brazil's political opportunity structure. In essence, the constitution secured four broad transformations in the balance of central and local state power. The first three correspond to the basic institutional attributes of *democratic decentralization* (Manor 1999). The fourth was explicitly designed to promote local *participatory* democracy. First, local governments were given significantly more political autonomy from their district-level and national overseers. In a rare constitutional arrangement, municipalities were designated as "state-members" of the national federation on equal footing with states. They were free to develop "organic laws"—in essence, municipal constitutions that were made more responsive to local needs. A number of cities in Brazil including Recife and Porto Alegre organized mass public debates on the new municipal constitutions. Cities were also allowed greater discretion with regard to land legislation, particularly through "social use" and "social interest" laws that guaranteed broad rights to municipal government to regulate the use of empty plots of land, or to develop municipal policies to deal with squatters' settlements. Local autonomy in deciding land-rights questions would have important implications for the problem of urban poverty. The state-member status of municipalities would also mean that there would be ambiguities in the coordination of the decentralizing efforts because it would not be legally possible for states or the federation to "force" municipalities to carry out services.

Second, local and state governments were given greater fiscal autonomy from the union, as the constitution codified a number of mechanisms of transfer of resources toward subnational government. Traditionally, the principal source of funding for local government came from federal revenue-sharing arrangements. The 1988 Constitution shifted a significant number of resources toward states and municipalities, while increasing the number of taxes each could raise, such as vehicle, sales, and services taxes for municipalities. It also allowed for greater nondiscretionary transfers from the state and federal government to the local government. Five taxes were transferred to states, including ICMS (value-added tax); states were free to set their own rates and were given discretion on its use, save for a provision that 25 percent would be transferred to municipalities in the state. The two funds of nondiscretionary transfers to states and cities, the "participation funds" (FPM and FPE) were augmented by increasing the proportion of the income tax (IR) and industrial products tax (IPI) transferred to it; these funds would be distributed according to states and municipalities on a formula based on per-capita income and size.[5]

Third, local governments were given the responsibility (or coresponsibility) for a range of social services that were "municipalized" or restructured in ways that emphasized local provision. For example the 1988 Constitution formally recognized that cities would be responsible for health services, along with transportation and primary education. As discussed below, these devolutionary policies have led to mixed outcomes because of ambiguities regarding which level of government would be responsible and accountable for certain provision.

Fourth, local governments became *free to institutionalize channels of direct popular participation in public affairs.* The 1988 Constitution established legal provisos for participatory mechanisms calling for the input of popular councils in the development of social programs. Most notably, Article 29 of the constitution calls for "the cooperation of representative associations in municipal planning" (Brazil 1988). These general provisions fell short of actually instituting participation. In the case of health, for example, the constitution mandates the creation of health councils, but it was necessary for an additional law (Law 8142 of December 1990) to create the health councils. In urban planning, the City Statute (Law 10257 of July 2001) regulated the creation of councils.

Uneven Implementation of Decentralization

Two broad sets of factors contributed to the highly uneven implementation of decentralization. The economic context was one of runaway inflation and increasingly constrained public investments. Worries about the "runaway" spending of states (an increase in real terms of 33 percent between 1986 and 1995 while states' GDP only increased by 16 percent in the same period), and several subsequent federal bailouts triggered a number of moves designed to foster fiscal recentralization (Kugelmas and Sola 1999). The stabilization plan for the real implemented by Fernando Henrique Cardoso in 1994 included several recentralizing measures as well as attempts to curb the spending of states. This included curbing the amounts of tax transfers to states and the creation of a new tax on transfers. A fiscal responsibility law (the Lei de Responsabilidade Fiscal, the LRF) limited public sector spending, and another 1996 law (known as the "Kandir Law") curbed the amount spent by states and municipalities on personnel (Souza 2001). In this context of increasing fiscal austerity, local governments enjoyed limited administrative and financial resources to fulfill their new mandates, a squeeze that was especially severe for municipalities with limited independent financial resources.

Politics also contributed to uneven implementation. A crucial factor in the crafting of the new constitution was the fact that parliamentarians involved in the Constitutional Assembly reflected disparate regional interests, and there was a general consensus among them to weaken central authority (Montero 2001, 1998; Samuels and Abrucio 2000). This was reflected in some of the institutionally vague arrangements of the reforms. The constitution does not assign responsibility for provisions, but rather assigns "directives." Articles 198 and 204, for instance, assign directives for health and social assistance to municipalities, without specifying the responsible entity. There are, in fact, thirty such areas of "concurrent responsibilities" in Brazil (Araujo 1997; Medeiros 1994).

There is a wide-ranging discussion on the impacts of decentralization in Brazil. Institutionalists have tended to paint a decidedly mixed picture. Weyland, who has influentially argued that Brazil's political institutions effectively stymie equity-enhancing reform (1996), describes the impact of decentralization as having "mixed but largely disappointing results in terms of service delivery, popular participation, strengthened local elites, and reform initiatives" (Weyland 1999, 1006). Montero goes so far as to argue that the reforms have "tended to revitalize the power of traditional, patrimonial elites" (Montero 1997). If we set aside for a moment the difficulty of evaluating the quality of decentralization across five thousand-plus discrete entities that vary dramatically in their institutional, socioeconomic, and political profile, some general observations about the increased significance of municipal government can be made.

First, in fiscal terms, the significance of local government has increased measurably. By the year 2000, municípios and states accounted for more than half of public expenditures and were the dominant providers of health, education, and infrastructure. Municípios accounted for 31 percent of education expenditures, 30 percent of health and sanitation, and 69 percent of housing and urbanism (IBGE 2002) in 2007; their overall share of social spending increased from 11 percent in 1987 to 19 percent in 1996 (Souza 1996). The resource base of municipalities and states also increased in real terms by 161.5 percent between 1989 and 1995. Other analysts point out that these resource gains have not kept pace with the higher level of service provisioning that municipalities are responsible for, particularly in small municípios (Araujo 1997; Arretche 2000; Pont 2001; Souza 1996). Debates notwithstanding, local government has become an increasingly important arena for development and social provisioning.

Second, the evidence on the devolution of services is mixed, but it clearly coincides with an overall improvement in the quality of service provisioning. Clearly, given shortfalls in funding, the quality of local services has been plagued by coordination problems and highly uneven local capacity. Jurisdictional and fiscal demarcation between federal, state, and local levels is still marked by ambiguities, overlaps, and significant gaps. And the variation in the basic capacities of local government to plan, implement, and administer social services is as varied as the political, socioeconomic, and institutional landscape of Brazil. Despite these problems, most of the literature tends to point toward modest overall improvements and in particular to significant cases of local innovation.[6] Most notably, there has been a significant increase in the relative provision of education by municipalities, supplementing the decision-making autonomy given by the constitution with an increase in the capacity to carry out those decisions. Between 1996 and 1999, the number of children in municipal schools nationally increased by more than six million, bringing the proportion of all students in municipal schools to 40 percent from 31.8 percent (Afonso and Melo 2000). While it is difficult to demonstrate a direct causal link, it is notable that during this period of increasing decentralization of social services to municipalities overall levels of social development increased significantly. Adult literacy increased from 68.84 to 78.23 percent from 1991 to 2001, and infant mortality rates fell from 47.68 to 39.96 per thousand during the same period.[7] What is most striking and most telling about decentralization is that it has not been accompanied by increased regional disparities and indeed may have contributed to a narrowing of the social development gap. In terms of rates of school attendance, the poorest regions have all but caught up with the richer ones. In terms of health, between 1990 and 1998 infant mortality rates have decreased by more than 7 percentage points with the biggest drops coming in the North and Northeast.

Decentralization is a multifaceted process of instituting and strengthening the capacity of local government. During the 1990s there was little doubt that local government in Brazil was significantly strengthened, albeit very unevenly. Municipalities received more resources and were granted increased authority to govern over a wide range of areas. Implementation has been plagued by coordination problems, and the resource base often lagged behind the new mandates. But there is little doubt that the functional and authoritative surface area of local state government increased. This, in turn, raised the stakes for defining and building *democratic* local governance.

LOCAL DEMOCRATIC INNOVATION

This book focuses on the introduction of various forms of Participatory Budgeting in 104 municípios from 1997–2000, but it is important to emphasize that PB represents just one type of reform in urban governance during this period. The most significant reforms arguably came within the framework of the various councils that were mandated by the constitution. All Brazilian municípios are mandated to form various sectoral councils with representation of sectoral interests, government, and civil society in health, social services, and planning. These councils have been granted significant powers in shaping the allocation of federal monies, most notably the right to veto the municípios sectoral budget.

Participatory Councils

In terms of social involvement, influence, and breadth, the council process has, in fact, a greater reach than PB. Councils are not new, and some, such as the National Councils of Health and Education, date back to 1937, the middle of the Vargas years (1930–45). But if these traditional councils were dominated by corporatist interests and limited to a consultative role, the council structures born in the 1980s were much more inclusionary and specifically designed to be deliberative. In 1986, the National Council of Health Reform was created, and it changed both the council's composition (now, half of the participants were to be users of the health system) and its mandate (from consultative to deliberative and binding). This process was influential in shaping the text of the constitution around participation and became the model for other councils created in the 1990s.

During the Cardoso presidency (1995–2002), there were several efforts to promote additional participatory fora as a means to improve government programs and actions through what Brazilians call "social control." These added to the pressure of social and political actors for the introduction of participatory fora. Several federal programs came to define participatory fora as a prerequisite to accessing resources. One of the most important was the creation in 1996 of the National Program for the Strengthening of Family Agriculture that stimulated the creation of thousands of Councils on Rural Development (Schneider, Silva, and Morruzzi 2005). By the late 1990s most municípios in Brazil had activated legal provisions in the constitution to form municipal councils on health and education. This participatory thrust under the Lula administrations (2003–2010), with the introduction of Councils of Social Control of the Bolsa Familia Program are a requisite for municípios to be recipients of Bolsa Familia, Brazil's vast and highly successful conditional cash-transfer program.

Municipal Initiatives

Since the new constitution, reforms have also consisted of innovative programs at the municipal level in which some form of civil society participation was institutionalized. While these were often not radical programs that granted substantial decision-making powers to local groups, "decentralization and participation" became part of the municipal government plans of many capital cities in the immediate posttransition period (Nickson 1995). The room to experiment with governance reforms that came with decentralization and the diffuse sense that "participation" was useful, as well as pressure by local civil societies, led to dozens of participatory experiments in municípios in Brazil by the mid-1990s in the areas of education, health, the municipal budget, municipal planning, and environmental regulation (Campbell 1997; Kowarick and Singer 1994).

The classic challenge of social movements is that it is difficult to scale-up and institutionalize their demands. The key in the Brazilian context has been the formation of a social movement party—the Partido dos Trabalhadores (PT)—that was in effect able to serve as the focal point and to channel social movement demands. It emerged as the most distinct and consequential new political force of the time. With its deep ties to movements, the PT self-consciously projected itself as a vehicle for translating civil society demands into party platforms, with a specific commitment to the democratizing of state institutions (Keck 1992; Meneguello 1989). While state-level contests favored political machines and established powerful families, the first fully free municipal elections of 1985 opened space to many outsiders. The PT, representing the paradigmatic case of the "social turn," of the Left in Latin America increasingly took advantage of these spaces (Fox 1994). After winning a *prefeitura* in the limited 1982 elections, then two in 1985, and then thirty-six in the 1988 contests (including São Paulo and Porto Alegre), it won fifty in 1992 and a hundred and four in 1996. It has continued to grow dramatically since then, continuing to win municipal contests, some state elections, and finally the presidency in 2002.

The early experiences of the PT in power were not successes, but the commitment to participation was sustained because of demands of social movements, as well as an enduring leftist vision of popular power that animated cohort after cohort of elected officials. But this participatory thrust was very much tangled up in more mundane politics and very visible failures, like the practical collapse of the marquee administration of Luiza Erundina in São Paulo a few weeks before the 1992 election.

Acrimony within administrations, often the pitting the PT against its own social base—social movements and unions—were also endemic in early PT administrations. The PT's vision for participation was deeply ambiguous: Was participation an end in itself, or was it a means to broader social change? Was it to privilege organized bases of support, or was it to reach out to the rest of society? But a central problem for elected officials was how to make participation compatible with governance and reelection. In many cases, the party-administration-movement combinations that were meant to congeal in the popular councils proved unworkable and often led to open conflicts. In these cases, councils tended to privilege organized movements, which often came at the expense of the administration's legitimacy with the broader electorate. Upon reflection, many administrators came to reject the idea that PT governments should be instruments of mobilization. Eventually, new, more pragmatic, views of participation would become dominant as a result of these early trials.

The Emergence and Travel of a Tool-Kit

A centerpiece of a new, pragmatic view of participation that emerged within the PT by the mid-1990s was Participatory Budgeting, and a principal conduit for diffusing these ideas throughout the country was the National Forum of Popular Participation, or the FNPP.

By the end of the 1980s, there already was a certain amount of accumulated experience about participatory reforms, but little systematic "theorizing." While the PT itself had created a national department within the party dedicated to this, it was a national forum organized by NGOs in 1990 that became the central conduit for lessons about participation. In 1988 the Instituto Camajar in São Paulo carried out a seminar for newly elected mayors of the PT about popular participation, and the discussion group that emerged out of the institute eventually became the FNPP, the National Forum on Popular Participation in Democratic and Popular Administrations. The FNPP brought together NGOs, social movement organizations, PT administrators, and academics to debate popular participation. Early on in the FNPP, there was a debate between those who advocated "institutional councils" such as health councils and those who defended the Participatory Budget, which was then being tried in Porto Alegre. Partially informed by the experiences of the next few years, when several PT administrations failed, some spectacularly, the Forum settled on PB as a preferred prescription, and it became involved in tracking and disseminating PB practices.

It was Porto Alegre's model of Participatory Budgeting, which emerged out of a combination of experimentation, responses to external pressures, and a search for legitimacy in the absence of a reliable social movement base, that became the model administration and the central point of reference for other PB experiments. In its first fifteen years, PB evolved from what was an open-ended experiment into a sophisticated process of grass-roots demand-making channeled through sixteen local district fora and five thematic structures, and resulting in annual budgets comprised of thousands of projects.

The success of PB in Porto Alegre is undeniable. First, extensive research confirms that as an innovation in governance and municipal decision-making PB has improved the quality and the redistributive impact of service delivery and public infrastructure.[8] Second, the ability of the administration to consistently draw thousands of participants and to deliver results in a timely and transparent manner was rewarded with electoral support. In turn, the PT's electoral dominance for sixteen years kept local opposition at bay and allowed the administration to carry out a number of ambitious reforms, such as introducing land-use taxes targeted at wealthier citizens that have funded many of PB's projects. The political efficacy of PB in Porto Alegre stands in sharp contrast to many other PT administrations that self-destructed under political conflicts in the late 1980s and early 1990s.

A key early institutional design of the "Porto Alegre Model" was what administrators describe as the "open format" for meetings, which emerged out of disappointments with civil society-mediated fora early on. The original broad concern with increasing popular participation in government and with the "inversion of priorities" (reversing the traditional pattern of spending public monies in Brazilian cities that privileged wealthier areas) led to initial attempts to dialogue with organized civil society, the "natural allies" of a PT administration. This format of *civil society representation* was dominant in many other PT administrations and is the implicit formula of "council democracy" that guided other PT administrations. Civil society-mediated participation, however, was prone to political difficulties and crises of legitimacy, when PT administrators were caught between charges of "clientelism of the left" (as seen by local media) when they met the demands of civil society, and "class treason" (as seen by their allies) when they did not. Open participation in the local fora that decided on the budget became a way for the administration to generate legitimacy for its redistributive platforms among the broader voting public as well as with allies. Two other important elements of the "Porto Alegre Model" are "self-regulation"— that is, that participants themselves decide on the rules of the process, and "self-determination," that its participants, and not administrators, decide on how the entirety of the capital budget (new investment) is spent.

The net result in Porto Alegre was a transparent participatory system with broad participation from among the city's poorer citizens that was widely perceived as legitimate and citizen-run, and that was successful at managing conflicts over competing demands. The benefits of Participatory Budgeting in this version are a mix of good governance (transparency, increased resources, the reduction of clientelism), social justice (redistribution of resources), and civic goals (legitimacy, dialogue, cooperation, and solidarity). All of these attributes are, of course, attractive to both local state officials and politicians seeking an advantage in Brazil's highly competitive party system (Wampler 2007a). Scholarly research has also helped make the case for PB. The case-study literature is particularly rich and has linked PB to redistributive outcomes (Calderón et al. 2002; Lebauspin 2000; Pont 2001; Pontual 1997; Pozzobon 1998), increased governmental efficiency (Marquetti 2002), increased civic activity, and a transformed political culture (Baiocchi 2003b).

PB became widely recognized as central to the "PT formula" of combining redistribution with broad-based participation, and by the mid-1990s, the PT had become more adept at negotiating the political difficulties in implementing the process. The "PT way of governing" was one that combined social justice goals with transparency, broad participation, and effective governance, and it was on this basis that the PT expanded its electoral influence in municipal governments throughout the country in the late 1990s. Participation, far from being an instrument of destabilizing the bourgeois political system as had been imagined by some in the mid-1980s, became instead central to a strategy of good governance. Twelve cities introduced PB between 1989–92. Thirty-six did so between 1993–96, at least 104 adopted PB between 1997–2000 (according to surveys done by the FNPP),[9] and the number jumping to 150 between 2001–2004. The pattern of adoption of PB, first in São Paulo state, then in the South, and more recently in some places in the Northeast follows the evolution of the PT—by far the most, and perhaps the only programmatic party in Brazil—which gained a following outside of its home state of São Paulo during the same period (Singer 2001).

But as the visibility and success of PB has increased, other political parties have begun to adopt the platform. While early on the vast majority of PB experiments were conducted by the PT by 1997–2000 half of experiments were carried out by other political parties, though still mostly by left-of-center parties.[10] The presence and electoral victory of a left-of-center party has not been enough. Internal ruling party fights and difficult relationships with municipal unions have sometimes been disabling to administrations attempting to implement PB. In the city of Betim, Minas Gerais, for example, where the administration carried out PB from 1997–2000, its inability to negotiate with its own bases of support cost it considerable legitimacy and eventually rendered the administration unviable. The story the PT in São Paulo from 1989–92, is another example of administrators' inability to negotiate internal pressure within the PT and eventually being completely immobilized (Couto 1995).

BOOTSTRAPPING LOCAL DEMOCRACY

Participatory Budgeting diffused rapidly for a variety of reasons. In addition to the FNPP, other NGOs like IBASE were instrumental in monitoring and promoting Participatory Budgeting to progressive administrators. Fundação Getúlio Vargas, Brazil's elite public policy institute, as well as NGOs like Pólis in São Paulo, were also proactive in documenting and publicizing municipal best practices, including PB programs. If PB had distinct political origins in urban social movements, by the 1990s it had developed a strong support base in policy circles and precisely at a time of intense creativity and experimentation in municipal governance reform. It was therefore only a matter of time before local participatory experiments that worked came to be known as "cities that work," or "islands of efficiency" (Figueiredo Júnior and Lamounier 1997). Participatory Budgeting itself was promoted as having a number of potentially beneficial impacts on city government. A "How To" guide from FNPP proposes that Participatory Budgeting

> can be an efficient instrument for important political, economic, and social achievements: greater transparency in the elaboration and execution of the budget; more social control of the budget and of public finances; the creation of a new standard for distribution of resources that would permit meeting the needs of the poorer population; changes in the system of *arrecadação* that permit the increase of municipal resources; fighting clientelism and corruption; the increase of legitimacy of municipal administration; the sharing of power between authorities and society; the strengthening of cooperation and solidarity; the affirmation of the culture of dialogue and of the mutual commitment between government and population; mobilization of organized and unorganized social sectors; education for citizenship; and the broadening of the public sphere.[11]

Our own earlier research also finds that the introduction on PB in Brazil in 1997–2000 was positively associated with the redistributive and development outcomes. Based on a statistical analysis that compared PB municipalities with all other municipalities, and controlling for a range of socioeconomic, fiscal, regional, and other variables, we found that adoption of PB was positively associated with increased municipal spending in health, with improved fiscal standing of municipalities, improvement of service provision in some areas like access to drinking water, and improvement in some human development outcomes such as poverty and enrollment rates (Baiocchi et al. 2006). However, we note the difficulty in isolating the effect of local governance, let alone PB, in Brazil's complex federalist structure, in which many different levels of government often overlap.

Even if there are strong empirical grounds to believe that the adoption of PB does lead to more inclusionary and more effective forms of local governance, we are still hardly in a position to answer some of the larger questions concerning the relationship between such reforms and democratization that we posed in the introduction. The problem here is that both parts of our relationship are, in fact, moving targets. On the one hand, what is actually meant by PB has varied dramatically. The basic structure adopted by municipalities generally included a yearly cycle with district-level meetings, concurrent meetings of a main budget council, and somewhat less commonly, municipal thematic meetings. According to Teixeira (2002), many experiments began as exact copies of the Porto Alegre experiment, down to the names of the municipal departments responsible for the process, only to be modified after a year or two. There has, quite predictably, been enormous variation in the institutional design of PB across cities. In Santo André, São Paulo, at the Council of the Budget, municipal department heads have the same number of votes as councilors (Carvalho and Felgueiras 2000). In Belo Horizonte, only 50 percent of capital expenditures are turned over to PB, and in Recife, district-level priorities are chosen at the same time as delegates (Azevedo 1997; Boschi 1999; Somarriba and Dulci 1997). The findings from our eight cases (see Chapter 3) highlight just how much local initiative goes into defining how much decision-making is afforded participants and how this decision-making takes place. We also show that while PB did result in measurable improvements in the quality and inclusiveness of governance, it did so to quite varying degrees.

On the other hand, the specific contexts in which PB has been embedded and its effects on civil society are as varied as local conditions in Brazil are heterogeneous. As we have already seen, the adoption of PB more or less tracks the evolution of the PT. It is also highly correlated with socioeconomic development. Taking the set of cities with self-designated PB experiments as a starting point, it is apparent that cities with more than five hundred thousand inhabitants in the South and Southeast were overrepresented, and smaller municipalities away from the more developed regions have seldom had such reforms. Participatory Budgeting has evolved geographically, moving away from its original home in the state of São Paulo, where the majority of experiments took place in the 1989–92 tenure, to the South, where a number of experiments went underway in the 1993–96 period, to a move to the North and Northeast where experiments took place in a significant way in the 1997–2000 period. Cities such as Porto Alegre and Sao Paulo have densely organized civil societies, with long histories of social movement mobilization; cities in the Northeast often have weak civil societies, with little or no social movement mobilization. It is against this kaleidoscopic background that local alliances of civil society, the PT, and administrators have experimented with Participatory Budgeting reforms.

In the next three chapters, we confront these two challenges to making generalizations about the impact and effects of PB. Drawing on the framework developed in Chapter 1, we present the design of our natural experiment and our paired case studies, before turning to an analysis of governance in PB cities (Chapter 4), and the impact of PB on civil society (Chapter 5).

3 ASSESSING THE IMPACT
OF PARTICIPATORY BUDGETING

THREE LOGICS OF INQUIRY

Participatory Budgeting stands out not only as one of the most important experiments in participatory democracy in recent times, but also represents a clear and distinct effort to institutionally transform state-civil society relations. In this chapter we introduce our eight case studies and review and assess the impact of PB. As we explain in detail, the paired-city design of our research project allows us to control for a wide range of factors and to isolate the impact of PB. In the paired analysis, we find that the four cities that adopted PB experienced significant changes in their budgeting processes that marked a rupture with past practices, whereas in our control group—that is, the four cities that did not adopt PB—it was more or less business as usual. In this chapter we report these findings in detail. In the next two chapters we focus exclusively on our PB cities, first examining the variation in institutional design across our four cases and then assessing the impact that PB had on the composition and activities of civil society.

Assessing and explaining the impact of any institutional reform poses unique challenges and even more so when the reforms have the stated ambition of changing the very nature of politics. PB in Brazil has received significant academic attention. But developing a comprehensive understanding of the impact of PB, and more generally when and how state-civil society relations can be transformed, has proven elusive. In designing our study, we identified two specific problems. The first was the inherently limited generalizability of the single case studies that have dominated the literature.[1] The challenge here was both to get beyond single case studies and also to address the problem of selecting on the dependent variable, that is, only focusing on successful cases. Looking at the case literature, an obvious problem is that the cities where PB was, in fact, introduced may be unusual, which raises questions about whether any inferences that are drawn regarding the "empowering" effects of PB can be meaningfully extended to other contexts. The second challenge was recognizing that "Participatory Budgeting" is a moving target, and its "impacts" even more so. Not only is there a wide diversity of arrangements that go under the umbrella of PB, but these arrangements are themselves products of diverse contexts and interact differently with those contexts. As PB has expanded beyond Porto Alegre and the first cohort of larger Southern and Southeastern cities like São Paulo, the range of contexts in which PB has been adopted has become ever more diverse. As PB reforms have been copied in the process of diffusion throughout Brazil, they have also been transformed. Twelve cities introduced PB in 1989–92, thirty-six in 1993–96, at least one hundred and four in 1997–2000 (the period covered by our study), and at least one hundred eighty-three in 2001–2004. Within the general template that PB stands for, there is variation in how much decision-making is afforded participants and how this decision-making takes place, ranging from arrangements that empower PB delegates to directly formulate the budget to more consultative arrangements (Grazia and Ribeiro 2002, 41–56).

To address these challenges, our research design sought to control for confounding variables and to isolate the impact of PB, while at the same time preserving context-rich explanations. As such, rather than seek "representative instances" of Participatory Budgeting from which to *generalize*, we sought to understand instances of participation in their contexts so that we might *extend* our insights.[2] Anchored in the critical realist traditions of social science, our goal was to make claims about processes and mechanisms in particular contexts in a way that gives us leverage to think both about other contexts and theoretical issues. In doing so, we engaged in three distinct logics of inquiry.[3] To address the different contexts we first utilized "matched pairs"—a methodology of comparing very similar pairs of cases, where one has the intervention of interest (in this case, PB) and the other does not. This "quasi-experimentalist" logic is designed to hold constant certain key factors such as size, political environment, and region that might have a confounding effect on our outcome, in order to be able to better isolate the actual impact of PB reforms. The second logic of inquiry is contextual. We treat each of our cases individually, with real attention to context, history, and actors. As we detail below, team members conducted extensive fieldwork in each of our sites, and for each case we have developed detailed profiles and analyses. Our data as such consists of a series of case studies, and throughout the book we strive to preserve as much of that context as possible, as evidenced in our use of detailed quotes. The third logic was comparative, where we treated each of the PB cases as representative of a trajectory, attentive to configurations of actors and institutions in shaping the direction of the trajectory. Because these were comparisons within a national context, this was akin to what has been termed the "subnational comparison" method which, Snyder (2001) argues, is the closest approximation in the social sciences to a natural experiment and has the advantage of increasing the probability (especially compared to intercountry studies) of obtaining valid findings in small-N research.

Taken together, our three logics of inquiry provide a comprehensive analysis and explanation of the impact of PB as a historical process of sociopolitical reform: in the first logic, we exploit the similarity between pairs to make a causal statement; in the second, we exploit the uniqueness of each case to tell a story about process; and in the third, we exploit the differences between a subset of cases to make statements about the importance of configurations in shaping trajectories. In the next section, we describe the research we undertook and the three logics of inquiry.

The Matched-Pair Analysis

This study goes beyond the existing, case-based literature on participatory democracy by evaluating the impact of participatory reforms through a series of carefully constructed matched comparisons between PB and non-PB municípios. Our matching rule was to pair PB municípios with non-PB municípios based on similar, but not identical, electoral outcomes in the 1996 election. The pairs consist of a município where the PT came to power with a small margin of victory and subsequently implemented PB, with a município in the same region and similar size category where the PT's vote share was only somewhat lower but translated into a small margin of loss for the PT, resulting in the nonadoption of PB. As the PT is very much a party born of civil society and Brazil's social movements of the 1980s (Keck 1992), our working assumption is that two municípios in which the PT garnered similar vote shares will be similar in terms of the local tradition of political activism and the composition and strength of civil society. (As we shall see later, this assumption is born out by our findings on the preexisting state of civil society in each pair.) In matching municípios in this manner, we also tried to control for scale and geography. The size of a city impacts a range of fiscal and governance issues. Geography matters, especially in Brazil, because of highly uneven patterns of spatial development. Pairing municípios with similar PT vote shares, similar population sizes, and from the same region thus allows us, within the limits of a natural quasi-experimental design, to compare municípios with similar political, social, and economic contexts, but with large differences in institutional reform (adoption or nonadoption of PB). This, in turn, makes it possible to cleanly identify the impact of institutional reform.

The paired analysis addresses two key methodological concerns that have not been fully dealt with in the existing research. The first is the need to appropriately construct the counterfactual in implementing the evaluation so as to address concerns regarding the possible confounding effects of unobserved (to us) or hard to quantify features of the context (for example, history of social movements, and so forth), or what, in the evaluation literature, is termed selection bias. To our knowledge, there has been no attempt in the existing literature to directly compare PB and non-PB municípios. There has, in other words, been no effort to control for possible selection bias. A second concern regarding the existing research is that it does not adequately take account of possible heterogeneity in treatment effects. By this, we mean the possibility that the effects of institutional innovations such as PB might vary with the institutional setting and the political, socioeconomic, and historical context. Even when the existing research has plausibly controlled for selection bias by focusing on before-after comparisons (of a variety of outcomes) within selected PB municípios, there remain concerns about the external validity of the results obtained because of the possibility of heterogeneous treatment effects.

The choice of the PT vote-share matching rule is central to the research design and needs to be fully explained. Our working assumption is that vote shares for political parties, especially for a programmatic party such as the PT that has well-defined ideological and policy positions, are likely to reflect (and hence capture) important aspects of the underlying sociohistorical and political economic context. In other words, our maintained assumption is that two municípios in which the PT garnered similar vote shares are unlikely to differ much in terms of those aspects of the local context—for example, a tradition of political activism, the degree to which clientelistic relations are engrained in the political culture—that might otherwise confound an evaluation of PB. On the other hand, small differences in vote shares can lead to large (discontinuous) differences in political outcomes—for example, which party ends up controlling the municipal administration—which in turn leads, in many cases, to large (discontinuous) changes in policy such as the introduction of PB. A matched comparison of municípios with similar vote shares but large differences in political outcomes that coincide with large differences in policy therefore provides some hope of cleanly identifying the impact of the difference in policy, which in our case is the introduction of PB. Under the maintained assumption that vote shares capture the relevant aspects of the local context, our research design is therefore a variant of the regression-discontinuity design, originally proposed by Campbell (1969) and subsequently applied and refined in a variety of settings (for example, Angrist and Lavy 1999).[4]

Following this design we selected five pairs of município: one in the South, two in the Southeast, one in the Northeast, and one in the North. This roughly follows the pattern of adoption of PB in Brazil in 1997–2000. A quantitative analysis revealed that a PT victory was the variable most closely associated with the adoption of PB and confirmed our assumption that the PT is critical to any explanation of PB. In order to select pairs, we identified all municípios in Brazil where the PT had won or lost by an absolute difference of less than 10 percent in the 1996 election. This yielded 274 municípios, which we then divided by region and then again by size, and finally by the electoral strength of other political parties, and lined up into columns of adopters and nonadopters of PB. From this roster we sought to identify pairs where the PB adopter was a PT município, and where a matching nonadopter had a similar absolute difference in vote shares, a similar size, and a similar configuration of other significant political parties. This yielded a roster of twenty-three PB adopters, each with a possible match with between one and five other municípios. From this roster we selected our pairs, keeping our regional distribution in mind and following the principle of greatest possible similarity between pairs.

The municípios that we paired reflected national patterns: those in the South and Southeast were more economically developed, wealthier, and had higher Human Development indicators than those in the North and Northeast. The regional distribution of the pairs—one in the South, two in the Southeast, and one in the Northeast—roughly follows the pattern of adoption of PB in Brazil in 1997–2000. The paired municípios and results for the 1996 elections are presented in Table 3.1. Here we report all five pairs, but for presentational reasons we do not discuss the pair from the North, São Miguel do Guaporé and Mirante da Serra, in the rest of the book.[5]

The Fieldwork

The paired research was conducted by teams of investigators in the various regions of Brazil. The teams gathered primary data such as rule books and financial data, and they interviewed key respondents in each município. Key informants

Table 3.1 The Matched Pairs

	PB Municípios							Non-PB Municípios					
State	Município	Electorate Size	PT Vote Share	PT Margin	Winner	Runner-up	State	Município	Electorate Size	PT Vote Share	PT Margin	Winner	Runner-up
NORTHEAST													
PE	Camaragibe	72,544	0.404	0.07	PT	PSDB	CE	Quixadá	43,032	0.440	-0.08	PSDB	PT
NORTH													
RO	São Miguel do Guaporé	8,119	0.412	0.02	PT	PMDB	RO	Mirante da Serra	8,181	0.464	-0.02	PMDB	PT
SOUTHEAST													
MG	João Monlevade	44,365	0.466	0.06	PT	PSDB	MG	Timóteo	43,064	0.491	-0.02	PSDB	PT
SP	Mauá	196,121	0.487	0.13	PT	PSDB	SP	Diadema	220,292	0.442	-0.01	PSB	PT
SOUTH													
RS	Gravataí	109,612	0.408	0.02	PT	PDT	RS	Sapucaia do Sul	76,836	0.361	-0.07	PDT	PT

Sources: TSE 1997; IBGE 2002

included administrators at various levels in the 1997–2000 administration, including officers in charge of budgeting, planning, and popular participation, as well as the mayor and heads of municipal departments. It also included legislators from the ruling and opposition party, leaders of civil society organizations, local unions, business organizations, and political party heads. For each município we interviewed between twelve and sixteen key respondents. The questionnaire consisted of a mix of open-ended and closed questions, and it was divided into three parts, part of a research process we describe in Appendix A. The first part explores the historical conditions and sociopolitical context of local government in 1996. We posed a series of questions about how government was run, who the key actors in government and civil society were—including especially detailed questions about civil society actors—and the general conditions of the economy and society at the time. The second part addressed the nature of governance in 1996–2001 and focused in particular on what role, if any, participatory mechanisms, including PB, played in shaping the nature of governance. In this section we re-posed basic questions about actors and institutions of local governance, but specifically focused on identifying changes, and in the cases of PB-adoption, the actual design and workings of PB. Our strategy here was process tracing, that is, documenting and evaluating the entire participatory input chain, from the first articulation of a demand to the actual budgetary allocation. This included very detailed questions about the "chain of sovereignty," that is, how demands were formed and then passed up from one actor or institution to another. The third part was more specifically focused on the impact of changes in governance. We focused both on identifying institutional changes and what impact these had on the local character of civil society. We re-posed many of the specific questions about the strength of character of civil society that were posed in part 1.

THE CASES

Before developing our comparative analysis, we present brief sketches of each of our cities, both before and after the observation period (1996–2000). Appendix B presents some selected development indicators for each of the municípios. Here the cases are presented in pairs, with the PB city always followed by a parenthetical (PB).

We begin with Mauá (PB) and Diadema, two midsized industrial towns in the state of São Paulo that are by far the most politically developed pair in our sample. Both are located in the band of industrialization that surrounds São Paulo—widely known as the ABC region. This is the historical heartland of Brazil's powerful labor movement. What marks them as somewhat unique is that they are among the birthplaces of the New Unionism of the 1980s, and Diadema is considered the birthplace of the PT. Diadema has an especially active and "combative" (the specific term used by our respondents) civil society, so much so that the movement sector has actually been wary of institutionalizing participation. In Mauá (PB), the victory of the PT in 1996 ushered in PB, but as we explain later, a "bifurcated" civil society quickly became dependent on the PT. In fact, this pair produces our most unusual and counterintuitive outcome. Diadema emerges as a case of noninstitutionalized empowerment where citizens have significant voice but largely through contentious politics. In Mauá (PB), the adoption of PB resulted in a form of dependent participation that led to a weakening of the agency of civil society. This is our only pair in which the PB city fared less well than its counterpart.

Diadema and Mauá (PB) clearly had the most mature and developed democratic structures in our sample, specifically marked by the early and strong presence of the PT. By the mid-1990s, both had well-developed political parties and predominantly associational modes of intermediation. In the case of Diadema, it is clear that the PT makes up the nucleus around which politics are organized, with all other political parties organizing in opposition to the PT. In 1996 the PT lost the election to the Brazilian Socialist Party (Partido Socialista Brasileiro, or PSB), a programmatic left-wing party. Strong and independent civil society organizations have more or less broken the hold of clientelistic practices allowing for more associational forms of engagement. Even though Mauá (PB) has developed a competitive political party system, it is still far more mired in past political practices than Diadema. The political field in Mauá (PB) in effect opposes the programmatic PT to a number of traditional oligarchical parties dominated by three families linked to the real estate sector that ruled until 1997. Though the presence of an organized opposition has limited traditional-style clientelism, recent municipal governments have resorted to practices of control and tutelage of social organizations.

Gravataí (PB) and Sapucaia in the state of Rio Grande do Sul have the distinction of being cities on the periphery of Porto Alegre. The municípios are very similar along a range of key socioeconomic and political factors. Both have solid industrial bases and significant revenue sources. Both are confronted with the problems of rapid urbanization, and in particular a concentrated and impoverished low-income population with little access to urban infrastructure. Until 1996, both cities were microcosms of Brazil's political culture.

On the one hand, political power was vested in fragmented oligarchical parties whose electoral support was built on the strength of clientelist politics. In Gravataí (PB), the Democratic Labor Party, or the PDT, which had ruled in 1989–92 and closely contested the PT in 1996, owed its support primarily to its control over the city's neighborhood associations. During the PDT administration, the mayor assiduously cultivated relations with the neighborhood associations, which in return limited their activities to the presentation of specific demands through personal relationships between association presidents and politicians, and carefully avoided more conflictive initiatives based on collective action. Similarly, in Sapucaia do Sul, community organizations were fully integrated into clientelistic political structures forgoing any capacity for autonomous social action. The debilitating effects of civil society's dependence on political society are graphically captured by a respondent: "During campaign season, the incumbent Mayor would distribute dentures, glasses, cups, T-shirts with his name on them, all paid for with money from the Prefeitura. He would go into the slums and give out campaign leaflets with writing on the back that said, 'Give the bearer of this note a hundred tiles and a hundred bricks.'" On the other hand, Brazil's protracted democratization struggle has produced a wide, diverse, and sophisticated slate of civil society actors, in particular active public employee unions. Though kept at a careful distance by traditional political parties, this more "combative" section of civil society (combative being a term widely used in Brazil and by many of our respondents) significantly increased its political activity in the state in the 1990s. Indeed, it was the support of unions, especially metal workers whose territorial base extended outward from Porto Alegre and teachers who were part of a statewide union, that brought the PT to power in Gravataí (PB). A similar support base fell just short in Sapucaia. The discontinuity associated with the "accident" of PT victory (electoral outcomes were decided by less than 1 percent) is particularly marked here. Gravataí (PB) adopted PB and developed, as we review in detail in the next chapter, the most institutionalized, robust, and Participatory Budgeting processes of all of our cases.

João Monlevade (PB) and Timóteo are both in effect "company towns" in the industrial belt of Minas Gerais, an area known for the influence of steel companies in town life. Both municípios are also known for labor union activism and PT sympathies. João Monlevade (PB), literally built by the Belgo-Mineira Steel Company, is today described by some as a "leftist town" because of the strong presence of the PT, which first ran an administration in 1989–92, with backing from unions and community movements. Business interests as well as the influence of the steel factory itself organized against the administration. Timóteo, similarly, is a city that is politically defined by organized commercial interests that orbit around the steel factory, as well as a history of labor militancy. Timóteo also had a PT administration in 1989–92. Civil society in both towns was defined by largely clientelist dealings with the administration, with the presence of outsider new social movements such as the movement for accessible housing and the movement of domestic workers. By 1996, both municípios were marked by polarization between PT and anti-PT forces and a tradition of "alternation" in power since 1989, when the PT managed to elect mayors in both. But in neither case had the evolution of party politics marked a full rupture with the clientelism of the past. The municipal government of 1993–96 in both cases engaged society through carefully selected organizations, offering specific benefits to politically friendly organizations. In Timóteo, for example, the municipal administration of 1997–2000 sponsored the Community Council where, once a month, presidents of neighborhood associations could have privileged access to administrators. In both towns, informants described the importance of *abaixo-assinados*, or petitions to powerful politicians, as a way to have social demands met.

Camaragibe (PB) and Quixadá are in the northeastern states of Pernambuco and Ceará. The Northeast is, of course, infamous for its low levels of development and for the political dominance of traditional oligarchs. Well into the 1990s, politics in both cities were dominated by traditional families that had governed for generations. Political party polarization revolved around powerful personalities, and the engagement of civil society organizations depended entirely on party patronage. Thus, despite the fact that social movements and the Catholic Church in particular had begun to mobilize the poor in the 1980s, as an organized sector, civil society was largely prostrate. The one exception to the pattern was the health movement in Camaragibe. A movement activist—Paulo Santana—was appointed as health secretary in the PSDB government in 1994, and taking advantage of national developments, he opened a participatory space in the form of health councils. The popularity of these councils helped build support for the PT, which then won the 1997 election.

All of our cases are midsized towns with adult populations of 71,000 to 351,000. All in some sense typify their regions, with three pairs located in the industrial belts of the more industrialized states. The Northeast pair is quite representative of that region in terms of the importance of local powerful families in municipal politics. Reviewing our pairs, we can make certain generalizations about the state of democratic politics and governance in the late 1990s.

Taken as a whole, the pairs reflect the heterogeneity of politics in Brazil, consisting of increasingly competitive party systems that pitted new political formations, most notably the PT and its more ideologically defined brand of politics (though with great local variation in the degree of programmatic development), against a colorful array of traditional as well as reconfigured oligarchical parties. But with the possible exceptions of Diadema and João Monlevade, political society in 1997 was still largely reflective of the traditional political order, marked by elite domination and little effective representation of popular groups. Diadema was the birth place of the PT and home to an exceptionally strong union movement. João Monlevade also had a strong union movement, and other aligned movements played an important role in the national transition to democracy. In Diadema, the PT was in power from 1983–96 and nurtured close ties to civil society organizations, which in turn exerted significant influence over policy. Yet even in this unusual instance, these links were strictly of the political brokerage kind and dependent on the PT remaining in power.[6]

The institutional setting of all our cases displays even less variation than the political field in 1997. This is not surprising given that local government is constituted by national law, and that political institutions in Brazil have generally been elite-dominated and clientelistic. Existing municipal legislation, moreover, empowers the executive at the expense of the legislature. It is quite clear that again with the exception of Diadema, national-level reforms introducing participatory structures had yet to take effect in these midsized towns. As we shall see in more detail in the next chapter, the institutional surface area for civil society participation across all our cases was very narrow. Before 1997, the only point of access to policy-making was through the mayor or powerful councilors tied to the mayor's party. In all eight municípios elected councils were generally seen as little more than a rubber stamp. Our respondents did report that some participatory structures—most often health councils—were operating before 1997, but none of these were deemed to have a tangible impact on policies or budgeting. João Monlevade had had an experiment with Participatory Budgeting in the early 1990s, but this was discontinued by 1993 and left little trace of routinized popular input. None of the eight municípios had any kind of popular forum for deliberation or consultation, although Diadema had created eighteen sector-based management councils that served as points of discussion for civil society organizations. The very narrow surface area of the local state and the general dominance of local elites also inflected the institutional process. This was characterized by various forms of clientelism organized either through personalistic networks (generally in the smaller municípios and those in the Northeast) or through highly organized forms of state sponsorship of intermediate associations, such as registered neighborhood associations beholden to the mayor's party.

In sum, only one of the eight municípios, Diadema, afforded civil society some space and opportunity for direct engagement with the local state, and even in this case, openings were limited to the political field, that is, mediated by the PT. In the other seven, it was in every sense business as usual, with governance either controlled by powerful, traditional patronage politicians, or by political parties that built their support through clientelism. None of these municípios had yet to expand access to policy-making and budgeting beyond the office of the mayor. Moreover, it is important to bear in mind that the narrowness of the political field and the insulated nature of institutional process existed despite the significant presence of the PT—a party that is more or less a proxy for social movement activation—in all eight municípios.

THE IMPACT OF PB

Having set the political and institutional stage for our eight municípios in 1997, we now turn to our analysis of the institutional impact of PB by examining the extent to which participatory governance was introduced between 1997–2000 in all of our municípios. The analysis focuses on the degree and effectiveness of participation by civil society in governance by posing two fundamental questions. First, what are the mechanisms and the actual spaces where participatory inputs—both those tied to PB and other processes—take shape? Where, in other words, are collective preferences formed? As we saw in Chapter 1, democratization and accompanying institutional changes—including the decentralization initiatives of the late 1980s—have created a wide range of new participatory spaces in Brazil. These spaces are all the more significant given Brazil's long-established traditions of clientelism and elite-based politics. Yet precisely because of the well-developed skills and tactics of elites in circumventing the rule of law and the norms of democratic practices, as well as the high and manifold "transaction costs" that subordinate groups face in engaging the political arena, we are interested not just in the form of the new institutions but also the actual practices. The mere existence of PB structures does not translate into participation as such. New institutional spaces are particularly susceptible to elite capture. It is as such vitally important to actually examine the functioning of participatory spaces, including their social composition, their linkages to the formal decision-making process, and their internal deliberative qualities.

Second, to what extent are participatory inputs translated into concrete outputs? This latter question has largely been neglected in the literature on participatory democracy. Most studies of participation generally focus on documenting participation itself, but only rarely evaluate the "chain of sovereignty," that is, the extent to which participatory decision-making is binding on actual government decisions. We address this question specifically through process tracing, that is, documenting and evaluating the entire participatory input chain, from the first articulation of a demand to the actual budgetary allocation.

To address these two questions, we evaluated the type of governance found in each município drawing on four criteria. The first two criteria capture the nature of participation, that is, the specific modalities through which citizens engage the local state, and the third and fourth criteria capture the extent of actual governance that results from participation, that is, the extent to which citizen inputs actually impact on public choices. First, we considered the mode of representation: How is popular representation in the budgeting process organized? This is a basic distinction made by participatory theorists and refers to a distinction between participatory and representative forms of engagement. Four possibilities emerged among our cases: none, direct, delegated, and mixed (direct and delegated). Direct refers to participation by citizens in open decision-making fora, such as neighborhood assemblies. Delegated refers to instances in which delegates are given a role at the municipal level in shaping the budget. It is important to underscore that by delegated we refer only to new forms of representation (in most instances what are called "delegate councils") and not to the elected city council structures (formal representative structures). In all cases where direct participation occurred, delegates were also elected to represent the community in the delegate council. The category of mixed refers to this combination.

Second, we considered the formalization of process: What are the rules and procedures governing participatory inputs? This is an important dimension because even a direct process (as above) would have a very different character if it were informal, that is, not rule-bound. Three possible categories exist: none, formal, and informal. Formalized processes were those in which there were explicit and widely known rules that gave participants a reasonable sense of future outcomes from their participation. Informal processes were those in which there were no such rules, or in which participants were not aware of such rules.

Third, we considered decision-making power: To what extent are citizen inputs translated into budgetary outputs? This is a central dimension to understanding whether participation is "empowered" (Fung and Wright 2003) or not. Three categories emerged: none, consultative, and binding. Given that participatory processes have no legally binding authority, "binding" in this context is a matter of influence and was evaluated on the basis of the observed degree to which municipal authorities took citizen demands into account. Nonetheless, for us "binding" referred to participatory processes in which the citizen mandate was expected to be translated into an actual governmental decision, while "consultative" referred to instances in which the results of citizen discussion had the status of a recommendation which was then subject to another, more authoritative decision by an authority. In "binding" decision-making the failure to translate a citizen mandate into a government decision would be considered a violation of the process by participants; in "consultative," participants would accept such an outcome as part of the process.

Finally, we addressed the scope of discussion: Over what range of governance functions (or domains) did participatory processes have influence? This dimension captures whether participation is limited to investment decisions, or if it is broader and involves other government policy domains (such as the provision of social services, for example). Four categories emerged: none, making general demands, budget, policies, and mixed (budget and policies). *Making general demands* refers to expressing needs, *budget* refers to actual discussion of projects and costs, and *policies* refers to the modalities of coverage and delivery of government departments. Mixed refers to both budget and policies. For each of our PB cases, we document and evaluate the institutional design of participation and the chain of sovereignty in detail in Chapter 4. Here, we provide an overview of how our paired municípios fared when assessed against these measures.

Based on the responses provided by our informants and on careful review of all collected documents, we categorized each municipality according to each of our four criteria. As Table 3.2 clearly shows, the study period (1997–2000) was one of significant change in the institutional forms and practices that govern citizen engagement in our selected municípios. Thus, seven of the municípios introduced some form of participation in budgeting affairs during this period (for reasons explained below, the form of participation in Diadema does not fall within our categories). Only Quixadá had no form of participation. Since there is a perfect correspondence of "binding decision-making power" with "mixed scope of discussion," the outcomes can be summarized in a shortened form, in Table 3.3.

Table 3.3 shows that cases fall into three clusters. The upper-right-hand corner, which we characterize as full PB, represents the greatest expansion of participation in that it involves direct and representative forms, and that these are binding in nature. In the three cases in this box, the process was formalized (F) and demands were mixed, impacting both the budget and policy more generally. The upper-left-hand corner, which we term partial PB, represents cases where direct and representative participation was introduced, but where decision-making power was limited to a consultative function. The lower-left corner represents the narrowest form of participation, which we term state-controlled participation, in the sense that it is both only consultative and delegated.

Table 3.2 Participatory Governance, 1997–2000 (PB municípios in bold)

Município	Type of Participation	Formalization of the Participatory Process	Decision-making Power	Scope of Discussion
Camaragibe/PE	Direct and Delegated	Formal	Binding	Mixed
Quixadá/CE	None	—	—	—
Gravataí/RS	Direct and Delegated	Formal	Binding	Mixed
Sapucaia do Sul/RS	Delegated only	Informal	Consultative	Demands
Mauá/SP	Direct and Delegated	Formal	Consultative	Demands
Diadema/SP	—	Informal	Consultative	Demands
João Monlevade/ MG	Direct and Delegated	Formal	Binding	Mixed
Timóteo/MG	Delegated only	Formal	Consultative	Demands

Table 3.3 Synthesis of Participatory Governance, 1997–2000 (PB municípios in bold)

Decision-making Power / Mode of Participation	Consultative	Binding
Direct and Delegated	Diadema (I) Mauá (F)	**Camaragibe** (F) **Gravataí** (F) **J. Monlevade** (F)
Delegated only	Timóteo (F) Sapucaia (I)	

* I = Informal F= formal

* Quixadá does not appear here since no form of participation was introduced.

As might be expected, all of the PB cities saw the introduction of direct forms of participation. Three municípios—Camaragibe, Gravataí, and João Monlevade—experienced the maximum degree of participation and control over public goods: the form of participation was both delegated and direct; it was formalized; it was binding on municipal authorities; and it covered a wide scope of governance functions (budgeting and policies).

Examining the PB cases, we see that the process was to varying degrees formalized. However, it is also quite clear that the introduction of PB does not always ensure that citizen inputs are translated into concrete outputs. In our assessment, only in João Monlevade, Camaragibe, and Gravataí did the participatory process qualify as binding.

Among non-PB municípios, there was less participatory governance, and generally, it tended to be less direct and less binding. Quixadá had no spaces for participation in the formulation of the budget. In Timóteo and Sapucaia participation was only delegative and inputs were largely of a consultative nature and limited in scope to the expression of demands. Diadema was the only non-PB city in which direct participation took place. The form of participation here was not organized through PB. It was, rather, the result of contentious demands by a highly organized civil society. We discuss each of these three clusters as well as the Diadema exception below. We begin with a discussion of Quixadá, our case of no participation, followed by the cases of state-controlled participation, then followed by the cases of partial PB and full PB.

Business as Usual

Quixadá was the one município that did not introduce any significant form of participation in 1997–2000. Like all Brazilian municipalities, it had a federally mandated health council, but according to our interviews even this council was not active in the period. In fact, this period marked a reversal of the earlier administration, which had introduced some participatory initiatives under a program dubbed "The Mayor with You." Having outpolled the PT by a razor-thin margin, the centrist Brazilian Social Democratic Party, or the PSDB, administration that came to power in 1997 was led by a long-standing local powerbroker, Francisco Mesquita. Serving his second term for a second party (formerly the PDT), Mesquita ran a government characterized by a complete lack of transparency and monitoring of the budgetary process. In this relatively small town of forty-three thousand voters, the administration actively nurtured personalized attention to demands and concentrated all decision-making in the mayor's immediate circle. Among civil society organizations, the only one to have access was the Federation of Neighborhood Associations, whose president was on the payroll of city hall during the 1997–2000 period, according to both city hall employees and civil society activists of the time.

A large majority of respondents in Quixadá reported that the influence of elites *increased* during the 1997–2000 administration, and most described it as "more closed" to citizen influence than before. According to former administrators, the mayor's inability to meet campaign promises was behind the deliberate effort to close down channels of direct communication. Contact with the government for average citizens took place through informal means, sometimes through chats the mayor would have with individuals in the course of other activities. According to a former department head of his administration, these "caused problems for the administration" because these promises, often made arbitrarily and for personal reasons, had the effect of undoing previous plans.

Perhaps most telling of the lack of transparency in the city was the fact that the budget preparation was *outsourced* to a consultancy based in the capital city of Fortaleza despite being the formal responsibility of the Department of Planning and Finances. The annual budget, according to a former employee of the administration, was a "piece of fiction" without connection to the actual expenditures and which was quickly drawn up one or two weeks before the legally mandated date. New projects were always defined "from the mayor's office."

State-controlled Participation

The cases of Timóteo and Sapucaia underscore the importance of carefully examining the nature of participation. In both cases, new forms of participation were introduced in 1997. Specifically, delegates to a citywide council were given a direct role in consulting on the budget. But from our interviews it is very clear that in both cases participation was carefully controlled, even orchestrated by the local state, and that the process as a whole had the effect of weakening civil society (as we shall see in the next chapter). Indeed, in contrast to the ruptures we have identified in the PB cases, there were significant continuities between these participatory schemes and earlier clientelistic forms of mobilization. In both cases, delegates to the citywide council were selected by politicians.

In Sapucaia, the mayor appointed the president of the Unions of Neighborhood Associations of Sapucaia do Sul (UAMOSSUL) as the director of community relations and exerted tight control over neighborhood associations that participated. In 1997–2000 the appointed director was a four-term councilor from the ruling party, the PTB. The government also began directly funding community organizations and incentivized the creation of associations in areas where other entities already existed but acted in the "incorrect form" (that is, conflictual action and not supporting the PTB).

In Timóteo, as a response to the fact that PB had been a campaign promise of the opposition, the administration introduced a consultative participatory system. It consisted of a series of meetings between the mayor and residents in various neighborhoods in the city at which a list of priorities was created. Participation was, however, controlled by the presidents of neighborhood associations that have long been tied to the mayor's political machine. These meetings were held in each of the city's seven districts, from where an "indicative list of actions" was then forwarded to the planning department, with ten projects being chosen for execution. These were announced at a final municipal meeting with representatives of the various organizations that participated in the earlier phase. This decision was made without any deliberation, and projects executed "according to the financial resources available to the municipal government." The lists of demands are registered in acts of the meetings, but there is no elaboration of single plan or document that combines the various demands, nor the formation of a forum that accompanies their execution. The control of the meetings by presidents of associations, the lack of deliberation in the meetings, and the lack of transparency in the overall process distinguish it from the consultative participation, the "partial PB" we describe below.

Partial PB—Consultative Participation

Falling short of the cases that are full PB, that is, binding participation, are two cases that we label "consultative participation." In both cases that fall into the upper-left-hand box of Table 3.3—Diadema and Mauá (PB)—delegative and direct forms of participation were instituted, but citizen engagement remained largely consultative. In both cases, there are opportunities for civil society organizations to directly engage the state, but the chain of sovereignty is not ensured. In the absence of clearly defined criteria by which civil society inputs are translated into authoritative decisions, the impact of participation is uncertain.

Measured against full PB in which citizens are de facto (if not de jure) empowered to shape the budget, this form of participatory governance clearly falls short of the participatory ideal. There are good reasons why consultative processes are often dismissed as a rather hollow form of participation. While they can provide the government with useful information and some legitimacy, they provide citizens little effective leverage over government decision-making, especially in contexts such as Brazil where elites routinely flout democratic norms. As we shall see in Chapter 4 in the case of Mauá (PB), consultation can also have the effect of demobilizing civil society.

One should not be too quick, however, to dismiss *consultative participation* as not contributing to popular representation. The PB ideal of *binding participation* is, in fact, quite rare even in the most "developed" democracies. Indeed, insofar as civil society is judged to have an important role in Western democracies, its impact has more to do with the "politics of influence" (Cohen and Arato 1992) than with binding authority. Most discussions of the politics of influence generally focus on fairly diffuse mechanisms, such as opinion formation through the media, and efforts to sway decision-makers through the "strength of the better argument"—most famously in Habermas's rendition of deliberative democracy—and rarely examine the institutional conduits through which such influence translates into outputs. If anything, the form of *consultative participation* observed here represents a more forceful mode of influence because it specifically creates fora in which opinions can be discussed, formed, and publicized. Even if such opinions are not binding, there are a number of ways in which the open and public expression of demands can increase the leverage of civil society. First, it provides an opportunity for groups traditionally excluded from the decision-making process to form and express choices. Second, to the extent that such choices are well publicized, they provide new points of accountability for politicians and officials. Third, the public articulation of direct demands can to some extent short-circuit traditional patronage politics by giving greater visibility to public, rather than private demands.

These points can be further developed by examining the case of Diadema. Diadema falls into the "consultative participation" category even though it is not a PB city. Here, the influence of citizens is not in a formal structure, but rather in the overall strength and contentiousness of civil society (which we examine in Chapter 5). In Diadema, a PB was attempted during the first two years of the administration as result of social movement pressures. Participatory Budgeting was poorly designed and failed in its own right, but not without triggering new social movement demands.

Despite the failure to institute participation, social movement activists were able to pressure the administration into publishing an annual "budget book"— a notebook that listed projects for each district and neighborhood and information on the municipal budget—as well as organizing training courses on the budget for citizen activists. Social movements were also active in starting participatory councils on health, social services, and education, where citizens monitored and impacted service delivery. Ultimately, the promise of a PB had the effect of mobilizing organized sectors, which dissatisfied with stillborn participatory attempts, demanded more access and decision-making into governmental affairs. Movements were able to gain influence, not through the creation of a regular forum, but through sporadic but organized contention. This is very much an instance of the politics of influence, albeit predicated on the strength and militancy of a highly mobilized civil society. What is important to underscore here is that that citizens can exert greater influence over decision-making even in the absence of institutional change.

Full PB: Binding Participation

Gravataí, João Monlevade, and Camaragibe are all cases of binding participation. In all three the mode of participation is a mix of direct and delegated participation. Gravataí, for example, combines direct participation in microregional and regional plenaries with instances of representation (forum of delegates and the council of PB). The process is extremely formalized, with a very detailed set of procedures and rules that define the roles, responsibilities, and criteria for the distribution of resources and the manner in which delegates are chosen. In terms of decision-making power, PB there is binding. In all three cases, the process of PB empowers the council of PB to deliberate and decide on the public works and services the population demands, and as such, the process is de facto binding. Finally, the scope of discussion encompasses both budget decisions and policy. There are, however, significant differences among these cases, which we examine in detail in the next chapter.

CONCLUSIONS

The cases we have examined represent extremely complex institutional reforms that display highly uneven levels of implementation and impact. Through our paired analysis we have tried to isolate the impact of PB and to identify and typologize the actual forms of participation. Before moving onto a detailed analysis of the specific institutional forms of participatory governance that emerged (addressed in Chapter 4) and their impact on civil society (Chapter 5), we can draw some initial findings.

First, what is most striking about our findings is that change appears to be the norm. At the start of our period of observation in 1997, most of our municípios were being governed as they have long been governed, by traditional elites operating largely independently of any effective mechanisms of popular control. With the exception of Diadema, our midsized and semiperipheral municípios seemed to have been largely untouched by national-level institutional reforms, and most had witnessed little of the effervescence of social movements so familiar in larger Brazilian cities.

Yet, beginning with the new administrations of 1997, seven of eight municípios introduced some form of participation. Four of these were, of course, our selected PB cities, but even among our control group, three of four took a page from the participatory playbook. Even if some of these initiatives were hollow at best, and dressing up old tactics of political control in new garb at worst, it is still striking that governments from three different non-PT parties felt compelled to move in this direction. If nothing else, this underscores just how powerful a legitimating principle participatory democracy has become in Brazil.[7]

Because of the controlled nature of our sample—pairing similarly structured PB and non-PB cities—we can also draw some lessons about the impact of PB. In all of our pairs, the city that introduced PB experienced significant changes in how processes of state-civil society engagement have become instituted. In all four cases, new fora for direct citizen input into the budgetary process were created and rules for citizen engagement were formalized. In the more successful cases, the instituted process had the effect of making citizen input binding on government decision-making.

Just how careful one must be in unpacking what participation means is underscored by our findings for Mauá (PB) and three of our control municípios. In Mauá (PB), the introduction of PB was limited to a largely consultative function, and while consultation can have democratizing effects, it falls far short of the participatory ideal. Even if on paper Timóteo and Sapucaia created new participatory institutions, in practice elites remained firmly in charge of the budgeting process and if anything established greater control over civil society.

Finally, the case of Diadema underscores that even in the absence of institutional reform from above, an organized and engaged civil society can impact governance. In this respect we need to recognize that institutional reform must be more broadly understood as resulting from the balance and interaction between political and civil society. Having established in the broadest terms possible that the introduction of PB can and does transform state-civil society relations, we now turn to analyzing both the variations in actual forms of PB and the causes underlying that variation.

4 REPRESENTATION BY DESIGN

"THE CHALLENGE OF BEING GOVERNMENT"

Camaragibe, our PB city in the Northeast, was host to a conference called "The Challenge of Being Government" in December 1996. Attended by the incoming government team, academics, and community activists, the conference was emblematic of concerns of newly elected progressive administrators throughout the country. In the case of Camaragibe, in particular, the winning PT ticket had run on the promise of instituting popular participation based on the health councils that had been operating in the município. Teresinha Carlos, who would become the mayor's chief of staff, recalls that they were inspired by a number of different prior experiences in Brazil, in particular, Porto Alegre, where a delegation had visited. The hope was to develop something new that learned from "all that had already been developed" (Oliveira 2003, 100).

The challenge of "being government"—of making good on campaign promises to institute popular participation in a way that took account of local realities was something that administrators in all of our PB municípios faced. They drew on what was then already a rich repertoire of experiences by progressive mayors, but they did so at a time when thinking about the meaning of popular participation was changing. The idea that local PT governments should be instruments of popular mobilization had given way to more pragmatic understandings that the PT should focus on governing well. Further, several failures at instituting participation now served as cautionary tales that simply deciding to institute participation was not enough. There was a growing realization that for participation to work, institutions needed to be carefully designed to foster the kinds of settings that promoted broad, inclusive participation but did not degenerate into disruptive contention. By 1996 PB had become *the* principal PT formula for accomplishing this. As a blueprint, it had been applied successfully in dozens of cities by the time of the conferences and discussions of late 1996. Its central innovation—open meetings leading to binding decisions on urban infrastructure—seemed to have traveled well, often extending support for PT administrations' redistributive platforms among the broader voting public while at the same time shielding administrators from charges of "clientelism of the left."

As we described in Chapter 2, the "cohorts" of cities with PB tended to be larger cities in the South and Southeast, often with histories of social movements.[1] But by the 1997–2000 cohort, the one under study here, the experiment had spread to different contexts. Our PB towns were not seen as ideal for PB in at least two ways. First, they suffered from a paucity of resources available for any kind of program revolving around urban infrastructure. The fiscal years of 1996 and 1997 had been especially difficult ones for Brazilian municipalities, and for small and midsized towns in particular owing to their inability to independently raise funds. The second difficulty had to do with the lack of organized allies in civil society. João Monlevade is perhaps somewhat of an exception, with its history of progressive unionism, but the rest of our PB cities had measurably fewer organized and autonomous civil society organizations than the cities that served as the model for participatory budgeting blueprints. While in all the cases there *were* progressive sectors of civil society, in every case many of these actors moved to city hall with the PT victory, thus initially weakening organizations.

For participatory institutions this lack of partners in civil society makes for a particular challenge. While PB meetings are open to *all* participants, from within organized sectors or not, in previous successful PB processes civil society organizations played important mobilizational and aggregative roles: drawing participants, building interest in the participatory institutions, processing demands, and carrying out important community negotiations ahead of formal deliberations. That is, these organized actors played exactly the critical mediating role between state institutions and civil society that democratic theorists have specifically assigned to secondary associations (de Tocqueville 1839/40; Warren 2001; Cohen and Rogers 1995). These were functions administrators of other successful experiments had learned to value.[2] One of the issues the architects of the four cases had to deal with was how to carry out this mediation in contexts marked by weak civil societies. As we shall see, this challenge yielded very different answers.

These answers emerged from a great deal of what Sabel has referred to as "institutional bootstrapping," or the possibility that improved institutional designs emerge from pragmatic experimentation by those in charge of the institution. According to Sabel, bootstrapping is the process by which institutions "can be rebuilt, again and again, by changing combinations of public and private actors, in light of the changing social constraints" (Sabel 2004, 7). That is, within a broad progressive mandate ("the challenge of being government"), but with a great deal of local autonomy to implement this programmatic vision, local proactive administrators adapted and fine-tuned the "blueprint" of PB (the Porto Alegre model) as needs arose, or jerry-rigged entirely new versions of PB. While scholars have often pointed to the creativity of social movements and civil society actors, attention to these forms of "democratic experimentalism" (Dorf and Sabel 2006) points to both the partial viewpoints and creativity of actors within government.

In this chapter, we return to the central question discussed by participants in the 1996 public seminar: How did these administrations meet the challenge of "being government"? The focus of this chapter is thus the range of institutional reforms in the four municípios where Participatory Budgeting was introduced. As we have discussed in the last chapter, three of the municípios (Gravataí, Camaragibe, and João Monlevade) were cases of "full PB"—binding and formal decision-making with elements of direct and delegated participation, and Mauá was an instance of "partial PB"—a consultative version of the former. We discuss each case with three different but interrelated analytic frames in mind: democratic experimentalism, the chain of sovereignty, and forms of mediation. Democratic experimentalism refers to the agency of local actors in introducing new forms of governance and focuses attention on identifying the specific ecology of political actors—administrators, activists, politicians—that underwrites institutional agency. The chain of sovereignty refers to the processes and the effectiveness with which participatory inputs—preferences formed and expressed in various fora—are translated into concrete outputs. We closely examine the new and adapted institutions that emerged in our four cases and draw on our interviews to reconstruct the processes of decision-making and to access the degree to which the "instituted process" of PB maintains an unbroken chain between democratic demands and public allocations. Forms of mediation refers to identifying the specific actors and mechanisms through which civil society, in its various manifestations, engages with the local state.

THE BASIC FEATURES OF PARTICIPATORY INSTITUTIONS

Participatory Budgeting is intended to be a conveyor belt that translates popular inputs into government actions; thus, it tends to involve complex institutional arrangements. In each of the cases, as we will see, the institutional arrangement that eventually emerged was quite different, though all in dialogue with a "basic blueprint" of PB that had been circulating among PT networks and provided the starting point for most of the PB experiments that took place at the time in Brazil (Teixeira and Albuquerque 2005; Avritzer and Wampler 2005; Wampler 2009).[3] In a simplified form, this blueprint is a yearly cycle of decentralized assemblies where participants and their representatives choose and debate projects that will make their way to a final municipal budget and ultimately be implemented. All of our cases shared some of these basic features, which we present here for the sake of the clarity of exposition.

Projects are probably the basic unit of concern for most participants. These are discrete government actions that have a specific cost. In most of our cases these are urban infrastructure projects, such as the paving of a particular road, or the construction of a park or school. Sometimes these projects can engage other areas of government action—such as health or social work, and sometimes PB can be related to longer-term concerns, such as the municípios' overall planning and development. This balance tended to vary between towns that focused exclusively on urban infrastructure projects (Gravataí), to those that included an element of strategic planning in the PB process (João Monlevade), to the case of Camaragibe where urban infrastructure was of secondary importance to other areas of policy, notably health. All of the processes, however, eventually deal with specific projects to be implemented in the following fiscal year. There is often a publication that details the decisions of the PB participants ("Planned Projects"), and there are sometimes monitoring committees of delegates who follow their implementation.

It is worth clarifying that Participatory Budgets make decisions over the *capital expenditure* portions of municipal budgets. Budgets can be generally divided into operating expenses (or fixed costs), the portion of the budget dedicated to maintenance of functions including government employee salaries and benefits, and capital expenditures, or new investments. In general, operating expenses far outweigh capital expenditures in any particular year. In 2000, among our cases, municipal governments allocated between 6 (Mauá) and 15.8 percent (João Monlevade) of their total budgets to new capital investments. According to our interviews, the capital budget was subject to the Participatory Budgeting process. But, in real per-capita terms, these were small but significant expenditures: in 2000, per resident this amounted to a low of R$15 (or about US$8) in Gravataí and a high of R$43 (or about US$21) in João Monlevade. These expenditure levels are roughly comparable to similar sized cities in other middle-income countries, though dramatically lower than larger Brazilian cities like Porto Alegre or São Paulo.[4]

All of the PB processes are organized along a yearly cycle. Designed to match the municipal budgeting cycle, processes are organized around a schedule of government-sponsored meetings that begin early in the year—around March or April, ending in November. All processes begin with assemblies, or open meetings, throughout the town, ending when a series of selected projects is forwarded either to a forum of delegates elected by the assemblies for further debate, or directly on to the municipal legislative body for inclusion in the yearly budget. It is in these assemblies that most of the democratic discussion and deliberation takes place, and throughout the year assemblies have different purposes: early on they serve the purpose of informing participants about the process and about available resources; later, particular projects are proposed and debated, and representatives are chosen. The last assemblies are devoted to making the final decisions on the budget. How binding those decisions are varies, with Mauá being the one case in which the PB process was limited to consultation.

There is a structure of decentralization and representation in all of our PB processes. All of the municípios are divided into districts for the purposes of Participatory Budgeting. In our municípios assemblies were organized in districts with populations that ranged from the rather large average of sixty-nine thousand (in Mauá) to a very small average of twenty-nine hundred in the microdistricts of Gravataí. The ultimate destination of projects is also organized by district, often with explicitly redistributive formulas to determine what portion of resources are devoted to each. How this was done varied somewhat by municípios, but in every case, poorer areas received a greater share of resources. Each município also had a distinct way of scaling-up preferences from lower levels. All four of the PB processes had delegates, or district representatives, that serve one-year terms. Delegates were usually elected early in the yearly cycle and performed important functions such as negotiating the distribution of resources within districts. There is sometimes a second-tier of representatives (budget councilors, in Gravataí, for example) that monitor implementation. Exceptions to this general format are those of Camaragibe, where delegates serve four-year terms, and Mauá, where there are additional representative spots reserved for heads of neighborhood associations and business interests.

Gravataí's Participatory Budgeting cycle serves as a good example of how the process works. The budgeting cycle, as shown in Figure 4.1 below, begins in March of each year. It begins with a first round of assemblies in each of the city's fifteen districts, where there is an accounting of the previous year's projects, and the number of delegates per district is determined. This is followed by meetings within the districts in neighborhoods, or "microdistricts," where participants raise ideas for projects, and these are voted on and rank-ordered in priority. In addition delegates are then elected to carry out the work for the rest of the year. Subsequently, there are meetings between April and October where much of the work is conducted. There are internal planning meetings of the administration that determine the costs of chosen projects as well as the amount of resources dedicated to each of the fifteen districts. Delegates also go back to their districts and have meetings where the distribution of resources by neighborhood within each district is determined. Given that each neighborhood has already selected and rank-ordered its projects earlier in the year, this distribution essentially determines which projects will be planned for the next fiscal year. Then, in a second round of assemblies in each district, the planned projects are announced and councilors who will monitor their implementation are elected.

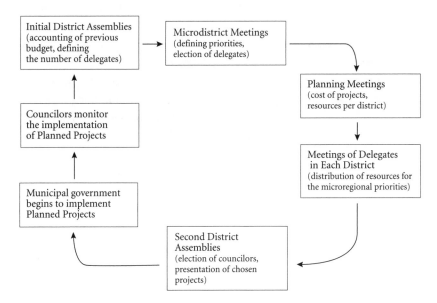

Figure 4.1 The Participatory Budgeting Cycle in Gravataí (1997–2000)
Source: Gravataí 2000

GRAVATAÍ'S PARTICIPATORY BUDGET

Gravataí's Participatory Budgeting process was, at first, closely modeled on the institutions of neighboring Porto Alegre, but it evolved to become a simpler process whose signature feature was its massive participation. By the year 2000, more than twenty thousand participants attended the assemblies throughout the town, or almost 10 percent of the total population. In Gravataí, because organized civil society was essentially absent from the process, if not openly antagonistic, during this period it played little or no role in drawing participants or processing demands, and the participatory process relied instead on the active and intensive intervention of city government to make it work. City hall employees divided the town into eighty-five microdistricts and coordinated meetings in each at the beginning of the cycle. It was a massive and complex experiment in inclusive participation that depended on a concerted effort by administrators who had to facilitate hundreds of meetings a year. In contrast to our other cases, it was a simpler process limited to infrastructure demands and with fewer opportunities for participants to innovate the process itself or to engage in longer-term strategic planning discussions. But, as we discuss below, it was also a transparent process with ample room for participants to debate decisions and to make binding choices on the budget.

PB was introduced in 1997 by the administration of the newly elected mayor Daniel Bordignon (PT, 1997–2000), fulfilling campaign promises. The high-profile successes of PB in Porto Alegre had made it an attractive campaign issue, with most candidates in the 1996 election making some mention of participation. According to recollections from civil society activists, the town had, in fact, had some experience with participation in budgetary matters, through a consultative process in the early 1990s where neighborhood association presidents had been invited to city council "to make proposals" before the annual budget was passed.

Key staff positions to design and run the participatory process were filled by veteran administrators from Porto Alegre, and the process launched in March 1997 was essentially copied from that city. The calendar of events, the rules of the process, and even the names of bureaucratic positions associated with PB were essentially the same. From the outset, however, administrators were concerned that the town's residents would be unable to self-organize for the process. Accordingly, Gravataí's participatory process was significantly adapted to become much more decentralized and simpler than Porto Alegre's.

Each of the town's fifteen districts was further divided into five to seven neighborhoods or "microdistricts." As one organizer put it, the idea behind the eighty-five microdistricts was to "go inside the neighborhoods to make plans" so as to "bring things closer to those fractions of the population who are always excluded from this process." The most important and unique feature of these neighborhood-level meetings is that their decisions *are considered binding.* The process is very direct. After a first assembly in the yearly cycle, meetings are held at which residents propose projects that are then displayed on a blackboard and voted on, as described by several of our interviewees. These proposals are aggregated to the district-level, where later delegates decide on the distribution of resources per neighborhood. Following this distribution, projects are selected for the district, respecting the original rank-ordering of the neighborhood. The idea is that after the original neighborhood meetings take place, "no one can alter the community's vote."

This streamlined system of direct participation at the most local level followed by aggregation is designed to be simpler than other versions of the PB process, such as Porto Alegre's or the ones we describe below for João Monlevade or Camaragibe. In contrast with those places, there were no discussions and votes on overall priority areas (such as deciding on the relative priorities of street paving versus housing versus health, and so on). There was also no discussion on the distribution of resources among districts. In Gravataí, 30 percent of the overall budget under discussion was divided equally among the districts; the remaining 70 percent was divided according to the population of each district. The highly devolved format of Gravataí meant that the role of councilors was limited to monitoring the implementation of projects, with no opportunity to revise the overall rules of the process or engage in longer-term strategic planning.

From our interviews, it is clear that the search for a streamlined institutional design that was "closer" to the population was largely the work of administrators who were especially aware of the potential difficulties of developing a participatory scheme in Gravataí. Gravataí's politics had long been dominated by a form of patrimonialism commonly associated with the Brazilian Northeast, but prevalent throughout the country in middle-sized and smaller towns. The lack of credible civil society organizations meant that much of the intermediation for PB would have to be done by city hall itself. The design thus aimed at building a participatory process that was direct, transparent, and efficient and that largely *bypassed* organized civil society.

In terms of transparency, the Planning Department, which was responsible for PB, attempted to insulate itself from organized interests, both in and outside of government. Given a long history of government resources flowing to rent-seekers, this initiative was understood as a key strategy for legitimizing PB. As one government official told us, he "received a lot of pressure from government colleagues. Department heads wanted their streets paved. To the point that people were trying to overstep the PB." To shield the process from internal interference, an independent structure was created outside of the Planning Department. Similarly, monitoring committees were established that tracked the contracting and execution of projects but also had the purpose of "making the community feel engaged," according to a civil society activist. Finally, there was a concerted effort to ensure transparency by carefully documenting meetings and decisions, so that "everything that was discussed was recorded in the minutes and became available to everyone," according to one participant.

Keeping the chain of sovereignty intact made a clear difference. During the four-year period under study, expenditures in health and sanitation as well as in social services increased significantly both proportionately and in absolute terms. Social service expenditures increased to 10.76 percent in the 2000 budget from 1.58 percent in 1996; likewise, health expenditures increased to 11.15 percent from 2.15 percent of a total budget that increased in real terms. Despite being a poor municipality with a per-capita budget a fraction of neighboring Porto Alegre's, the administration registered some improvements in access to basic education, adult literacy programs, and in the building of new health clinics.

The Limits of Gravataí's PB

Though by far the most participatory and binding of our sample, Gravataí's PB was not without its problems. The institutional design, which relied so heavily on devolving decision-making authority to microdistrict assemblies suffered the classic problem of decentralized decision-making: an overemphasis on local projects and services. Even as the design made it possible for citizens to directly engage with local problems, resulting in high levels of participation, it made it much more difficult to formulate citywide demands. Addressing such needs was, in general, limited to specific areas that were funded independently and not subject to PB approval. Thus, projects such as schools, whose reach extended beyond a microdistrict were difficult to propose. One respondent recalled that "people came to discuss projects for the microdistricts. They came to propose the drainage of their own neighborhood's street. There were a few people who tried to create a more general discussion, one that was universal for the municipality. In this system that was difficult." Indeed, this tension between local-level demands and the need to address broader issues is one that had also plagued PB in other cases. In some cities it was resolved by introducing citywide "thematic councils" that were specifically designed to address sectoral issues. In João Monlevade, as we are about to see, the problem was addressed by introducing a strategic planning component to PB. But in Gravataí, the emphasis of PB, born largely from the political imperative of having to break with particularly corrupt state agencies and clientelistic relations, was on direct participation. The result was a process that was markedly weighted in favor of neighborhood-level issues.

Though this highly localized process of demand-making had its obvious drawbacks, this very direct and government-mediated version of PB did produce a quite dramatic rupture with past practices. The difference with the past is, moreover, not only in the actors (citizens with no prior associational engagement) and the processes (direct participation), but also in the actual practice of citizenship, and more specifically in how choices are formed. This point bears emphasis because it is at the core of the difference between representative and participatory democracy. In light of the direct and binding chain of sovereignty we have described here, we can assert that the participatory demands processed through PB in Gravataí are not the reduced form of demand-making posited in pluralist democratic theory (that is, representatives aggregate the interests of their constituents). The participatory structures of PB represent a fundamentally different mode of making choices, one that occurs through iterative processes of public discussion. Based on our key respondent interviews, we do not have enough information to evaluate the degree to which the microdistrict assemblies met the very high standard of engaged, equal, publicly oriented speech posited in deliberative democracy theory. No doubt the deliberative quality of these local publics varied. And certainly, in the process as a whole, there were moments where mobilization and bargaining were important, particularly at the district and municipal levels. But there is little doubt that the outputs were the product of participation by ordinary, and certainly previously voiceless, local citizens, and that this local decision-making is by design. This difference between expressing choices through representative structures and *forming* choices through a local public process is precisely what distinguishes representative from participatory democracy (Avritzer 2002; Habermas 1996). Participatory democracy implies learning effects, active problem solving, and the willingness to change a priori choices in light of open discussion. These practices are critical, as associational democracy theories argue (Warren 2001; Cohen and Rogers 1995), in nurturing the democratic capabilities and normative commitments of citizens.

PARTICIPATORY BUDGET—JOÃO MONLEVADE

While Gravataí's PB process stands out for its focus on local investments and massive participation, João Monlevade's PB process is distinctive because of its focus on strategic planning as well as some of its innovations, such as the "Priorities Caravans" that we describe below. PB in João Monlevade was not just about local (neighborhood-level) demands; it also emphasized citywide demands, by integrating participation with strategic, longer-term planning. This created a more complex and extended chain of sovereignty, but also one that confronted the problems of parochialism inherent in the Gravataí model.

PB in João Monlevade emerged from a much richer history of participatory experiences than was the case in Gravataí. João Monlevade had previously experimented with social participation during the first administration of Leonardo Diniz Dias (PT, 1989–92). That administration had launched an incipient PB process and also introduced a number of councils for sectors as varied as the elderly, health, and transport. These councils did not survive the subsequent administration (Germin Loureiro, PMDB, 1993–96), but nonetheless were important symbolic and policy resources for the social movement activists who helped elect the PT in 1996.

When PB was introduced in 1997 it was coordinated with a larger administrative program that sought to integrate social participation with planning and, in particular, to ensure that larger, citywide investments, and not just local priorities, were subject to participatory inputs. The coordination with planning was also a response to a crippling inherited debt.

In its first year, the incoming administration inherited "an almost bankrupt" city government, with high debts and little margin for investment. The first months of the administration were dedicated to surveying possible means for reducing costs and increasing fiscal capacity. In order to reduce costs, administrators introduced several measures to increase internal control over expenditures. To increase fiscal capacity, municipal property tax rates were updated and efforts to monitor compliance were stepped up. Through these measures the administration increased its budget for PB projects for 2000 to almost $4 million Reais (US$2 million), almost 16 percent of the total budget, up from 6 percent in 1997.

As with PB in Gravataí, PB in João Monlevade was both binding and involved direct participation from the first year of its operation. This is reflected in an institutional design that has some similarities to Gravataí's. As in Gravataí, this town of sixty-six thousand was divided into six districts, which each held assemblies where general demands were raised and where delegates were elected. Unlike Gravataí, there were no microdistricts, and delegates played a more prominent role in later stages of the process. The delegates met repeatedly to first rank-order demands in order of priority. A second set of delegates then monitored the projects. Participation increased over the years. In the first year, seven hundred fifty participants attended the process, and fifteen hundred attended in its fourth year. Some of the municípios' previously excluded groups—such as the homeless movement (*Movimento dos Sem Casa*)—became active agents in the municípios' planning and were able to include items such as housing projects as an important priority.

As we have described, João Monlevade was a city in which social movements were particularly strong. Civil society organizations capitalized on the institutional space of PB and used their capacity for mobilization to stimulate participation among the population. Organized movements were particularly influential in electing delegates, in helping generate demands, and were especially involved in strategic planning through the Municipal Plan of Development. One participant recalled that "each organization had people directly involved in the budget's planning." In this sense, the result approximates what was observed in Gravataí: channeling social demands through PB, thus eroding traditional forms of claim-making. However, in contrast to Gravataí, participation in João Monlevade was heavily mediated by preexisting social organizations and less dependent on government officials, as evidenced by the recollections of a former city official:

> We saw that certain groups were organized. Groups like the Neighborhood Associations. These people, because they were organized, were better able to put forth their issues. They were able to have a greater effect. They capitalized on their right to be involved in budgetary decisions. They arrived there with defined interests. They arrived saying: "We want this and that." They were accustomed to making claims and knew how to maneuver in PB.

The Evolution of an Integrative Strategy

While participation in João Monlevade for the first three years was limited to choosing urban improvement projects, in its fourth year it was adapted and expanded to include "thematic discussions" and a more explicit discussion of the town's long-term development goals. As PB evolved, it was scaled-out to include larger, citywide projects. Organizers recalled that at a certain point they had realized that there was a need for PB to include not only local projects but also "works that affect the city as a whole. So we defined some of these projects, and proposed them to the PB participants who would choose them." These larger and much more costly projects were proposed by the administration as part of the strategic plan, but were submitted to PB for consideration. Bringing strategic investments into the purview of PB had the effect of expanding discussion beyond local concerns to cover issues that had a more general character, such as the discussion on strategic planning or investment in a downtown redevelopment program. In its fourth year, PB evolved to encompass a conference on municipal development and the opening up of more opportunities for community oversight over municipal affairs.

By the fourth year, roughly half the capital budget was allocated to local projects and the other half to strategic planning. This ring fencing of the budget had the advantage of clearly demarcating the administration's citywide priorities from popular demands, ensuring that the later would be safeguarded and reducing the endemic conflicts that had plagued so many other PB experiments. The careful integration of planning and participation also had the advantage of more effectively linking preferences and proposed projects to actual budgets. Because PB fora had to formulate priorities within well-defined budget constraints, the common problem of overdemand and the subsequent frustration with local governments' inability to fund all demands was averted. The PB process was also further insulated from political interference by developing a clear formula for distributing resources to districts. This formula predetermined the amount of resources for each of the five districts in proportion to the population, overall levels of poverty, existing infrastructure, and service levels. According to one of the city planners "a little more went to the needy areas, a little less to areas with good infrastructure."

Based on our assessment of all eight municípios we studied, it is clear that in comparative terms João Monlevade was highly effective in executing planned projects. This no doubt reflects the overall care and thoroughness with which the PB process was designed. Our respondents, however, also highlighted the impact of two institutional innovations: the "priority caravans" and the "Monitoring Committees." In the caravans the delegates traveled together in buses to visit each district in the município and the proposed project sites. The goal of

the caravan was to offer delegates information relevant to the process of deliberation on the priority projects by allowing them to come directly in contact
with the reality of the intervention. Also, the caravans allowed the delegates to
develop a more publicly oriented understanding of the budgetary process by
exposing them to problems and challenges across the entire city. This had the
effect of undergirding a more deliberative logic to the budget discussions. By
exposing all the delegates to the full range of problems in the city, the caravan
provided a shared point of reference for making and defending criteria for pri-
oritizing projects. This explicit effort to create a sense of public interests was
judged by one respondent as "perhaps the greatest gain for the community. To
get to know the município, see the difficulties of others." Or as one PB delegate
simply put it, "Now, instead of demanding without knowledge, we got to know
the city as a whole."

The Monitoring Committees played a critical role in completing the chain
of sovereignty—that is, in ensuring the participatory inputs were translated
into outputs. Composed of dedicated delegates, the committee went to work
after projects had been selected and "monitored the process and could demand of the mayor to know what happened to last year's projects," according
to one participant. As another recalled, "If something didn't seem right, you
now had the authority to call the proper authorities, ask them to send an en-
gineer." Committee members we interviewed emphasized how well organized
and transparent the process was, and the senior official responsible for internal
auditing reported that his office's data showed that in the years of PB, 95–98
percent of projects were implemented.

PARTICIPATORY ADMINISTRATION—CAMARAGIBE

Of all the cases discussed in this book, Camaragibe's "Participatory Administration" is probably the best known in public administration circles in Brazil. It is
a prize-winning PT administration that garnered distinction in the late 1990s
for a novel and creative approach to participatory governance. In addition to
several other national and international awards, in 2000 it received an award
from the national Public Administration and Citizenship Program for the accomplishments of the Participatory Administration. Awards were granted for
the especially impressive accomplishments in the policy areas regarding children and health.[5] The município's community-based public health approach
has achieved the status of international "best practice" for its success in developing a participatory approach to public health and its very concrete outcomes.

Child mortality, which is normally a "sticky" variable, was practically *halved* in Camaragibe between 1997 and 2000. Similarly the participatory education policy led to an increase in primary school attendance to almost 100 percent from 72 percent four years earlier. Innovative approaches to governance also extended to economic sector development, including professional training programs.[6]

As with all our cases, the government plans justifying participation invoked ideas of citizenship, empowerment, and better governance. But the idea of a "Participatory Administration" (in contrast to "Participatory Budget") is distinct. According to city documents, it has at its root the principle that the responsibility for the "management of all public affairs is shared with the population." Thus, all areas of public administration are supposed to be open to direct public input and oversight.[7] Part of the distinctiveness of Camaragibe lay in its distance from the South and Southeast of the country—the geographic center of PT activity and NGO networks. Camaragibe's administrators thus invented much of the institutional design anew and relied on its own previous local participatory experiences, especially experiments with health councils.

Unlike Gravataí and João Monlevade, Camaragibe developed participatory institutions that did not revolve exclusively around the budget. The scope of participation was much broader. Rather than controlling the budget, the process intervened in the governance of all the municipal departments that served citizens directly: Social Services, Education, Public Works and Planning, Health, and Culture. The particularity of this design reflects the pragmatic choices of administrators to channel participation *away* from new investments and *toward* areas of governance such as health which rely on external funding, and where management of services is more important. Camaragibe is the poorest municipality in our sample, and its city government is the one with the least fiscal capacity.[8] Urban infrastructure needs far outweighed the available capital budget. In 1997 less than 20 percent of the population was connected to the municipal sewage line, and more than one-third lived in areas at risk of landslides. Yet, despite the lack of resources and the overall economic underdevelopment of the city, Camaragibe evolved the most complex set of participatory institutions in our sample.

The Evolution of the Process

The evolution of the Participatory Administration in Camaragibe is closely tied to the political trajectory of Paulo Santana, who became mayor in 1997. Santana, a highly respected activist from the health movement, had served as the head of the municipal health department for a year (1989–90); during that time, he had launched a Municipal Health Conference. That conference in turn resolved to establish the Health Council. Then-mayor Arnaldo Guerra (PTB, 1989–92) dismissed Santana and dissolved the council. Local activists mobilized around the issue of the council, and the council was reinstated in 1993 under the next administration (Mayor João Lemos, PSB, 1993–96), when Santana was reappointed to head the Health Department. As head of the Health Department, Santana continued to meet with activists of the health movement, who insisted on increasing the scope of participatory policies and decentralizing health provision (Teixeira 2002, 5). From then on, the Municipal Council became more active in intervening in municipal health policy, and in 1994, it implemented the Health Conference.

But it was during the 1996 electoral campaign that the proposal for a Participatory Administration emerged. The current administration did not have the approval ratings to name a successor from within that party, and Santana emerged as a candidate. An initial participatory exercise (the "City Forum") involved a neighborhood-by-neighborhood diagnostic exercise that generated the basic outlines of the plan for the Participatory Administration. This was understood as an *alternative* to Participatory Budgeting as practiced in many Brazilian cities. As Teixeira notes:

> The objective was not to elaborate something similar to the Participatory Budget, with the population discussing the application of a volume of previously defined resources. Another path was chosen: a model of participatory administration in which the residents indicate a set of priority actions for municipal governance and, after learning of the amount of available resources, prioritize those demands. (Teixeira 2002, 6)

Once elected, Santana's team sought partnerships with several advisory institutions, including the Recife-based Josué de Castro Center, a progressive social science research institute.[9] These advisors helped further the earlier "diagnostic" work of the campaign process by continuing to carry out research in the town's five districts. The next step, as proposed by the advisory committee, was the mobilization of the community. There were visits to civil society organizations and an intense advertising campaign to mobilize participants for a series of workshops to prepare them for the eventual Participatory Administration. These "Organizational Capacity-building Workshops" (Capacitação) sought to develop the "participatory consciousness" of the population as well as its capacity for self-management and technical decision-making. In April 1997 the Participatory Administration was introduced to the population in the First City Forum, attended by thousands of participants.

The Role of Delegates

Shortly after that first City Forum, citizens in the town's five districts came together to elect one hundred twenty delegates (one for every thousand residents) for a four-year term. Their charge was to mobilize the community in their district, make the administration aware of the needs of their district, and keep its population informed of the status of the municipality and the workings of the administration. Tenório and Filho quote the statutes approved in the 2000 City Congress that define the role of delegates:

> To discuss, within their districts, local necessities and to pass to the population information about the city plan; to participate in ordinary and extraordinary meetings with the administration and with sectoral councils; to mobilize the population and local organizations for plenary meetings; to participate in the training program on the public budget; to organize with the administration the map of social needs for each district. (2006,102)

The title of the Participatory Administration planning seminar that we quote at the start of the chapter, "The Challenge of Being Government," became more than just a slogan and took on a literal meaning. If the role of intermediation between the local state and society in Gravataí was taken up by city administrators through the structure of meetings at very local levels and by organized civil society in João Monlevade, in Camaragibe this role fell to the delegates. These volunteers were in effect tasked with functions normally associated with governmental roles and with an unusual (by wider PB standards) term length of four years. Yet they were clearly distinguished from normal representatives as underscored by the official literature of Camaragibe's Participatory Administration that emphasizes that delegates are—in contrast to elected city councilors—"unremunerated." After being elected, delegates took a course in public budgeting, and a statute of delegates was created, as were standing committees of delegates on particular topics and an ethics committee of delegates to monitor each other (Camaragibe 2000; Tauk Santos 2002).

The Yearly Cycle

In contrast to the aggregative and linear yearly cycle that characterizes our other PB cases, the process in Camaragibe is more complex, marked by parallel but interrelated cycles of meetings, assemblies, and fora. It brings together two parallel institutions, the Council of Delegates that focused on urban infrastructure and a structure of councils that worked on specific policy areas.

The Council of Delegates functions in a manner roughly similar to the PB cycles described above. The delegates meet with administration experts early in the year to discuss the amount of resources available for infrastructure investments for the year. After collecting demands from the town's five districts in a series of assemblies, the delegates and experts meet for several weeks to determine which of those demands were technically viable and could be met within the available budget. Delegates then reported this information back to residents in their districts. Finally, delegates called an assembly in their respective districts to vote on priority projects.

In addition, Municipal Councils (principally in the areas of health and education) were integrated into the participatory structure.[10] There, as in other cities in Brazil with councils, representatives from the relevant unions, from the administration, and from society debate the management of sectoral policy. But in Camaragibe, the councils also proposed projects. Sometimes these projects emerged from councilors themselves, but sometimes they emerged from yearly or biannual conferences that each council sponsored.

These conferences—open to all citizens—were designed for deliberation on the specifics of particular policy areas. The respective municipal departments were supposed to operationalize and implement the priorities formed at the conferences, under the monitoring of the respective council. According to a former participant, the conferences are not simply consultative, but rather places where "policies of health, education, and social assistance were deliberated. This policy was then followed by the corresponding department." Conferences in effect serve to link social demands to local government and were active in a range of sectors including health, social services, education, culture, children and adolescents, women, and public safety. The impact of the conferences is, moreover, extended by the councils, which serve as standing fora for monitoring the implementation of conference resolutions.

Based on the inputs from the Council of Delegates and the Municipal Councils, the city prepared a list of proposed actions for the next fiscal year. The Plan of Projects was then presented and discussed publicly in a municipal assembly called the City Congress. This assembly was open to all citizens, but the right to vote was limited only to the one hundred twenty delegates, the councilors from the Municipal Councils and representatives of formally registered social organizations. Being a space for promoting actions that the city government is publicly committed to, the City Congress served as a tool for delegates to hold the government accountable to the participatory process.

The Limits of Camaragibe's PA

One of the limits of the Participatory Administration process was that there was not a one-to-one correspondence between the Plan of Projects and the annual budget. The Plan of Projects represented a list of desired works, but did not specify in which year the works would be implemented. A former city official described the resulting gap in implementation: "If the municipal government is able to obtain resources, projects will happen faster. If the resources aren't obtained, projects will have to be funded by the government's own resources and everything takes longer." The Plan of Projects also sometimes incorporated projects that were considered priorities by the municipal government, even if they were not raised in participatory fora. One former participant recalled that "[Certain institutional projects] are presented as proposals in the City Forum, each year. In this sense, they are not presented as a question to be debated, but as a question to be presented as a decided fact." To some, this meant that the discussions about projects were too removed from the budgeting process itself, since delegates could not compose the whole budget as is the case in many cities with PB. For many of the participants, this represented less than full citizen control of the budgeting process. One former delegate recalled that:

> This was a contradiction in the process because the delegates were invited to discuss the management as a whole, discussing the problems of management, the investment plan, proposed actions, but ... the process of accountability and development of the whole budget did not involve the delegates. So, you are invited, but you are not involved in the process of composition of the budget.

Though many of our respondents commented on the gap between the participatory process and final budgeting and implementation, they all nonetheless viewed the process as binding. Implementation was sometimes delayed for what were generally sound fiscal reasons and the government did on occasion push through it own priorities. But overall, the oversight of municipal finances through the councils and the publicly discussed Plan of Projects meant that the administration was in effect bound to complete the projects that emerged from the participatory process.

A second limit of the Participatory Administration has to do with its reliance on delegates. Delegates played an unusually prominent role in the Participatory Administration; with their four-year terms and broad mandate, they took on roles normally associated with government officials. During the first two years of the administration there were instances of delegates defining the priorities of demands for their districts without formal authorization of those populations. This was corrected with the introduction of new rules making delegates fully accountable to their districts. Nonetheless, delegates continued to play a very important role throughout the years of the Participatory Administration. This meant that, on the one hand, tensions with the local city council over authority tended to be more conflictive than in other cases of PB. As one of our informants described it, "Initially, city councilors were shocked with the idea of having delegates in the Participatory Administration. They felt that the delegates would replace their jobs. So, during the first four years they were always questioning things." And on the other hand, because delegates tended to be community leaders who then became full-time volunteers with the administration, there was a danger of subordinating social movements to the administration. One former participant recalled that city hall "really involved the movements' leaders," but sometimes "the movements followed, to a certain extent, the promises formed through the local government rather than their specific claims."

Camaragibe represents an important departure from the basic blueprint we described earlier in this chapter. The process instituted in Camaragibe was, in fact, much more about *participatory governance* than participatory budgeting. In some respects, the process penetrated more deeply into the machinery of local government, even as it afforded the administration more discretion in budgetary matters than in our first three cases. The chain of sovereignty was less direct and more diffuse, but it was also more encompassing. This difference can be ascribed both to Camaragibe's much more restricted budgetary position and its greater reliance on external funding, as well as to the practices and orientations developed through its own local experience with health councils. As with our three earlier cases, we again find clear evidence of pragmatic adaptation to local conditions and heavy reliance on preexisting experiences with promoting participation. Both these points highlight and help explain the extraordinary heterogeneity of actual institutional design behind the idea of PB.

MAUÁ'S PARTICIPATORY BUDGET

"The Listening Budget"—Former Participant

The introduction of PB by the administration of Oswaldo Dias (PT, 1997–2000) marked an important departure from traditional practices. In previous administrations, the Societies of Friends of the Neighborhood (SABS) had routinely been invited to present their demands directly to the municipal mayor. But as our interviews made very clear, this was a limited type of engagement with the local state: participation was restricted to the presidents of SABS who had party affiliations with members of government; discussions did not produce any promise from the government to attend to collective demands; and meetings were ineffective in producing concrete results in terms of providing access to public projects and services.

As was the case in Gravataí, in launching PB the PT administration borrowed directly from the basic blueprint we described earlier, though adapted to the local reality of fiscal deficits. For example, in the first year, the assemblies that were held in Mauá were not empowered to raise demands and identify priorities. Instead, the administration held more than forty assemblies in the first months of its government primarily to publicize the financial straits of the municipality.[11] Faced with a financial shortfall and unable to carry out new investments for the first year, the administration held off on carrying out more ambitious reforms while trying to "put its house in order." Subsequently, the administration did introduce some reforms, but the PB that emerged revolved around district-level meetings with a limited consultative function. Delegates elected at these meetings attended a "participatory council" at which they communicated the priorities of their districts and neighborhoods to the administration but had no say over the budget. One delegate described it, jokingly, as "conselho escutativo" (a "listening council," which is a play on the Portuguese "conselho participativo").

The resulting institutional design was nonetheless quite complex and directly addressed both problems of representation and integration. The cycle begins with neighborhood meetings in which information concerning government actions (availability of resources, projects to be implemented, accounting of past projects) were disclosed, delegates were chosen (one delegate for each twenty participants attending the meeting), and demands for district-level projects and services were heard. The thirty-nine neighborhoods were aggregated into six districts. For the first year in which delegates were elected (1998), thirty-six hundred residents participated in the PB process. Then, in a parallel structure, meetings were held with representatives of organized sectors took place to gather their demands. The sectors included associations from commerce and industry, the Catholic Church, the evangelical church, and neighborhood associations. Finally, parallel thematic meetings were organized to integrate noninfrastructural demands.

As elaborate as these structures were, our interviews revealed a very contested interpretation of both the substance of the Mauá's PB and the overall logic and practicality of PB. Most notably, our informants decried the absence of actual deliberation over the budget. As one city hall employee in charge of budgeting surmised, "The Participatory Budget has no bearing here [in the elaboration of a budgetary proposal]. . . . What do we do? We call on the councilors of the budget and tell them how much will be spent and for what causes. But, they have no direct participation here." Administration officials responsible for PB's implementation presented a series of arguments to justify limiting participation to a consultative function. First, they pointed to the pragmatic issue regarding the risks associated with the introduction of a deliberative process in the context of the financial shortfall the city was experiencing. Specifically, they expressed the concern that such a process could result in demand overload, with important political costs for the government. As one official put it, "We receive requests, but we don't vote on them. We don't do this, because the process of voting on issues that are prioritized presents problems. We don't work with that logic. We respond to a logic of having data and doing what we can." Second, officials argued that limiting participation to consultation made it possible for the government to meet the electoral promise of introducing participatory fora and at the same time provided the opportunity to address social demands while being conscious of budgetary limitations. This pragmatic adaption to the lack of resources was one of the arguments for a purely consultative PB model. In this sense, interviewees critically examined the idealization of Porto Alegre's PB model, saying that deliberation on the budget is a fiction, "it's impractical, it's impossible!"

The case of Mauá represents what may very well be the modal response of most state actors—be they bureaucrats or politicians—to the idea of binding participation. The concern officials expressed with subordinating government action to the deliberation of participatory fora was rationalized largely on the claim that social demands tend to be particularistic and fail to take into account the wider issues (financial, technical, political, administrative, and so on) which determine the capacity of the government to respond to those demands. In this managerial view, the municipal executive, as the bearer of a global vision of the municipality and armed with the requisite knowledge to define priority actions, cannot be subordinated to the participatory forum's social demands, especially when the demands are generally parochial, such as "demands from a group or segment that doesn't have a macro vision" or demanding "ambulances, when the hospitals are not functioning." From this vantage point, PB is conceived as a consultative complement, rather than as a substitute, to representative structures duly formed through the electoral process. That is, PB is the place for the government to present its government plan, and PB councilors are "a thermometer. We put our proposal out there, and we see the reaction."

If Mauá's PB did not constitute an effective participatory forum, what, if any, effects did it have? First, as a consultative forum, PB produced a channel for the expression of social demands, informing the municipal executive of specific issues determined by the population to be priorities. Such issues, after an assessment by the government of the validly of their "real" urgency, could then become the basis for intervention by the municipal administration. In addition to acting as a mechanism for listening to the population, Mauá's PB constituted a channel for direct communication between the municipal executive and the population, allowing for dissemination of information and encouraging some government accountability. In fact, many interviewees identified this as the principal characteristic of Mauá's PB: providing a space to publicize the situation faced by city hall (especially its financial limitations) and to publicize the proposals made by the government to the council. Accountability and the transparency of information concerning the municipal government were, in fact, the core functions of the meetings held in districts, the Popular Council, the thematic meetings, and those with the neocorporatist sectoral fora. In sum, PB helped process and organize information, but in its formal structure it had no effective leverage on how local government used that information. This is the critical assessment that the respondent cited earlier arrived at when he pronounced PB a "Listening Council."

But PB also had a second effect that was much more democratic. Critics of deliberative democracy often dismiss it on the grounds that talk is cheap. Yet, even in the absence of clearly defined mechanisms to bind government decision-making to PB-generated preferences, there is little doubt that the talk generated by PB did influence government. Mauá's PB created an institutional channel for mobilization and collective claim-making, one that a relatively well-organized civil society (which we describe at length in Chapter 5) was able to take advantage of. The various fora that constituted PB in turn become spaces in which demands could be heard and in which conflict would some-times arise, requiring effective responses from the municipal executive. In most cases these conflicts emerged in response to proposals made by the municipal executive. The fora in effect instituted a process of exposing government action to criticism and counterclaims. In this sense then, PB did constitute a sensor, if not a direct link, through which civil society could exercise its influence.

CONCLUSIONS

Drawing on our analysis of the *actually instituted process* of PB in our four cases, we can make the following observations. First, insofar as PB has brought tradi-tionally marginalized or dependent groups into the process of decision-making as citizens rather than as clients, it has in effect expanded the demos. Thus, as they evolved, the forms of participatory democracy introduced were a pointed and self-conscious break from the past in two respects. On the one hand, they bypassed traditional forms of political mediation such as clientelism and boss-ism and created a parallel chain of sovereignty based on new spaces and chan-nels of citizen engagement with the local state. On the other hand, by care-fully specifying the rules and processes of participation and linking civil society inputs to specific forms of governance these participatory reforms marked a break with "spontaneous" civil society mediation. PB, it should be noted, is it-self an expression of the demand for the deepening and expanding the rights of citizenship that emerged from Brazil's powerful urban movements of the 1980s and 1990s (Dagnino 1998; Holston 2008). Having made this point, we reiterate that translating the new norms of citizenship into concrete capacities required political intervention and careful institutional design.

Second, if PB deepens democracy by bringing new actors into the demos, it also broadens the range of issues that are subject to democratic authorizations. A range of local government decisions and resources that were once the exclu-sive purview of local elites, are now, to varying degrees, open to direct forms of public scrutiny and deliberation. Of course, such public participation could be limited to advancing particularistic or parochial demands. This was obviously the paramount concern of officials in Mauá and is also revealed in the local-ism of demand-making in Gravataí. But participation, as we have emphasized, is highly artifactual and the logic of demand-formation is highly contingent on the actual process. Thus, as Abers (2000) and Baiocchi (2005) have both shown in careful, detailed analyses of the actual functioning of deliberative popular assemblies, the process of deliberation does for the most part encourage more public-mindedness. In our cases, specific institutional designs such as the introduction of thematic fora, the "Priorities Caravan" or a careful integration of local demand-making with strategic planning did have the effect of promoting more encompassing forms of governance.

Third, in its ideal-typical form PB represents a form of instituted participatory democracy that is in effect a hybrid of direct democracy and representative democracy. PB structures and processes parallel, but do not supplant formal electoral representation. The PB budget is formed through a combination of direct participation—neighborhood assemblies—and delegates who carry neighborhood mandates to the budget council. But final authorization of the budget rests with the legislative assembly (specifically, the municipal council). In formal terms, such a chain of representation would appear to be inherently unstable given the lack of legal authority accorded the PB process. Yet, the fact that in our three successful cases the process was judged to be, in fact, "binding" points to just how powerful the legitimacy-producing effects of a deliberative process can be.

If each of the four cases represents unique institutional designs that were bootstrapped responses to different contexts, each also illustrates the trade-offs between different choices. Table 4.1, below, summarizes each of our four cases.

Gravataí is the clearest case of a borrowed blueprint and of the advantages and limits of government mediation. Here, Participatory Budgeting was patterned after the Porto Alegre model, but was creatively adapted to local conditions, specifically the perceived lack of local civil society capacity. In Gravataí, collective actors played no role in the mediation of demands, and PB meetings were held at the microdistrict level, with some microdistricts having fewer than three thousand residents. Participation was massive and inclusive owing to the presence of government facilitators at every stage. Residents in effect mediated and represented their interests themselves. But if this case represents the most direct form of participation, it also by design limited the role of collective organizations in mediating demands. The institutional design also limited the possibilities of negotiations between local units and narrowed demand-making to local infrastructure and local projects. A final weakness of this design lies in the possibility of the "colonization of the life-world," or more specifically the degree to which state influence can crowd out civil society initiative. Most notably, the dominance of government officials in running PB ruled out the possibilities in Gravataí for innovation in the process itself by civil society organizations.

Table 4.1 Summary of the Four Cases

	Gravataí	João Monlevade	Camaragibe	Mauá
Origins	Transplanted from Porto Alegre	Previous experiences, PT discussions	Invention and previous experiences with health councils	Originally borrowed from Porto Alegre, but changed to emphasize financial constraints
Levels of Participation	Massive (25,000/238,000) 10.5%	Low (1,500/66,000) 2.3%	High (8,500/ 128,000) 6.6%	Low (3,600- 20,000/417,000)
Decentralization	High (85 microdistricts)	Low (5 districts)	Low (5 districts)	Low (6 districts)
Scaling-up	Aggregation	Combination of aggregation and inclusion via social movements, debates among delegates	Integration of demands of fora on infrastructure and city councils	Combination of aggregation with inputs from organized civil society
Role of Mediators	None (government)	Social movements are most important	Delegates play extremely crucial role	Formally organized civil society plays a role
Focus	Infrastructure, local demands	Infrastructure and long-term strategic planning combined	Participatory Administration as a whole.	Informational
Strategic Planning	None	City congress on development	City forum	None

In João Monlevade, Participatory Budgeting had been trial-tested in a previous administration (1989–92), and by virtue of the national reach of its social movements, administrators had participated in national discussions about effective tools for participation through fora like the National Forum for Public Participation. The PB process that emerged in João Monlevade was very much an innovation based on previously successful ideas. In particular, here the participatory process greatly emphasized strategic planning and the involvement of participants at levels beyond the generation of neighborhood demands. So in addition to efforts at generating a discussion about the city itself, participants were involved in all stages of budgeting, including monitoring. Organized civil society played a key role. Associations and movements mobilized citizens, helped process demands, and offered suggestions for improving the process. In João Monlevade, Participatory Budgeting reforms were shaped by the long history of social movements, and these social movements and their umbrella organizations continued to play an important role in mediating demands in the Participatory Budget. These autonomous organizations not only provided a counterweight to the government's role in PB, but also they played a crucial role in recruiting participants to the process and in shaping demands. The upside of the design of João Monlevade's PB is that it secures the greatest autonomy for civil society and enhances its innovative role. On the downside, the process is potentially less inclusive. Voluntary organizations, by definition, do not encompass the entire population and can be selective in the interests, identities, and preferences they represent.

In Camaragibe, a município far less plugged into national circuits than João Monlevade and Gravataí, the participatory blueprint for the Participatory Administration was a highly local invention based on the previous experiences of Health Councils and a pragmatic response to a lack of available funds for investments. The emphasis was on governance, broadly conceived, and civil society activists played a very prominent role in the mediation of demands. This took place through a complex institutional design where councils and local fora were convened to debate policy (in the councils) and infrastructure demands (in the fora), and all converged at a municipal city forum. Participation was high, but in a unique twist, delegates were elected for a four-year term at the start of the process and played the role that the government officials played in Gravataí—drawing participants, helping filter demands, negotiating scaled-up demands. In Camaragibe, associations—neighborhood associations and movements linked to health and housing, among others—played important roles in the mediation of interests. This is evident, for example, in the privileged role that delegates (who, according to our interviews, tended to come from movements) played.

Finally, we have the case of Mauá, where Participatory Budgeting was limited to consultation. The PB process was a complex one, but a shallow version of the Porto Alegre blueprint, limited in its design to providing legitimacy for the administration. The consultative process itself was substantial, but one in which participatory inputs could be overridden by administrators with little justification. This was a case in which the chain of sovereignty was broken. Despite this, as we have also discussed, this was a process that served some important democratic functions, such as creating a space for discussion and negotiation between civil society and government officials.

5 MAKING SPACE FOR CIVIL SOCIETY

Our paired analysis of four municípios that adopted PB and four that did not has so far revealed two broad findings. First, cities that introduced PB experienced a shift in the form of engagement from traditional forms of discretionary and personalized engagement to more participatory and institutionalized modes, albeit with varying degree of success. Second, in carefully reviewing the actual process of participation that was instituted in each of our four cases of PB we found enormous variation. The manner and degree to which the chain of sovereignty was preserved in each case was tied to very different institutional designs. But if these institutional designs have a strong bearing on how demands are processed—and specifically on how participatory inputs are translated into concrete outputs—any analysis of the democratic effects of the introduction of these reforms begs a second set of questions: How did PB, in its various institutional manifestations, impact civil society itself, in particular the capacity of civil society to autonomously form and aggregate democratic demands? As we argued in Chapter 1, the quality of associational life is in no small part an artifact of the institutional environment. Institutional reforms as such not only can transform the quality of governance but also can have an independent effect on the quality of associational life. In this chapter we evaluate the effect that the introduction of PB has on civil society. We do so by specifically comparing the state of civil society before and after the reforms in the pairs of cities. Our analysis reveals that PB reforms do indeed open up spaces for civil society, but that this impact is contingent on the preexisting state of civil society. In particular, the extent to which civil society had the capacity for autonomous organizing before the introduction of reforms makes a measurable difference to the type of state-society relations that emerge. We then discuss each of our cases of change and show how each of these corresponds to different instances of *affirmative democracy* and *mobilized democracy*.

CIVIL SOCIETY IN 1996

Before developing our comparative analysis, we present brief sketches of the status of civil society in each município before 1996. Conceptualizing and measuring civil society is notoriously difficult. In Brazil, there are no reliable official registers of CSOs, and such data would in any event tell us little about the capacity and autonomy of these organizations and hence of the overall quality of associational life. Given the theoretical concerns what we reviewed in Chapter 1, we opted for developing a qualitative picture of both the internal and relational dimensions of local civil societies through interviews with key respondents. In the section of our questionnaire that focused on civil society, we asked our respondents nineteen separate questions designed to assess five different criteria. Specifically, we first asked about the density of civil society organizations, how long these organizations had been active, and their relationship to each other. We then probed the nature of civil society's ties to political parties and to the state, including the specific channels and modalities of interaction with political society.

In order to develop a picture of the state of civil society in our eight municípios that is analytically and comparatively useful, we present our findings using the relational model of civil society and democratic regimes presented in Chapter 1. The model disaggregates local civil society along two axes. The horizontal axis is self-organization, which refers to the degree to which collective actors in civil society are capable of independently organizing, that is, mobilizing their own resources and forming their own demands (self-determination). Civil society organizations (CSOs) are classified either as *dependent* when they do not have the capacity for self-organization and self-determination without external support, or *autonomous* when they have the capacity for self-organizing and self-determination. The vertical axis is the mode of engagement and refers to how CSOs make demands on the state; we identify two modes: *institutionalized* (rule bound and transparent procedures of demand-making), and *discretionary* (discretionary demand-making contingent on loyalty to broker/patron). The four possible combinations produce four different types of democratic regimes: affirmative, mobilized, prostrate, and bifurcated. Our qualitative evaluations of the condition of civil society prior to the reforms is presented below by pairs and summarized in Table 5.1

The first point to note is that all of our pairs, with the exception of Mauá and Diadema, fall into the same cell. This underscores the robustness of our selection criteria, especially our assumption that the percentage vote share of the PT com-

Table 5.1 State-Civil Society Relations Before 1997

Degree of Self-organization Demand-making	Dependent	Autonomous
Institutionalized	Affirmative Democracy	Mobilized Democracy Diadema (movement democracy)
Discretionary	Prostrate Democracy Camaragibe Quixadá Gravataí Sapucaia	Bifurcated Democracy Mauá Timóteo João Monlevade

* Cities are presented as pairs, with the exception of Mauá and Diadema, which fall into different cells.

bined with region is a good proxy for the state of civil society. Camaragibe and Quixadá are in the northeastern states of Pernambuco and Ceará, respectively. The Northeast of Brazil is infamous for its low levels of development and for the political dominance of traditional, landowning oligarchs. Well into the 1990s politics in both cities were dominated by traditional families. In Camaragibe and Quixadá civil society was poorly organized and with some exceptions, most notably the progressive church in the case of Quixadá, subject to clientelistic control. In our scheme, civil society is dependent and can only engage with the state through discretionary processes, thus producing a democratic regime classified as *prostrate*. Also in the same cell before 1997 are the cities of Gravataí and Sapucaia in Rio Grande do Sul. Along a range of key socioeconomic and political factors the municípios are very similar. Both have solid industrial bases and significant revenue sources, but they are confronted with the problems of rapid urbanization and a concentrated and impoverished low-income population with little access to urban infrastructure. In both cities, political power was vested in fragmented oligarchical parties whose electoral support was built on the strength of clientelist politics. In both places, civil society organizations were instrumentalized by political parties. In Gravataí, for example, since the late 1980s mayors have successfully used associations characterized by scant autonomy, little representativity, and a general lack of resources to build political support.

Mauá and Diadema in São Paulo are midsized industrial towns. Diadema has an especially active and "combative" (the specific term used by our respondents) civil society, so much so that it has actually been wary of institutionalizing participation. Diadema's CSOs, which included neighborhood associations, the *moradia* movement (homeless/housing movement), health organizations, unions, church organizations, and samba schools, demonstrated a particularly high level of organization, specifically the capacity for autonomous demand-making. Diadema represents the prototype of a *mobilized democracy*, although it should be emphasized that engagement was more contentious than institution-alized (and that as such might better be described as a *movement democracy*). We classify it as "institutionalized" because of the routinized access of social movements to the local state and the background expectations—after many years of successful demand-making, that those demands be met.

Mauá's civil society, though born of the same social movement history as Diadema's, was divided between CSOs closely tied to and dependent on the state and more autonomous CSOs commonly described by our respondents as the "combative" sector. The associations tied to the local ruling party, the PSDB, worked very closely with the city government between 1993–96 through the traditional mode of *assistencialismo*, or social service-oriented organizing, including a milk-distribution program (Alvarez 1993). The "combative" or movement sector had roots going back to the pro-democracy mobilizations of the 1980s and in particular the progressive church. Because this sector was entirely excluded by the ruling elite-based parties, they adopted and developed sophisticated modes of contentious politics and established a significant presence in local neighborhoods, often engaging in intense conflict with the more traditional "friends of the neighborhood" types of associations.[1] Mauá, in other words, had a *bifurcated democracy*.

João Monlevade and Timóteo are both "company towns" in the industrial belt of Minas Gerais, an area known for the influence of steel companies on town life. Both municípios are also known for labor union activism and PT sympathies.

Both had relatively dense civil societies, with active neighborhood associations, community clubs, unions, charitable organizations, and a plethora of organized business interests. In both, João Monlevade and Timóteo however, there was a bifurcation between those organizations and associations that engaged the state through clientelist arrangements, and new social movement organizations and militant unions that held a more combative stance. Both municípios, like Mauá, can be characterized as having *bifurcated* democracies.

THE IMPACT ON CIVIL SOCIETY

The character of civil society at the end of our study period (2000) was assessed in the same manner with which we established the pre-1997 character of civil society (see Table 5.1). The before and after comparisons are represented in Ta-

ble 5.2 (below) using our typology of state-civil society relations and our char-
acterizations of resulting democratic regimes. All of our cases are represented
at both time points, with PB cities in bold and arrows indicating a change in
regime in the 1997–2000 time period. In 1996, all pairs appear together except
for Diadema and Mauá, the one pair where civil society was not isomorphic
to begin with. As the PB literature would predict, all of the municípios that
adopted PB (and experienced a measurable change in the institutional setting)
experienced a change in civil society (indicated in Table 5.2 by a shift in the cells
they occupy). In contrast, the municípios that did not adopt PB experienced no
measurable change in civil society (and do not have arrows in Table 5.2). The
impact of PB is clear; what is less clear are the direction, quality, and mechanisms of that impact. We unpack these relationships through extended narra-
tives of grouped cases.

As illustrated by the arrows in Table 5.2, all the PB cities experienced some
change in the condition of civil society and hence in their democratic regimes.
The table makes clear that PB mattered more for improving the mode of engagement than for improving the self-organization of CSOs. Specifically, the
arrows in the table point to three different pathways: Gravataí and Camaragibe
shifted from cases of *prostrate* democracy to *affirmative democracy*; João Monlevade shifted from a *bifurcated democracy* to a *mobilized democracy*; and Mauá
shifted from a *bifurcated democracy* to an *affirmative democracy*. The arrow for
Mauá is a dotted line to underscore that this case comes with significant qualifications. Before examining each of these cases in detail, we briefly summarize
each of the non-PB cities.

Table 5.2 Changes in State-Civil Society Relations, 1997–2000

Degree of Self-organization *Mode of Engagement*	*Dependent*	*Autonomous*
Institutionalized	**Affirmative Democracy**	**Mobilized Democracy** ◄ Diadema (movement democracy)
Discretionary	**Prostrate Democracy** **Camaragibe (PB)** Quixadá **Gravataí (PB)** Sapucaia	**Bifurcated Democracy** Mauá (PB) Timóteo **João Monlevade (PB)**

* PB cities are in bold.

* Cities are presented as pairs, with the exception of Mauá and Diadema, which fall into different cells.

THE PERSISTENCE OF CLIENTELISM

We begin our analysis by focusing on the case that experienced no institutional change (Quixadá) and the two cases that experienced only limited change in the direction of delegative participation (Timóteo and Sapucaia). These were all non-PB municípios, and in all three there was little change in the activity and condition of civil society. In all three cases, however, the presence of the PT and increased political competition alone created pressures for institutional reform.

In Quixadá, a previous PT administration had established a "City Hall and You" program, which had created greater expectations for participation. During the 1997–2000 period, however, civil society remained highly dependent on clientelistic ties to local government and CSOs were able to do little more than funnel some demands to officials in exchange for personal allegiance. As one respondent described it, "There wasn't any space for debate and the population had more demands. The government could not meet demands and closed itself off." One respondent noted that the administration would not "even dialogue to say no."

In the cases of Timóteo and Sapucaia formal mechanisms of non-PB participation were introduced, but participation was carefully controlled, even orchestrated by the local state. This form of participation had the effect of weakening the autonomy of civil society, while strengthening those organizations engaged in clientelist exchanges with the ruling party. In Timóteo, as a response to the fact that PB had been a campaign promise of the opposition, the administration introduced a consultative participatory system called PROPOR, which relied heavily on neighborhood association presidents tied to the mayor's political machine to create a list of priorities. Participation in this system led, according to our respondents, to "an increase in dependence," because "you had to tow the line of the [government-sponsored] Community Council to get anything." In Sapucaia, the mayor introduced a participatory scheme that was little more than a vehicle for clientelist cooptation. The mayor met weekly with presidents of neighborhood associations, and participants did report that individual demands were sometimes met by the mayor: "There was a neighborhood that wanted pavement with the presence of one resident, and the mayor delivered it." Nonetheless the local state retained control of associations, with the head of the local Union of Neighborhood Associations having a job as a community liaison in the municipal government. In sum, despite a formal system of participation, CSOs in Sapucaia and Timóteo remained very dependent on the government.

MOVEMENT DEMOCRACY

Of all our cases, Diadema is most unique. This is the one case where, even in the absence of institutional reforms, a well-organized and combative civil society did manage to have input into city governance. As noted earlier, the preexisting level of organization in Diadema's civil society as well as its trajectory after 1997 were exceptional in our sample. Despite the absence of formal participatory channels, civil society exerted significant pressure throughout the period. Through contentious activities like demanding access to city hall accounts and demanding improved health delivery, civil society here remained in our mobilized democracy cell. Because the contentious mode did secure significant influence, civil society became self-sustaining. This case exemplifies how a well-organized civil society can exert significant influence over the state even in the absence of institutionalized participatory structures. However, since participatory channels of engagement were not institutionalized, but rather were the result of a balance of power in which movements had significant influence, Diadema might be more accurately labeled as a case of movement democracy (underscoring the importance of the contentious capacity of civil society) rather than a mobilized democracy.

In response to movement pressure, the administration that was elected in 1997 introduced a PB-like process that was quickly abandoned in 1998. Social movements increased activity demanding access to municipal finances. Activists were eventually able to pressure the administration into publishing an annual "Budget Book"—a notebook that listed projects for each district and neighborhood as well as information on the municipal budget. Social movements were also successful in demanding that councils on health, social services, and education be given a more active role. Ultimately, the *promise* of a PB had the effect of mobilizing organized sectors that were dissatisfied with stillborn participatory attempts and that demanded more access to decision-making in governmental affairs. Movements gained influence, not through the creation of a regular forum, but by reorganizing themselves around sector-specific issues and sporadic contention. For example, the housing movement organized land occupations throughout the four years, leading in some instances to negotiations that led to the development of new public housing units.

The few opportunities for participation in Diadema did not diminish the agency of a well-organized civil society that had clear demands and the expectation of eventually achieving participation. As one of our respondents noted, the recalcitrance of the municipal administration only led to more organization because if "you find it [the door to city hall] closed, with no space for discussion you become more organized. You think, I can't get in with fifty, next time I'll have to bring 100 people."

BUILDING AFFIRMATIVE DEMOCRACY

In two of our cases we see a change from prostrate to affirmative democracy that resulted from PB reforms. In other words, there was a change from a dependent civil society engaging the local state through discretionary processes to a dependent civil society engaging the state through institutionalized processes. This process describes two of our cases, Gravataí and Camaragibe, where PB also promoted greater inclusion of traditionally marginalized social groups. In both cases, PB created a formal channel of interaction between civil society and the state with clearly defined and publicly known rules that broke with the practice of discretionary demand-making that had fueled clientelism. In both places civil society had a precarious existence prior to PB, with many CSOs entangled in clientelist practices. PB reforms occasioned a transformation of those practices as well as a greater inclusion of underprivileged participants in governmental decision-making.

These changes have not, however, led to a strengthening of civil society's capacity for self-organization. We have classified this mode of engagement as dependent because in one case (Gravataí) participation in PB processes was driven directly by government officials, and in the other (Camaragibe), the new collective actors who emerged remained dependent on government initiative. In the absence of civil society organizations capable of autonomous organizing, participation remained entirely dependent on the participatory process and specifically on the support of the administration. Though civil society remained dependent, there has been, as we shall see, a fundamental rupture with past practices, a rupture that justifies reclassifying these cases from instances of prostrate democracies to affirmative democracies.

Gravataí illustrates this point clearly. As we saw in Chapter 4, participation in PB was high during the four years in question. Participants were mostly drawn from among the urban poor in irregular settlements. Most of the participants came from *outside* of organized civil society, as what few organizations existed opposed the PB process. In Gravataí, the participatory process itself became the only site of public discussion and association. The story of Camaragibe's Participatory Administration (PA) is similar. The PA introduced significant spaces for direct and binding participation, including councils on health, transportation, education, and planning. Existing movements, such as the health movement, saw their voices dramatically amplified. New collective actors also appeared in civil society, including the gay movement and the black movement, and achieved greater visibility through participatory proceedings. But even as civil society become more active, it still remained dependent on the state. Our respondents all noted that civil society *reacted* to openings established by city hall, rather than taking independent initiatives. This relational dynamic is complicated and is explained in detail in the next two sections. In making sense of the logic of affirmative democracy while acknowledging is ambiguities, we also draw a distinction between the mediated form that characterizes Camaragibe and the direct form that characterizes Gravataí.

MEDIATED AFFIRMATIVE DEMOCRACY: CAMARAGIBE

The 1980s: Fragmentation and Personalism

The case of Camaragibe is characterized by a change in the mode of engagement, which, despite the institutionalization of mechanisms of access to public policy, tended to reproduce a relationship of civil society dependence on the local state; though as we saw in Chapter 4, this relationship was mediated by delegates. To understand this result requires a reconstruction of the trajectory of the transformation.

Camaragibe is a relatively new municipality, formed in 1982. Its first mayor, Carlos Lapenda (PMDB, 1982–88) was from one of the traditional oligarchical families. During this period engagement with local state institutions was through traditional practices of clientelistic mediation, either through city councilors or the mayor himself. A direct effect of this mediation was to fragment and isolate associations. As one key informant noted, "So the associations were much more individualistic. . . . I spoke directly with the mayor. And the mayor listened or he didn't. He said, '—What I am able to do, I will. And what I am not able to do, I will not do. What I can do, I'll do. And what I cannot do, I won't do.' . . . We complained because we had no sanitation; we complained because the transportation did not work; we complained because we did not have paved roads."

During this period neighborhood associations became involved in the implementation of specific social service programs, especially the distribution of food from state and federal government. This practice increased the control that the local administration could exercise over associations since it had the power to select the associations to be included in the programs. In addition, this practice assigned the leaders of the selected associations with access to important resources. Association leaders not only had access to the goods to be distributed, but also the possibility to choose who would receive such public goods, thus strengthening their positions. As one civil society respondent recalled, "What gave the association the most strength at that time was that the state government distributed milk." In his view, "people would engage with the association in search of something," and as associations were able to distribute goods, they "could become stronger." Other civil society interviews confirmed that this kind of practice was "common in the city" and done "in order to win votes."

During the 1980s, other civil society activity was limited. Though progressive sectors of the Catholic Church were active, several interviewees underscored the limits of this support and the absence of CSOs doing political and organizational work. In addition as was the case in Diadema and João Monlevade, in the context of low levels of local economic development, unions in Camaragibe were weak and incapable of mobilizing forces in civil society. In fact, with the exception of the Rural Workers Union, the majority of unions were formed no earlier than the 1990s and tended to be limited to representing demands of their constituents. Finally, the Workers' Party (PT), which played an important role in organizing CSOs in other municípios, had a rather limited role in Camaragibe. As one party organizer put it, "It only became important in municipal politics after we won the elections in 1997."

In the absence of actors able to become interorganizational mediators, civil society in Camaragibe in the 1980s was characterized not only by organizational weakness and clientelistic practices, but also by fragmentation, or in our terms, the lack of a space of collective mediation of demands.[2] In this "culture of everyone for themselves," as one activist recalled, for example, "The [Municipal] Employee's Union had almost no relations with the [neighborhood] associations." Because so many neighborhood associations had privileged access to channels of power, competitive relationships with other associations was the norm, and according to one respondent, "community leaders were always a little possessive . . . you could not create an association because there was already one and if another appeared it would result in conflict." In sum, in the 1980s civil society in Camaragibe was trapped in a vicious cycle: the prevalence of clientelistic modes of engagement, which encouraged the search for direct links with the mediators and individual politicians rather than through collective action in civil society, tended to fragment civil society and further entrench clientelism.

Breaking with the Past

The governments of Arnaldo Guerra (PTB, 1989–92) and João Lemos (PSB, 1993–96) which proceeded the introduction of PB in 1997 would set the stage for the participatory innovations of Mayor Paulo Santana's administration. These prior administrations began a transformation that broke with the vicious cycle described above by introducing new modes of engagement.

These governments were formed by a composition of the center-left parties, including the PT, which attempted to break the iron grip of the Lapenda family over local politics. As coalitions, these governments were marked by significant internal political and ideological diversity. On the one hand, this diversity made possible the introduction of some participatory governance innovations. On the other hand, it created conflicts that resulted in the departure of members of the government. Most notably conflicts around the installation of the Municipal Health Council in 1989–90 resulted in the resignation of the future PT mayor and secretary of health, Paulo Santana. The Guerra and Lemos governments introduced more or less formal mechanisms of social participation including meetings with leaders of organizations to gather "the demands of the people." In addition they created the Municipal Health Council and other fora for civil society organizations and government representatives to debate policy priorities. However individual and direct contact between the representatives of civil society and clientelist intermediaries remained the predominant form of addressing demands.

The key innovation that opened the gates to governance reform was the creation of Municipal Health Council, which was introduced by the municipal health secretary, Paulo Santana and launched with much fanfare in 1989 with the First Municipal Health Conference, a space for community activists and health professionals to debate future health policies. Santana was removed from the position after one year, and the Health Council was abandoned. He was reinstated in 1993, when he reunited key players from the 1989 meetings and once again reinstated the Municipal Health Council, which began to emerge as a space for the articulation of collective demands. One municipal employee recalled, "The project of popular health created a leadership group from the base. So you had the leading neighborhood associations, local leadership of the union movement, small businessmen, and teachers." One key feature of the council was its Family Health Program. It created a network of "community health agents" that operated across the city, but especially in poor neighborhoods. In their comprehensive and intensive contact with the population, the community health agents became, along with the actors involved in participatory fora of health, key to Paulo Santana's electoral victory in 1997. As a participant at the time described it, "All of the activity around health helped Paulo Santana a lot as a candidate."

The PT Victory and Introduction of the Participatory Administration

With the introduction of the various fora that made up the Participatory Administration, which we described in Chapter 4, previous modes of clientelistic engagement lost much of their traction. However, given the preexisting configuration of civil society in Camaragibe, the institutionalization of participation was very much led by the administration. The leadership of community movements, "instead of being autonomous and going to the prefeitura to discuss proposals and demand changes [in the participatory process], placed so much trust with the government." Thus, while the PA did break with clientelism, it did not increase the autonomy of civil society organizations.

The institutionalization of participatory fora significantly reduced the costs of participation of civil society activists, many of them delegates, who could now focus on the fora and claim the position of spokespersons for interests groups and social demands. As one respondent observed:

> The Municipal Health Council began to hear all the people's dissatisfactions, expressed through their leaders. Then came other councils. And they all operated like ombudsmen. Indeed, the councils function today, too, as ombudsman. This provided the people with a space to voice their dissatisfactions and satisfactions, without them having to go to the street. When you, as community leaders, want to mobilize a neighborhood to form a protest, it becomes difficult because the people lack a culture of mobilization. So who ends up raising demands and making suggestions? It is the leaders themselves, listening to the people of the neighborhood. So I would say that the work of movement leaders today is more raising issues than it is about mobilization.

Institutional participation, in sum, substituted for the work of organizing and social mobilization. Some of our respondents took an even more critical position, arguing that organizations had became less willing to challenge government because earlier "the community critically raised more issues and made more changes," but now the posture became "if I support you and believe in you, then I will be left unable to hold you responsible for anything." This shift to institutional participation, without the existence of autonomous and socially rooted associations, meant that community leaders, many of whom had become delegates, played increasingly important roles in mediating between administration and the population. This logic was strengthened by the specific design of participatory fora in which delegates played very prominent roles.

In addition, the design of the Participatory Administration tended to blur the boundaries between social organizations, political actors, and the local government. If in the past this blurring was the result of clientelistic relations, in the new context it was generated both by the closeness of delegates to the administration. This form of mediation nonetheless represented a critical break with traditional clientelism. In the past, mediation had been secured through personal networks and the exchange of highly discrete favors (loyalty in exchange for narrowly distributed rents), mediation was now embedded less in networks than in institutions and involved exchanges that were more transparent and codified. The blurring of the line between the state and social actors did, however, reinforce civil society organizations' dependence on the government, which led to, in a phrase used by a number of respondents, "a loss of identity." Respondents described a general confusion among civil society activists about what activities were part of "the movement" and what were "part of government."[3]

In the context of their fragile relationship with the municipal government, civil society organizations of Camaragibe and segments of the population involved in the various participatory fora did not find themselves able to form an autonomous and active political role during the administration of Paulo Santana. More specifically, the civil society actors were not able to construct a more symmetrical position in relation to state actors, who focused much of their power on the allocation of public resources. This form of dependence on the state is different than the clientelist past, however. Now there are institutional channels of participation and demand-making, public spaces of discussion and deliberation, and the state must account for its actions in public fora. This reduces both the discretionary and personalistic nature of traditional mediation. Nonetheless these changes coexist with what is still a marked asymmetry between the state and civil society, a basic tension at the heart of affirmative democracy.

DIRECT AFFIRMATIVE DEMOCRACY: GRAVATAÍ

The 1980s: Subordinated Civil Society

As in the case of Camaragibe, the municipality of Gravataí has been characterized throughout its history by a political context that offered few opportunities for the development of autonomous associations. Instead, the prevalence of clientelistic relations amplified political actors' strategies of control over so-cial organizations and resulted in social organizations' attempts to have their demands met by forming personal relationships and assuming a subordinated role to those political actors. The three administrations that preceded Dan-iel Bordignon's (PT, 1997–2000) government all actively sought to establish their control over civil society organizations. According to respondents' recol-lection the most common practice was to directly recruit organization leaders into government jobs, most notably presidents of neighborhood associations who were directly "invited to work in the prefeitura" or by paying them to be "community advisors." Another common tactic was the "distribution of vari-ous goods (food, medicine, utilities, etc. . . .), using neighborhood associations as intermediaries to the population," according to a civil society activist who also recalled that "Mayor Abilio dos Santos [PMDB, 1983–88] organized things by having little tickets. The person goes to him and asks for something—'I need this thing.' Take a little ticket. They were the famous little tickets. This relation-ship was clientelistic."

The mayor was eventually found guilty of using public goods for election campaigning and lost his right to run for political office for eight years. The PMDB was followed by the left-of-center populist Democratic Labor Party (PDT), a traditionally strong party in the state of Rio Grande de Sul. The PDT directly organized associations in regions of the city that had none, a strategy that paid off in the 1988 elections. According to a former city hall employee, Mariano Mota won the municipality for the PDT with the support of the com-munity movement at a time when "almost all associations were involved with the PDT." During his tenure (1989–92), however, the PDT attempted to exert direct control over associations while continuing to stimulate the formation of new associations in a manner similar to the strategy of other PDT mayors. In practice, the message was "join neighborhood associations and your sug-gestions will be heard," as one respondent recalled. Because associations were seen as appendages of the administration, which exerted direct control over the inner workings of associations and doled out favors to sympathetic associa-tions, the community movement remained narrowly dependent on a set of hi-erarchical and paternalistic exchanges. Moreover, because of partisan ties and mediation based on personal ties, these organizations were not deeply rooted in the neighborhoods they were supposed to represent. Thus, their dynamism and functioning depended directly on the support of the party, and when the party lost and a new party took power in 1993 the frailty of the movement was exposed as a stark decline in associational activity ensued. A neighborhood association director recalled that in the mid-1990s there were very few functioning associations, "a very small number, twelve, fifteen max . . . of regularized neighborhood associations."

In this context marked by clientelistic relations city councilors played the critical role of mediating between the public and the prefeitura, facilitating access to those individuals or organizations indebted to the executive. One community activist recalled, "I had a very strong relationship with the prefeitura. We became close with a councilman who was well positioned in the government. We received his assistance and were eternally grateful. . . . There was no institutionalized way of getting things done in the prefeitura. It was all based on pressuring individuals."

In this institutional environment, the associative fabric of Gravataí revolved around a logic of organizations attaching themselves to political mediators who monopolized access to public projects and services. Especially in the case of neighborhood associations, whose functioning revolved around demands and services, clientelism was the norm, leaving no room for the development of more autonomous and self-organized expressions of civil society. Associations "asked for a police patrol, a daycare worker, and an additional classroom. All small things." Dependent as they were on political patrons, the associations focused their efforts on cultivating their political relationships at the expense of organizing residents. Another effect of these paternalistic and subordinating relations was the fragmentation of the fabric of associations, resulting both from the direct involvement of organizations in partisan disputes and acute competition for particularistic access to public goods and services. The resulting breakdown of the solidarity between associations is best captured by one respondent's comment that at the time "each battle was for their neighborhood. I even say this: for their street. It was very common for people to ask. Because the association wasn't concerned with other areas."

A small number of organizations rejected these practices, but still remained isolated from the broader community movement. Some were associated with progressive elements of the Catholic Church through Comunidades Eclesiais de Base (CEBs, Ecclesiastic Base Communities). These associations were generally indentified with the PT and involved in political-organizational activities in some of the municípios' regions, in which social and political leaders were committed to collective mobilization and autonomous demand-making, but did not have the organizational capacity to challenge the dominant practice of clientelism. A second group of social organizations that deviated from prevailing clientelistic practices in Gravataí were unions linked to the Central Única dos Trabalhadores (Central Workers Union, or CUT), a group whose members were generally affiliated with the PT.[4] While these unions supported the candidacy of Daniel Bordignon, with the exception of the Union of Municipal Teachers, they were more focused on labor issues at the state and national levels than in municipal affairs. As such they had few interactions with community organizations.[5]

The Introduction of PB and New Modes of Mediation

The clientelistic configuration that dominated governance in Gravataí underwent a number of significant changes under the government of Daniel Bordignon and with the introduction of PB in 1997. First, discussion and deliberation on the municipal budget became public, which blocked the traditional personalistic channels of access to public resources and destabilized clientelistic networks of mediation. This, in turn, significantly weakened the effectiveness of traditional clientelistic brokers. Just how significant this relocation of public power was is evident from (as we showed in Chapter 4) the fierce opposition to PB from city councilors and the clientelistic leaders of the neighborhood associations during the first years of the PT government. This came to a head in 1997, when a block of city councilors threatened to overturn the decisions of Participatory Budgeting, but were pressured to comply with PB by a mobilization of PB participants.

Later, with the consolidation and legitimation of PB, a portion of these oppositional actors began to insert themselves in the PB process, shifting their traditional role of personalistic mediation toward mobilizing social action through a new mode of engagement. Some city councilors of opposition parties, recognizing that their hands were tied because no city councilor could vote against PB projects even started to participate in PB, "bringing people to the assemblies." The victory of Daniel Bordignon also affected the associative configuration of Gravataí because it brought some of the few prominent activists of the labor movement and social movements highlighted above into government, further reducing the already limited number of activists available for organization and social mobilization. The combination of having a significant portion of neighborhood associations assuming oppositional postures, in addition to the removal of unions from municipal political life, resulted in their being a very limited number of social organizations with the ability and willingness to act through a process of mobilizing social participation in PB. This "change in terms of the leadership of the union movement" that "did not have prepared replacements" hollowed out the few organizations that could have played a productive role in PB, according to one civil society activist. In the resulting organizational vacuum, the locus of participation shifted to interpersonal networks of family, neighbors, and friends.

Participation without organizational mediation was, as we showed in Chapter 4, an artifact of the institutional design of the Gravataí's PB, which virtually eliminated any form of delegated representation and transferred the process of deliberation to eighty-five microdistrict assemblies in which the people were directly involved. The intent to break with the mediation of social organizations was a result of pragmatic planning from the PT's management, which lacked significant support among local civil society. One of our respondents specifically pointed to this rupture and interpreted the establishment of direct relations between the population and the government as a mechanism for the democratization of public management:

> The PB's system, for me, continued to consist of a discussion pertaining to the paradigm of public management, breaking a kind of logic of assistance. The political party lost their position of being the messiah: "Vote for me and I will end up building a plaza in this neighborhood." The neighborhood association lost the ability to say: "Support our Association and we will bring things to your neighborhood." . . . That logic of leadership began to break and decisions begin to be shared directly by the population.

In sum, clientelistic forms of mediation and discretionary forms of demand-making gave way to institutionalized, public, and transparent claim-making through PB. Participation in PB was massive and drew subaltern participants directly into decision-making. The mode of engagement was in other words dramatically altered, shifting from clientelism to citizenship. But civil society remained quite dependent on the government and unable to counterbalance its power or to develop a more propositional stance. This was evident in the fact that participants were limited to forming and expressing local demands, but had no say in extralocal issues and could not transform the process itself. In sum, despite the large numbers of participants in Gravataí's PB, and the fact that decision-making in the PB was direct and binding, it is not surprising that many of our respondents came to the conclusion that during PB, as one member of the municipal government put it, civil society developed "significant dependence on the government's political actions."

Making Sense of Affirmative Democracy:
The "Curse of the Participatory Democracy Model"?

In both Camaragibe and in Gravataí participation opened up direct processes for participation, altering the mode of demand-making. Demand-making was described as less clientelistic, less geared to individual demands, and more inclusive. In Camaragibe and in Gravataí, the dominant practice prior to reforms among neighborhood associations was to seek individual negotiations around specific demands with city councilors. In both cases, respondents uniformly agreed that participatory reforms ruptured these clientelist links and ended the intermediary role that city councilors used to play in such negotiations.

If affirmative democracy in Gravataí and Camaragibe has made a positive difference, it is nonetheless a very fragile equation. Citizens must no longer forgo their political autonomy to engage the state (clientelism), but their engagement remains largely dependent on the initiative of local government. Whether relations were direct (Gravataí) or mediated by delegates (Camaragibe), in both cases they were characterized by the absence of any independent mediation by civil society organizations. In the absence of more established and autonomous civil society organizations, this high level of involvement with participatory institutions has produced ambiguous outcomes.

In both cases participation opened up direct processes for participation, altering the mode of engagement with the local state. In Camaragibe and in Gravataí, the dominant practice prior to reforms among neighborhood associations was to seek individual negotiations around specific demands with city councilors. In both, respondents uniformly agreed that participatory reforms ruptured these clientelist links and ended the intermediary role that city councilors used to play in such negotiations. But also in both cases, there is a profound ambiguity about the role of civil society. On the one hand, many respondents in both municípios interpreted this as a "strengthening" of civil society—more mobilization, more access to the state, and less clientelism. On the other hand, this access to the state takes place on terms set by the state. With a weak organizational base, the mode of engagement is one in which participatory democracy remains dependent on affirmative support by the state. This conclusion is clearly expressed in the following critical assessment *of a member of the government*:

> The subordination of social organizations was a curse for the participatory democracy model. I think the agenda of involvement is an agenda that has to

come from the people. And today, this agenda is the government. The popular movement, I think, has lost its autonomy. We see this in Camaragibe. It's not co-opted, but it is the logic of the government. . . . The participation of the popular movement in institutional spaces does the following: the governmental agenda is imposed on the popular movement.

Having said this, it should be reiterated that while civil society is not organized enough to establish its own autonomous settings for discussion and opinion formation, the state-sponsored settings of PB have promoted iterated processes of public discussion. The difference between expressing choices through representative structures and forming choices through public deliberation is precisely what distinguishes representative from participatory theories of democracy.

MOBILIZED DEMOCRACY:
TOWARD ASSOCIATIONAL AUTONOMY IN JOÃO MONLEVADE

João Monlevade stands out as the prototype of PB. In this working-class city on the outskirts of Belo Horizonte, the civil society mode of engagement moved decisively toward associational autonomy, or what we have labeled mobilized democracy, with the introduction of PB. In João Monlevade, the seesaw of clientelism and contention was displaced by a more institutionalized mode of engagement as new avenues of participation created by PB led to greater associational activity and as excluded, but autonomous, social sectors and social movements were able to become active participants in municipal decision-making. If the city can now be classified, like Diadema, as a case of a mobilized democracy (the ideal-typical form of democratic civil society) this outcome was clearly conditioned by antecedent conditions. In contrast to Gravataí and Camaragibe where an opening was predicated on tutelage, civil society here started from a position of autonomy vis-à-vis the state and political society before the 1997 period.

The degree to which an opening from above can be galvanizing for an organized civil society is underscored by the pace of change in João Monlevade. Elected by a coalition supported by social movements, unions, and social movement-oriented neighborhood associations, the PT administration took up participatory reforms within the first year of coming to power. During the first year, PB was expanded to include "thematic discussions" and a discussion of the city's long-term development goals. PB quickly evolved to encompass a conference on regional development and the opening up of opportunities for community oversight over a number of municipal functions. Participation expanded throughout the four years of PB, doubling in numbers to two thousand in the last year.

Respondents described a greater opening of the government to citizens, with much more oversight over government functions. Respondents were almost unanimous in the view that civil society had significantly increased its influence over the government. The nature of demand-making and problem-solving was markedly transformed during this period. In João Monlevade, previously combative social movements, notably the homeless movement and the movement of housekeepers, became involved in participatory processes and curtailed their protest activity without abandoning it completely, especially in the case of the homeless movement. Traditional neighborhood associations long accustomed to clientelist practices saw opportunities for favor-trading reduced.

The Associative Past and the Transition to Democracy

The município of João Monlevade's associational life centered around the Sindicato de Trabalhadores Metalúrgicos de João Monlevade (STMJM, Union of Metalworkers of João Monlevade), founded in 1951. Bringing together mainly workers from the local steel company, the STMJM had developed since the 1960s a strong practice of claim-making and efforts to insert its leaders into politics. The union carried out its first strike against the steel company in 1962, and shortly afterward, the president of the union was elected to city council. With the military coup in 1964, however, prominent leaders of the movement were arrested, and the union came under the control of the military. It was only in 1972 that opposition forces were again elected to head the union, and the union came to play a prominent role in the 1978 general strikes that marked the emergence of the so-called New Unionism period in Brazilian politics.

The STMJM played a nationally prominent role in the subsequent period of transition to democracy, even sponsoring in January 1980 the Meeting of Monlevade. This meeting brought together the principal leaders of the New Unionism movement, segments of the "progressive church," social movements and political groups from the Left, all with the goal of creating an alliance of social and political forces at the national level. This meeting was the founding event of the Associação Nacional de Movimentos Populares e Sindicatos (National Association of Popular Movements and Trade Unions, or ANAMPOS). ANAMPOS, in turn, led to the creation of the Central Única dos Trabalhadores

(Central de *Movimentos Populares*, or Center for Popular Movements, CMP) and the Workers' Party.

Another important actor in the context of intense mobilization, at the end of the 1970s and during the 1980s, were the activists associated with the progressive church, who founded the Casa do Trabalhador (Home of the worker), which would play an important role in training movement leaders during the next decade, through courses, seminars, and meetings. Casa also helped give rise in 1978 to the Domestic Worker's Association, which would later play a central role in supporting PB. Neighborhood associations, engaged in traditional clientelist practices of mediation, were also present in João Monlevade, but unlike in most of our other municípios, these were much weaker than the more autonomous segments.

Since the first elections in 1985, control of the município has alternated. The PMDB, linked to the business community and revolving around the figure of Germin Loureiro, ruled in the 1986–88 and 1993–96 periods. The PT, which was linked to the STMJM and to some of the "combative" segments of civil society, elected a former president of the union, Leonardo Diniz, to mayor in 1989–92 and another labor leader, Laercio Ribeiro, in the 1997–2000 term.

While the Loureiro years were marked by personalistic and discretionary forms of responsiveness to social demands, respondents highlighted the existence of channels for dialogue and a respectful relationship with "combative" organizations. This relationship can be illustrated by the subsidization, throughout that period, of a building for the Domestic Workers Association. One respondent characterized this period by noting that while the mayor "respected people's claims, he didn't want popular participation." Forms of pressure seemed, from time to time, to be successful in having influence. A hallmark of João Monlevade's "combative" social organizations was their early and direct engagement with politics and their ability to elect representatives at the local and national level through the Workers' Party. From the union movement came a federal deputy, a city councilor, and two mayors, while leaders of the homeless movement and the Domestics' Association elected a city councilor each in the early 1990s. Once inserted in political-administrative arenas, these social movement actors tended to capitalize on the opportunities and resources provided by their institutional positions to strengthen their organizations.

During the next few years, autonomous segments of civil society continued to intensify their activism, and the city was the stage for several rallies, protests, and land occupations by the homeless movement. In addition to this level of mobilization, there are a few important factors that help distinguish João Monlevade's civil society. First, unions—and especially the STMJM—played a central role in local civil society; moreover, in contrast to narrow trade unionism (which focuses on the interests of its represented occupational category), the STMJM was far more encompassing, concerned with a range of issues that impacted working-class citizens.[6] With support of the STMJM, the Community Radio was formed, with the goal of acting as a channel of public expression for those "combative" actors in civil society, like the homeless movement and the Domestics' Associations. Second, the progressive organizations like the STMJM, the homeless movement, and the Domestics' Association were linked to national counterparts, lending them symbolic and material support.

Scaling-up Civil Society: The 1997–2000 Period

As described above, the state of civil society in João Monlevade at the time of the introduction of PB was marked by both a high degree of organizational capacity, that is, the presence of well-entrenched and politically autonomous associations that had significant experience, and well-developed channels and repertoires, for pressing claims on the local state. This, in turn, meant that municipal government had a civil society interlocutor capable of mobilizing and influencing the local political dynamic. Civil society was not only capable of mobilizing but also pressing its demands on the local state and could do so largely because of a heightened and sustained capacity for contention. With the election of Laercio Ribeiro for the 1997–2000 period, and with the introduction of PB once again, civil society directed much of its efforts to working with the new institutional arrangements. For some organizations, there was a shift in practices away from "personal relations with constituted power" to "direct participation, through the channels of communication and participation."

In addition, however, some organizations (especially the homeless movement) maintained the use of collective action as a way of pressuring the city government to meet its demands or to question government decisions, leading one respondent to comment that "the cooperation between social movements and the PT prefeitura was not always so peaceful." One union activist recalled that "there were a lot of protests, demonstrations. The metalworkers union fought for better public transport, cheaper tickets, mainly for the worker. This revolutionized the city," while another recalled the "union made requests of the city," such as the "Center for Worker Support."

Examples of other contentious action included the homeless movement camping out in front of city hall to pressure for funds for municipal public housing and a protest that that local social movements mobilized against a proposed raise for municipal department heads in 1998. Several respondents remarked that protest activity increased in *intensity* with the PT administration, noting that "here in John Monlevade, even with the PT in power, we always seek the path of struggle."

Thus, in contrast to our other PB municípios, João Monlevade's civil society organizations were determined to preserve their autonomy from institutional politics. These organizations were specifically concerned with avoiding a situation in which their identification with the political parties generated a relationship of subordination, which could lead to a loss of legitimacy with segments of society that they sought to represent. That their legitimacy was preserved is evidenced by electoral success of the leaders of these organizations. This effort is clearly illustrated by a statement by one of the leaders of the homeless movement, who described a tension between the interests of maintaining the autonomy of the movement and the need to seize opportunities to improve the movement's institutional standing: "Today we find the need to have a place within the municipal government, especially if it is from the Left. To move from paper to action, the movements have to be there in the administration because they gain from an important experience. . . . [But] we had these moments of confrontation. It was a democratic confrontation. They understood, and we continued our trajectory of making claims."

The ability of social movement actors to preserve their autonomy from the PT government may be partly explained by the fact that major organizations were responsible for creating the Workers' Party in the município in the first place. In this sense, instead of the party instrumentalizing social organizations, the predominant view in João Monlevade is that the party is an instrument for the "combative" social forces to forward their political demands and proposals. Similarly, the PT government is perceived as a government ally, but one that is constantly reminded to accommodate the pressures of social forces and political opposition.

The case of João Monlevade clearly demonstrates the dynamic impact that institutional reform can have on civil society. An opening that was created from above in the opportunity structure allowed an already active and autonomous civil society to effectively scale-up without compromising its autonomy. Previously excluded civil society actors became privileged interlocutors, increasing their capacity for dialogue with the state, and transforming their practices. In João Monlevade, both clientelist practices and contentious action declined in favor of direct dialogue. The case of João Monlevade also illustrates the extent to which the preexisting autonomy and organizational capacity of civil society allowed CSOs to play a greater role in shaping the actual form of participation than in cases of affirmative democracy. This closer relationship between the state and civil society did lead some respondents in João Monlevade to express concern that civil society had become too "turned toward city hall." But in contrast to our cases of affirmative democracy, the prior self-organization of civil society has produced a much less fragile equation, with civil society organizations more able to negotiate the terms of the interactions.

The case of João Monlevade can also be used to underscore two more general points. Sociologists have long argued that social movements can have transformative effects, but they have rarely demonstrated when and how social movements can actually achieve the institutionalization of their demands. In João Monlevade contentious social movements not only helped shape political society by midwifing the PT, but also drove the process of making local government become more participatory. In contrast to much of the governance literature which tends to presume that "good governance" is only possible when administration is insulated from politics, in this case it is clear that contention and institution-building reinforced each other. A second point, however, is that social movements, or an active civil society, can hardly be transformative on their own. In order for an active civil society to have lasting effects, it had to both engage political society and to take advantage of openings in the structures of governance to push for institutional reforms. Civil society was in this respect every bit political and strategic, and not just normative. Change, moreover, required a particularly propitious local political ecology in which movement actors were able to converge horizontally and scale-up into political society.

DEMOBILIZATION:
THE PARADOXICAL CONTRACTION OF CIVIL SOCIETY IN MAUÁ

The case of Mauá is an important counterpoint to the trends described in our first three cases. As indicated by the dotted arrow in Table 5.2, its democratic trajectory has an ambiguous character. With the introduction of PB civil society experienced a contraction of sorts, moving from the position of having some autonomy but being limited to highly discretionary and clientelistic modes of engagement that characterizes a *bifurcated democracy*, to having a less autonomous civil society linked through institutionalized channels, or *affirmative democracy*. Before the PB reforms, CSOs had displayed a range of political practices, and while able to autonomously organize, they were partially linked to the state via clientelism. PB clearly reduced clientelism as a mode of mediation, but the autonomy of civil society was compromised in the process. This contraction was clearly linked to the institutional form of PB and the way it interacted with a deeply bifurcated civil society.

As we saw in Chapter 4, Mauá's version of PB, introduced in 1997, fell short of the participatory ideal (binding participation) and was largely consultative. Neighborhood plenary meetings had the limited role of educating participants about municipal finances and electing members to a citywide council whose primary role was to liaise with neighborhoods. Some PB councilors described being able to exert pressure on the administration in determining investments in areas like health and urban infrastructure, but overall civil society participants were clearly very critical of the process. Some jokingly referred to it to as the "listening council" rather than the budgeting council.[7] They were also critical of a perceived lack of transparency, the lack of direct response to community needs, and the lack of a clear decision-making mandate for the population.

Even though participation in PB drew thousands of participants, it was viewed as weakening civil society by a broad range of actors in civil society. Before PB, Mauá's civil society was clearly divided between traditional neighborhood associations invested in social assistance and grass-roots organizations based on social movement models. By effectively ending clientelist exchanges and introducing clear-cut rules, the new administration was seen as closing itself off from many neighborhood associations. On the other hand, respondents, including five who were active in PB and CSOs, also saw the "combative" sector declining after the introduction of PB. Before the introduction of PB demand-making consisted of protests, petitioning, and other forms of contentious action because there was no channel of participation. But with the introduction of PB, civil society was brought into government and effectively demobilized. As a movement activist noted, "People went to work in government, but nothing changed because they stopped making claims."

The Bifurcated Past

Civil society in Mauá was bifurcated between two segments that had contrasting modes of engagement with actors in political society. On the one hand, an important segment of Mauá's civil society—specifically the neighborhood associations, samba schools, and charitable institutions—engaged in a dense network of clientelistic exchanges until 1997. On the other hand, the 1970s witnessed the emergence of an autonomous segment of civil society characterized by its orientation to active engagement with the government based on the notion that public projects and services are rights of citizenship. The formation of this "combative" segment of civil society in Mauá was carried out by the same actors who built the PT at the time. In this sense, the PT in Mauá was as much an organizational actor as a space of interaction and articulation for those seeking alternatives to traditional clientelism.

This linkage between clientelistic relations and the implications of patterns of social organizations' activities is clearly illustrated by the case of the SABs. The SABs constituted a form of traditional organization in Mauá, marked in general by subordination to the municipal governments which provided them with the requisite resources to sustain their position as mediators between the population and political actors. In this sense, for example, the SABs were, for a significant period of time, an important instrument for the execution of the municipal government social service policies, as for example in the distribution of nutritional products and the emergency contracting of workers during periods of high levels of unemployment. One participant recalled that, "When the election time arrived, it was also the time in which families were afforded more milk, eyeglasses, and medical consultations. It was up to the Societies [SABs] to direct the benefiting population towards the ballots. . . . They gave milk on the condition that the recipients would in turn vote."

Moreover, the SABs were chosen by the municipal governments as official representatives of the population's demands, acting as privileged mediators of the personalized and discretionary distribution of those projects and services. This form of mediation was institutionalized to such a degree that the president of the Federation of Neighborhood Associations of Mauá's Residents was employed by the prefeitura to act as the recipient and guide of social demands. While respondents argued that "the Federation ended up having a certain kind of power within the city" because city hall "contracted their president," most respondents from civil society understood it as "co-optation" because it meant that "someone from the neighborhood associations was responsible to receive these social calls for change," but this "didn't have an effect." Others saw it as a hierarchical relationship that had the consequence of making the Community Federation a "representative of the Executive inside the communities." In addition, neighborhood associations received other more direct rewards, such as access to public areas for the construction of organizations' headquarters and grants from the municipal government for the support of politically allied organizations.

"Until 97," one of respondents recalls, "if they received a grant. The directors [of the organization] only had to justify how it was spent in order to receive money for the next year." These "sponsorship deals" resulted in a dependent relationship very similar to what we found in Gravataí and Camaragibe: the formation of organizations, often quite disconnected from the communities they were supposed to represent and defined by their personalistic mediation of their directors.

In some neighborhoods, however, alternative forms of organization emerged that challenged these practices. For example, in one neighborhood with an established association that received grants from city hall, residents nonetheless organized an alternate association to fight for paving. "We created a committee of residents, who split with the Society of Friends because we knew the society was an executive service." In this neighborhood, with the assistance of the progressive church, a residents' committee was formed which came into conflict with the existing association over who was the proper representative of the community, and eventually with city hall itself. A protest movement ensued, which after "marching together all the way to the city hall" had the effect of discrediting the neighborhood association "because they were tied to public power." In the context of contesting clientelistic relations, these actors struggled to develop a repertoire of protest actions, which combined presenting demands through available institutional channels and confronting local government through collective action.

Though not as central as activists from the progressive church, our respondents also highlighted the role of trade union activists (especially metallurgical, teachers, state, and oil unions). The Workers Party ended up being a space of coalition for these protest movements. It was recalled that "then [came] the PT, with a newspaper, disseminating this newspaper, calling meetings, holding discussions, the councilors of the party mobilizing the people in the City Hall, organizing movements . . . calling for reform, construction of schools, of health posts, the streets. These things ended up helping mobilization move along in a serious way." The strength of partisan organization led, over time, to a blurring of boundaries between activism in civil society and activism in political parties.

The Dias Administration and the Introduction of Participation

The victory of Oswaldo Dias and the PT in 1997 represented a strong blow to traditional clientelistic politics. The new administration directly confronted the material basis of clientelism by cutting off public resources for social organizations, which triggered strong reactions from organizations that had traditionally commanded these resources. "Before," one respondent recalls, "organizations were passive recipients" of money. But when the new mayor arrived and "said 'No one is going to get money. No organization will receive money.' Many organizations folded." In addition, channels of traditional personalistic mediation were blocked through the institutionalization of public fora for participation, most notably the PB. One participant recalled the difference,

> [Before] there was a certain necessary proximity with the government, a form of intimacy. First, you had to claim something, then form a protest, then collect signatures. Today, in the municipality, things have changed. The mayor doesn't need to wait for you to show up to make claims. He comes to you with the PB process. There is a representative of the district, a representative of the neighborhood organization, a representative of the people in government.

The reactions of social actors to the opening of institutional spaces for participation were diverse. The organizations involved in clientelistic relations interpreted this shift as a weakening of social organizations and, especially, their leaders as mediators. Accordingly, they adopted a critical posture in relation to the PT government and participatory fora. While presidents of neighborhood associations were "all invited, only 40% participated," according to one activist. Many actively opposed the PB process, complaining that earlier modes of engagement, such as petitions, ceased to be effective.

The less clientelistic civil society organizations, those previously engaged in protest activity, had a conflicted relationship to PB. On the one hand, their activists clearly identified the participatory fora as an achievement that opened governance to civil society engagement. As these organizations focused on PB, they turned away from more contentious activities, such as "organizing students, closing a school, throwing trash in the middle of the street, pounding a drum" and toward institutional participation. "Movements of noise," as one recalled, "were no more." But several activists expressed frustration at their inability to more meaningfully shape the discussion or set the agenda of PB meetings. As we described in Chapter 4, the PB process in Mauá was one with limited decision-making afforded to participants. This tended to delegitimize the process and the organizations that had originally supported it.

Further, fears that more confrontational actions could weaken the PT government and thus strengthen their political opponents constrained these organizations. The difficulty of working with the PT government while preserving movements' capacity for contention was expressed by several of our respondents, who argued that "today, there are few movements in Mauá and they have been totally weakened. . . . And you can't object to it because you are in the party." The movement of many social activists into government positions was in itself something that weakened "combative" social organizations, as "movement leaders, generally, became party leaders" and the rest of the "community leadership left to go to the government." One respondent summarized the problems of close ties between the government and the combative social sector:

> Whether you like it or not, when you're in the government you don't get to participate in a movement. And there aren't protests. Those who were allied to clientelistic politicians don't have a background in organizing rallies. Those who have that capacity are in government. Then there's that conversation of preserving the party, to not harm the government when your party is there.

The Mauá case is thus difficult to classify. PB reforms introduced a direct channel of communication between civil society and the state, though it was purely of a consultative nature, not allowing civil society to shape the terms of the discussion. As a space for what proved to be ongoing discussions of the financial state of the municipality, the plenary meetings no doubt fostered increased accountability. But the "combative" capacity of civil society was compromised. Clientelist sectors of civil society felt disconnected from authority, and combative sectors were demobilized. Participatory fora, in other words, curtailed the actions of both groups.

Mauá provides a perfect illustration of the zero-sum game between mobilization and institutionalization that informs—implicitly or explicitly—much of the social movement literature. There is little doubt that in this case bringing the movement into government did have the effect of taming contention and possibly even weakening movement autonomy (though CSOs did maintain significant organizational capacity). But the contrast with João Monlevade—where movement engagement with the state resulted in increased influence while preserving the capacity for autonomous action, underscores the fact that such outcomes are hardly a result of some inevitable, zero-sum logic, but rather are the product of specific local political ecologies.

CONCLUSIONS

The contrast between the paths followed by Mauá and João Monlevade underscores the very delicate nature of the balance between state and civil society. Political sociologists have been centrally preoccupied with this problem, but have failed to develop frameworks for examining this relationship in a dynamic and comparative perspective. We have attempted to address this shortcoming by developing a two-dimensional analytic model of civil society that takes into account both the self-organization of civil society and the general context in which it engages the state. If the first axis has been the subject of most research on civil society (especially in the social movement literature), much less attention has been given to the engagement question. We then specifically tested the extent to which institutional reforms impact civil society by comparing similar municípios in which one introduced PB and the other did not. Our findings can be summarized.

As the associational democracy literature has emphasized, institutional reforms can have direct impacts on how civil society organizes and represents itself. As our paired analysis shows, tangible change in the condition of civil society took place only in those cities that adopted PB. In three of four cases, these changes were in the direction of democratic deepening. In the case of Mauá, an improvement in the mode of engagement came at the expense of civil society's autonomy. As one might have anticipated, institutional reform mostly mattered for changing the institutional setting, that is, creating more meaningful points of interface between the local state and civil society. Thus most of the movement in Table 5.2 is along the vertical axes—the mode of engagement. Institutional reform did not have much of an impact on the self-organization of civil society.

If our findings point to the malleability of civil society over a relatively short time span, they also underscore what is often glossed over in the associational democracy literature, namely, the extent to which the impact of reforms depends on preexisting political and civil society configurations. Prostrate civil societies became more active, but only under the protection of an affirmative state. Those civil societies that were the most successful in scaling up as a result of PB *and* maintaining their autonomy were civil societies that already enjoyed significant self-organization. Mauá represents our cautionary tale. In Mauá, PB has actually increased control of the political party in power over civil society. Civil society organizations that once enjoyed a high degree of autonomy (but no opportunities for engaging the state) have compromised much of their self-organization in exchange for inclusion in the governance process.

Drawing together the findings from this chapter and the preceding one, we can now develop a fuller picture of our distinctive democratic regimes. What our case studies have shown is that different state-civil society configurations produce different democratic regimes. We have conceptualized state-civil society configurations along two axes: a horizontal axis of the self-organization of civil society and a vertical axis of the mode of engagement with the state. We have, in turn, linked each of the possible configurations to different democratic regimes. Our analysis of the impact of PB, moreover, revealed two distinct forms of participatory democracy. Thus a civil society that is autonomous and self-organized and can engage the state through institutionalized processes results in a *mobilized democracy*. A civil society that is weaker and more dependent on the state but can, following the introduction of PB, engage the state through institutionalized processes results in an *affirmative democracy*. An affirmative democracy is one in which the state plays a proactive role in enabling civil society to engage in the process, either through highly direct processes (such as in Gravataí) or more mediated processes (such as in Camaragibe). If a *mobilized democracy* in effect approaches the ideal-type form of participatory democracy, it does pose unique challenges. And while an *affirmative democracy* clearly falls short of the participatory ideal, it represents not only what is probably the most common real-world expression of an instituted participatory process, but also a very pragmatic adaptation by political elites (including social movement leaders) to the common problem of weak civil societies.

We want to unpack the participatory character of both regimes by further exploring how each can be characterized in terms of the twin dynamics of preference formation and the chain of sovereignty. Preferences are not given, nor do they emerge spontaneously. In Habermasian terms democracy is a process of "opinion-and-will formation" that is forged in the communicative spaces of civil society. Habermas has developed his theory of deliberative democracy in the context of what he assumes to be a highly pluralized, differentiated, well-resourced, and autonomous civil society (a condition he fully recognizes is historically and developmentally contingent). In the Brazilian context this cannot be taken for granted. The movements of the 1990s notwithstanding, most local civil societies in Brazil, including the majority of our cases, are fragmented, dependent, and lack the basic capacity of self-determination.

To the problem of preference formation we can add the problem of preserving the chain of sovereignty. If the former refers to the vitality and autonomy of communicative practices, the later refers to the institutional process through which inputs are translated into tangible outputs. Instituting PB can as such be said to be an effort to address both problems simultaneously, that is, to nurture communicative practices (for example, deliberated preferences that emerge from assemblies) and to ensure that communicative inputs are actually translated into real investments. In the last two chapters, we have discovered two things. First, far from being a theoretical preoccupation of academic observers, securing this overall chain of preference formation and sovereignty was something that preoccupied PB architects, administrators, and activists ("the challenge of being government"). In tackling this challenge, local actors bootstrapped a variety of institutional forms. Second, the key to understanding the workings of the chain lies in the role of mediators.

Each of our cases of an instituted participatory process is composed of a series of linkages between actors, processes, and fora. At each step, preferences and inputs are processed in different ways. They are at various times deliberated, bargained, aggregated, and coordinated. For example, the assemblies are in principle the arenas in which community priorities are deliberated. Citywide councils represent moments of bargaining between districts, but also instances of coordination. Delegates are sometimes simply called upon to transmit community preferences to a higher forum, or to actually help process and aggregate local preferences. And civil society organizations, where they exist and enjoy a sufficient degree of autonomy, also play a critical role. CSOs can alternatively push forward the deliberated demands of their memberships, aggregate and coordinate demands across a range of actors, represent the voiceless (for example, children), or represent sectors or issue areas that have weak stakeholders (for example, the environment). CSOs can represent these preferences and interests at various points in the chain, either as prefigurative forces that shape the preferences of participants or activists (including many delegates and architects of the process) or as active intermediaries between society and the state.

With these points in mind, we can once again briefly characterize the process in each of our cases of participatory democracy and link them to their respective democratic regimes. These are summarized in Table 5.3.

Table 5.3 Three Cases of Participatory Democracy

Direct Affirmative Democracy (Gravataí)	Mediated Affirmative Democracy (Camaragibe)	Movement Democracy (João Monlevade)
Least autonomous	Medium autonomy	Most autonomous
Most inclusive	Medium inclusive	Least inclusive
Least open to societal innovation in claims-making	Room for societal innovation but requires high level of coordination with state	Most open to societal innovation in claims-making
Problems of "colonization of the Life-world"	Problems of accountability/ or Delegitimation of civil society	Problems of representation

In Gravataí, the chain of sovereignty was short and direct (direct affirmative democracy). Very local assemblies made very binding decisions that traveled very quickly up through the chain. The absence of mediators, and most notably organized civil society, was compensated for by a proactive government. As a result, civil society did not develop a preference formation capacity of its own outside of the actual deliberative fora. Demands were as such the result of deliberation, but this was a rather compressed form of deliberation since actors entered the fora without prior experience of deliberation or prior opportunities to develop preferences. And since the chain was so direct, there was little opportunity for coordination with other needs and interests. Overall, the preference formation process and the chain of sovereignty left little room for innovation and favored narrow, highly localized demands. By contrast, because there were no preconditions to participation and because fora were dominated by ordinary citizens speaking for themselves (as opposed to representatives of organizations), the process was highly inclusive. What PB accomplished in Gravataí was to give citizens a direct and unmediated voice in the making of the budget. The local state affirmed citizenship by creating channels of binding engagement. The Achilles heel of the Gravataí model of direct affirmative democracy is, of course, the lack of civil society autonomy. Citizens have no alternative to the state's invitation to participate. Communicative power, in other words, remains entirely dependent on state power, and the life-world, in the absence of differentiated and autonomous associations capable of problematizing and transmitting issues to the public sphere, remains highly vulnerable to colonization.

In Camaragibe, the chain of sovereignty was longer and more complicated. The institutional design sought to combine local deliberated inputs with significant mediation and coordination functions at a higher level (mediated affirmative democracy). Community preferences were certainly deliberated, but delegates played a proactive role in shaping, processing, and translating the demands formed by assemblies. In some ways, delegates were as much agents of the state as they were delegates of the people. The complex institutional design and the strong mediating role assigned to delegates was a response to both the weakness of civil society and the perceived need to extend participation beyond the budget into administration. The fact that delegates were quite empowered in their engagement with the state, and that the process had so many points of contact with the state across a range of sectors, did allow for a lot of societal innovation, but also depended on a lot of coordination with the state. Since participation in local assemblies was not mediated by CSOs, the process was broadly inclusive. However, the strong role accorded to delegates in mediating between communities and the state did have the effect of narrowing inclusivity. And while it is certainly the case that the proliferation of fora and councils afforded civil society more opportunities for engagement and for developing more autonomous positions, the reliance on state-empowered delegates may have also counteracted that autonomy. Finally, because delegates were so dependent on the state and because the process allowed for so many points of intervention by authorities, public administration in Camaragibe did suffer from problems of accountability. The other side of this was that because of the perceived dominant role of the state in orchestrating the process, CSOs, even while being offered significant new opportunities of engagement, suffered from some loss of legitimacy. These seemingly contradictory outcomes—that both civil society and the state both suffered legitimacy problems even as they have become more intertwined—is driven home by the fact that the most articulate lament—"the curse of participatory democracy model"—came from state actors. Having worked hard to create spaces for political society, the architects of PB themselves were concerned that their interventions were possibly breeding complacency and lack of initiative on the part of civil society organizations.

In João Monlevade, a strong civil society, characterized by organizational autonomy and enjoying high levels of coordination among CSOs, was able to play an active role both in preference formation and in directly mediating with the state. Indeed, the role of CSOs here comes closest to approximating the ideal-typical case of the democratic effects of associations (Warren 2001). What is key here is that even before the instituted process of participation began, CSOs had already mobilized and aggregated interests. The input of civil society was as such much more autonomous and far less dependent on the state. This prefigurative role also allowed for more societal innovation, since civil society brought not simply demands to the state, but whole programs and policies. There was also a clear link between the active role of an organized civil society and the care with which the architects of PB built strong coordination functions (strategic planning) and processes (the caravans of delegates). Because strong and mobilized demand-making can overburden government and lead to conflict, the architects of PB had every incentive to build in coordination functions. And because civil society organizations were well coordinated among themselves (mediating publics) and highly sensitized to more citywide and encompassing issues and interests, they were open to participating in coordinating activities. The strong role of civil society did, however, also crowd out nonorganized forms of demand-making with the result that the process was, overall, less inclusive than in Gravataí and Camargibe. It was, in other words, much harder for individual citizens to get directly involved. We have interpreted the close and well-coordinated relationship between civil society actors and state actors as mostly synergistic, much as in Evan's model of embedded autonomy (1995). But we must recognize that such embeddedness runs the risk, in the absence of countervailing mechanisms, of becoming overly insular and eventually ossifying into a form of party-sponsored corporatism. In part, this is the concern that has led critics to claim that the process was politicized and to level the familiar (and somewhat self-serving) accusation that it was little more than a form of PT clientelism. Be this as it may, the line between embeddedness and synergy, and politicization and capture is indeed a fine one. More than any other finding we have presented in this book, this powerfully underscores the extent to which participatory democracy is a very delicate equilibrium.

CONCLUSION

Bootstrapping Participatory Democracy

The political theorist Mark Warren has observed that "Within democratic theory a remarkable consensus is emerging around Tocqueville's view that the virtues and viability of a democracy depend on the robustness of its associational life" (2001, 3). But why exactly is it so important to bring civil society into our understanding of democracy? Throughout this book we have tried to answer this complicated question, but we begin this conclusion by making a fairly simple assertion: civil society is critical to the quality of democracy because it supports collective action. This is the case in two quite different respects. First, civil society can facilitate the mobilization of underrepresented groups who, despite enjoying formal rights of citizenship, cannot process their claims through institutionalized channels. New collective actors that emerge in the associational spaces of civil society can thus help break through the self-reinforcing equilibrium of representative democracy in which those who have privilege (in terms of either formal rights or heightened capacities to use their rights) can use politics to reinforce that privilege. Second, a vibrant civil society can underwrite the collective problematization and processing of new issues and norms and through the medium of the public sphere (which itself is always constituted of multiple publics) reach new understandings of what we collectively value through argument and deliberation. Once we dispense with the surprisingly obstinate fallacy in liberal theory that politics are individual and that political action is a response to individual choices and preferences formed in some isolated bubble of rational calculation, then we have to recognize the fundamentally social character of political life. In this sense, civil society is critical to how actors come to collectively understand, process, and coordinate their needs, interests, preferences, and identities. In its normative ideal, democracy can then be conceived as a set of practices that links civil society to public authority. Deepening democracy, in turn, can be seen as a strengthening of that link and more explicitly as a process of "shifting the means through which collective decisions are taken away from money and coercive power and toward communicative power or influence" (Warren 2001, 67).

In making the case for participatory democracy it is important to reiterate two key qualifications. First, this is not about substituting participatory or deliberative democracy for representative democracy. Doing so is neither desirable nor possible. Rather, the concern is with (a) addressing the deficits of formal democracy and, in particular, repairing the broken chain of sovereignty, and (b) recognizing that there are both normative and functional reasons to link state power to the information, creativity, energy, and capacity for collective action of civil society. The second qualification is that if participation matters because of the way in which it brings civil society in, then we must be extremely attentive to actually existing civil society and its very delicate relation to the market, state, and social power. If this first qualification takes its cue from Habermas and his theory of communicative power, particularly his core idea that the systemic logic of the market and state have to be counterbalanced by the communicative power of civil society, then the second borrows from Bourdieu and invites a relentlessly critical, but not hopeless, examination of the actual forms, practices, and effects of civil society. As we have repeatedly noted, it is possible to identify a range of civil society formations that undermine citizenship, most notably the clientelistic practices that are the norm in democracies that suffer from low levels of institutionalization (O'Donnell 1993). But when civil society is voluntary, communicative, and publicly oriented, it does promote the quality of democratic practices.

This then leads up to two critical questions. First, under what conditions can democracy-enhancing forms of civil society flourish? Second, to what extent can democratic *practices*, nurtured in the bosom of civil society, be translated into democratic *effects*? Much of the literature on civil society has failed to tackle these questions directly, creating a huge gap between the normative promise of democracy and our empirical understanding of how democracy works. We have addressed these questions by carefully examining and evaluating the impact of concerted efforts to promote local participatory democracy in a specific context that would not, at first blush, appear to be conducive to participatory democracy.

The political science literature on Brazil has generally painted a rather dismal picture of the efficacy of Brazilian democracy, especially with respect to the style of local politics. The literature on Brazil until the 1990s points to what has typically been described as a dysfunctional political system dominated by clientelistic and oligarchical parties that rule but cannot govern. The problem of mediation of social demands has been acute, both in terms of the social conditions of Brazilian politics and the basic institutional characteristics of the electoral system. Pervasive inequalities and pronounced social and political exclusions (including highly circumscribed political rights before 1989) have promoted highly personalistic and hierarchical modes of political representation. Against this background an electoral system marked by malapportionment and an open-list PR system has resulted in poorly institutionalized parties. The sum result has been the dominance of political elites that thrive on discretionary power and routinely flout both the rule and norms of democratic process.

What is true at the national level is even more so true at the municipal level where politics have traditionally been dominated by powerful families or narrow cliques, and where the business of governing has essentially been one of highly organized rent-seeking. The problem is compounded by the extensive powers that Brazilian law extends to executive authority, most notably in budgetary matters. Taken together, these factors have encouraged rent-seeking, backroom deal-making, and overall poor governance at the municipal level. Sociologists and anthropologists have, moreover, pointed to severe forms of inequality and social exclusion as barriers to meaningful participation. It is against this backdrop that we have examined actual political practices and institutional reforms in eight midsize Brazilian municipalities. Our findings suggest that local politics and democratic practices are not as immutable as the broader literature claims and that changes in institutional environment can both improve governance and empower civil society.

A careful examination of the processes through which citizens engaged local government between 1997–2000 in our eight municípios revealed that PB cities provided for much more effective forms of engagement than their non-PB counterparts. The degree of effectiveness ranged from *consultative participation* in which citizens were able to express their demands in an open and organized manner (that is, in dedicated fora) and did influence decision-making, to cases of *binding participation* where citizens were directly involved in shaping the municipal budget. The scope of citizen influence ranged from making general demands to specifically shaping patterns of investment and service delivery. Though there was great variation between PB cities, there is little doubt they were all marked by an expansion of the opportunity structure for citizen engagement. Even the most restricted version of PB had the baseline effect of increasing the flow of information about municipal governance, creating spaces for citizens to voice their demands and subjecting what were once highly insulated and discretionary processes of decision-making to public scrutiny and even iterated bargaining.

Institutional reforms as such do matter. In the Brazilian context, PB emerged as a practical strategy of a broader movement toward participatory democracy. The reforms were born of civil society—specifically the gestation of social movements with a long history—and were politically facilitated by the emergence of the PT. The broader context mattered on two counts. First, it generated the repertoires and norms of reform. That is, when local actors sought to build more participatory forms of government they could draw from a wide range of experiences effectively diffused through dense social and political networks, supported by a range of formal and less formal NGOs and foundations. There is little doubt, however, that the PT provided the most important mechanism of diffusion. The broader context also mattered because of decentralization initiatives and constitutional provisions that encouraged participatory reforms.

But, as we have seen, the local context was critical to shaping outcomes. In each of our four PB adopters, the actual design of PB varied dramatically in both scope and mode of engagement. João Monlevade combined direct participation with a range of planning and coordination functions; Gravataí fashioned a set of processes that were very direct and required little mediation, but also made it much more difficult to coordinate at higher levels. Camaragibe built a system that went beyond the budget to encompass administration; its Participatory Administration resulted in a highly complex institutional design that combined fora with a range of coordinating institutions. The Camaragibe model required a high degree of mediation, specifically in the form of powerful delegates who were often closer to the state than to their communities. These differences reflected pragmatic adaptations by PB architects to local realities, in particular to the condition of local civil society. It is difficult to exaggerate the extent to which the implementing and impact of PB was in the most proximate sense an outgrowth of the commitment and innovativeness of these actors. In all three cases participatory democracy was clearly bootstrapped. But that bootstrapping took place against a backdrop of normative and institutional repertoires developed by social movements, and in the context of local political ecologies.

PB had a positive effect on governance, but what impact did it have on civil society? The literature on civil society emphasizes the importance of forming and nurturing autonomous civil society organizations and is often wary of institutionalizing engagements with government. Indeed, a consistent preoccupation in the civil society and social movement literature has been with the classic tradeoffs between institutionalization and mobilization. More recently, and in response to the celebratory tone of some scholarship on participation in the early 2000s, this preoccupation has been revived in some works critical of participatory development.[1] Of particular worry has been the impact of what Cornwall and Coelho (2007) have described as "invited spaces" of participation, those opened from "above."

To address this concern, we specifically examined the impact of PB on civil society itself, working with a typology of state-civil society relations outlined in Chapter 1. We worked with a two-dimensional analytic model of civil society that takes into account both the self-organization of civil society and the general context in which it engages the state. If the first axis has been the subject of most research on civil society (especially in the social movement literature), much less attention has been given to the engagement question. We then specifically tested the extent to which institutional reforms impact civil society by comparing similar municípios in which one introduced PB and the other did not. Our findings can be summarized.

As our paired analysis shows, tangible change in state-civil society relations took place only in those cities that adopted PB. In three of these four cases, these changes were in the direction of democratic deepening. Gravataí, Camarabige, and João Monlevade all graduated from the status of simple representative democracies in which civil society had little power, to the status of *affirmative* democracies in the first two cases and a *mobilized* democracy in the case of João Monlevade. That the introduction of PB does not inevitably deepen democracy is illustrated by the case of Mauá, in which an improvement in the mode of engagement came at the expense of civil society's autonomy. Overall, as one might have anticipated, institutional reform mostly mattered for changing the institutional setting, that is, creating more meaningful points of interface between the local state and civil society. Thus most of the movement in Table 5.2 is along the vertical axes—the mode of engagement. Institutional reform did not have much of an impact on the self-organization of civil society.

If our findings point to the malleability of civil society over a relatively short time span, then they also underscore what is often glossed over in the associational democracy literature, namely, the extent to which the impact of reforms depends on preexisting political and civil society configurations. Prostrate civil societies became more active, but only under the protection of a reformist state.

Those civil societies that were the most successful in scaling up as a result of PB *and* maintaining their autonomy were civil societies that already enjoyed significant self-organization. Again, Mauá represents our cautionary tale. In Mauá, PB actually increased control of a political party in power over civil society. Civil society organizations that once enjoyed a high degree of autonomy (but no opportunities for engaging the state) compromised much of their self-organization in exchange for inclusion in the governance process.

BEYOND BRAZIL

As one surveys the literature on participatory democracy, two impressions are striking. First of all, the range of experiments that are given the label of participatory is truly impressive, even disconcerting. First, such reforms range in scale from countrywide reforms, such as Bolivia (Van Cott 2008), Indonesia (Gibson and Woolcock 2008) and South Africa (Heller 2001), to highly scattered and localized initiatives (Coelho and Von Lieres forthcoming), not to mention participatory initiatives as part of development promotion (Cooke and Kothari 2001). Second, the scope of issues over which participatory reforms have been introduced ranges from city and even provincial state budgets, to particular policy areas (environmental management, the workplace, schools) to single-issue initiatives (voter reform in British Columbia, a specific development project). Third, participatory reforms have been initiated across an expansive spectrum of social and political contexts. This includes highly institutionalized Western democracies, democracies in the global South marked by the worst income inequality in the world (Brazil and South Africa) or by histories of pervasive social exclusion (Ecuador and India), and nondemocracies. Thus even in authoritarian China, local governments have experimented with a range of governance practices, including some limited instances of deliberative democracy (He 2006).

Given this range and complexity, it is inherently difficult to draw generalizations. We will instead sharpen our observations by examining two well-documented cases that are similar in scope, scale, and context: the Indian state of Kerala and South Africa. Our goal here is not to provide a comprehensive comparative analysis of participatory democracy, but rather to draw out from the comparative research and the existing literature some key lessons that emerge from our study of PB in Brazil. These lessons have less to do with developing a definitive statement on the causes, conditions, and effects of participatory democracy, than reflecting on some of the challenges of bootstrapping democracy. The lessons we want to focus on are the malleability of participation, local capacity and preference formation, political agency and new alliances, strategies of implementation, bootstrapping and blueprints, and bringing civil society in.

Kerala and South Africa lend themselves to a comparison with PB in Brazil. In both countries, participatory reforms were initiated as part of a broader process of democratic decentralization and were introduced in social and political contexts that bear striking similarities to Brazil. First, all three are robust and consolidated democracies in which competitive elections and all the basic institutions of formal democracy have been firmly established.[2] Second, in all three cases the challenges of surmounting accumulated inequalities and entrenched forms of social exclusion are enormous. Third, in all three cases social movements played a critical role in setting the stage for participatory reforms. Finally, in each case an identifiable agent of change—left-of-center programmatic parties—has created significant opportunities for promoting more democratic forms of local government.

The Indian state of Kerala (population thirty-one million) has long been recognized for its achievements in promoting social development (Drèze and Sen 1995; Heller 1999; Williams 2008).[3] But despite the strength of mass movements (most notably, organized labor) and a high literacy rate, Kerala, as is true of all Indian states, has been governed in a highly top-down fashion. Vertically organized state bureaucracies have exercised a virtual monopoly in service delivery and development, and local government—that is, municipalities and rural governments—have enjoyed very limited powers and virtually no resources to promote development. Until recently, the first level at which Indian citizens encountered a democratically constituted form of the state was at the provincial level, with the average Indian state having a population of thirty million in 2001. This began to change in 1993 with the passage of the 73rd and 74th constitutional amendments that gave new powers to local governments and mandated citizen participation in the form of *gram sabhas* (village assemblies). The amendments, however, left the details of implementation to states. States did institute regular local government elections, but for the most part failed to devolve significant responsibilities and resources downward. This was largely because political parties that rule at the state level depend on local powerbrokers that are directly threatened by democratic decentralization. But in Kerala, a coalition of leftist parties led by the Communist Party of India-Marxist (CPI[M]) returned to power in 1996 and almost immediately launched the "People's Campaign for Decentralized Planning" (the Campaign hereafter).

Inspired and informed by a statewide community organization—the KSSP (Kerala Sastra Sahitya Parishad, or the Kerala People's Science Movement), a fifty-thousand member organization with a long history of promoting local experiments in participatory planning and development—the CPI(M)-led government implemented what is in scope and scale undoubtedly one of the most ambitious participatory reforms ever undertaken. All 1,214 local governments in Kerala—municipalities and the three rural tiers of district, block, and *gram panchayats* (rural local governments)—were given new functions and powers of decision-making and were granted discretionary budgeting authority over 35–40 percent of the state's developmental expenditures. In addition to devolving resources, state officials sought to directly promote participatory democracy by mandating structures and processes designed to maximize the direct involvement of citizens in planning and budgeting.

Much as in the case of Brazil, the transition to democracy in South Africa was accompanied by powerful calls for institutionalizing participation. The anti-apartheid movement was spearheaded by a broad coalition of civil society organizations, but the mass element of the movement was dominated by what in South Africa were known as *civics*. These neighborhood associations initially emerged as community-based efforts at self-provisioning in black townships but in the 1980s became powerful vehicles of organized resistance to the apartheid state leading a series of boycotts and protests that were critical to bringing the apartheid government to the negotiating table. In their political form, civics were "frenetically participatory . . . maintained by wave upon wave of political activity, generated by the heady atmosphere of insurrection against an unpopular, racist regime" (Adler and Steinberg 2000, 11). The organizational forms pioneered by the civics—street and area committees that answered to popular assemblies—embodied "a distinctive notion of participatory democracy [and] an assertion that the democracy of the ballot box constituted a truncated and deformed form of citizen power" (Adler and Steinberg 2000, 8). Indeed, it has been remarked that the strength of the civics was such that South Africa stands out as the only case of democratic transition in which negotiations were not limited to the national arena and to political parties, but also took place at the municipal level where grass-roots organizations were directly incorporated (Swilling and Boya 1997).

At the time of its democratic transition, South Africa's foundational development document, the Reconstruction and Development Program (RDP), explicitly identified participatory democracy as a key objective and argued that all local development had to be based on the mobilization of civil society.[4] The umbrella organizations representing civics—the South African National Civics Organisation (SANCO)—played a key role in shaping urban policy, including the Local Government Transition Act, which constituted local government as an independent sphere of government and devolved significant budgetary and developmental powers to municipalities. Subsequent legislation, moreover, mandated a series of participatory processes in local governance. Most notably, all municipalities in South Africa must formulate an annual Integrated Development Plan (IDP) through a prescribed process that calls for broad-based community participation. In the early years of the post-apartheid South Africa, Community Development Forums (CDFs) were a ubiquitous phenomenon in townships, serving as popular assemblies in which local development plans and interventions were debated.

But the experiment with participatory democracy in South Africa was short-lived. Just two years after the transition, the African National Congress (ANC) government abandoned the redistributive thrust of the RDP and embraced a much more market-driven vision of development. Increasingly, the center came to see the local state more as an instrument of delivery than a forum for participation. As many commentators have noted, in the past decade local government has become increasingly insulated and centralized (van Donk et al. 2008). In the name of efficiency and more rapid delivery, the ANC has managerialized decision-making processes and reduced the quality and scope of participatory processes created under the RDP. A wide range of participatory institutions including the Community Development Forums have been dismantled or hollowed out, and municipal governance has been centralized into "Unicity" structures that have entrenched a bureaucratic and corporatist vision of urban governance (Beall, Crankshaw, and Parnell 2002). The privatization or outsourcing of many government functions, including the preparation of IDPs, and increased reliance on consultants has virtually crowded out community structures. In sum, the local spaces in which citizens can practice democracy and exert some influence over South Africa's very ambitious project of local government transformation (for example, de-racializing the apartheid city and closing the service gap between whites and Africans) have been hollowed out. With little room to effectively exert voice, township populations have increasingly resorted to contentious action including widespread "services protests" (Atkinson 2007). Most tragically, in 2008 a wave of xenophobic violence swept through townships and informal settlements, and many commentators pointed directly to the absence of genuine processes of democratic engagement as the underlying cause (Misao et al. 2010).

When examined in the light of the Kerala and Brazilian experiences, the demise of participatory democracy in South Africa can only be explained in terms of the balance between political and civil society (Heller 2009). In institutional terms, post-apartheid South Africa was well equipped to nurture participatory democracy. The constitution and relevant legislation provided legal support for participation, and by the comparative standards of developing-world democracies, including Brazil and India, local governments, especially the larger municipalities, enjoyed significant resources and administrative capacities (Heller 2008). Civil society organizations initially appeared well placed to support participatory structures. The terms of the transition, however, had produced a ruling party that not only enjoyed overwhelming electoral support (more than two-thirds of the vote in every national election) but also saw itself as the incarnation of transformative politics and as the sole legitimate heir of what it calls the National Democratic Revolution. So even as the RDP reserved an important role for civil society in the transformative project of de-racializing South Africa, the ANC viewed civil society's role as largely complementary to its own transformative agenda. As a truly hegemonic force, the ANC could in effect subsume civil society. This political logic, born of the broad and encompassing mandate that the transition conferred on the ANC and to the quite extraordinary state capacities inherited from the apartheid regime, explains why structures and processes that were originally presented as providing autonomous spaces for civil society participation in local government (such as Community Development Forums and IDPs) were quickly either brought under the control of party structures or substituted with more technocratic forms of decision-making.

In contrast, the political circumstances under which participatory democracy took root in Brazil and Kerala came against the backdrop of a crisis of political party systems and the Left's loss of faith in the traditional top-down, command-and-control transformative state. Viewed against the case of South Africa, this equation proved much more favorable for bringing civil society in. In Brazil PB was publicly presented as an alternative to the traditional local clientelistic state and as a means for dislodging oligarchical party control. In Kerala, the challenge was less public (supported as it was by a party-in-power), but the architects of the Campaign and its civil society progenitor, the KSSP, were determined to challenge the power of patronage politicians, especially what is locally referred to as the "bureaucrat-politician nexus of corruption." In PB the chal-

lenge to politicians was frontal: the PB process was designed to operate in parallel to the official budgeting process and to circumvent elected councilors. In
Kerala, the Campaign was designed to integrate locally elected panchayat officials, but to do so while carefully containing their discretionary powers through
participatory structures.

Another point of contrast with South Africa's vision of participation (at
least as shaped by the ANC) is that the PB and the Campaign both viewed institutional reform first and foremost as a means to providing new avenues of
mobilization. The emphasis, at least at the outset, was less on promoting development and extending service delivery and more on nurturing new forms of
state-citizen engagement and specifically on changing the way in which choices
about development are made. PB, as we saw in Chapter 2, was closely tied to
the new discourses of active citizenship that grew directly out of the democracy
movement. In the first wave of PB reformers led by Porto Alegre the goal was
explicitly to use government as a vehicle for social movements, but as we have
seen, second-generation PB experiments, including the four cases we have examined, were more concerned with "the challenge of being government" and
focused on bringing civil society into governance.

In Kerala, the political logic of the Campaign was succinctly summarized by
a key Planning Board official: "Politicians and bureaucrats want to hold onto
power and the only way to dislodge them is through a social movement" (Heller
2005, 94). The link between mobilization and development was made very
clear. Making his case for democratic decentralization, especially with respect
to Kerala's economic problems, the architect of the Campaign, T. M. Thomas
Isaac, writes that "defending the public infrastructure in education, health and
other sectors is no longer possible without improving the quality of their services. All these necessitate a reorientation of the mass movements towards direct
intervention in the development process in order to improve productivity or
improve the quality of services" (Thomas Isaac and Franke 2002, 45). A perma-
nently mobilized civil society thus emerges as the primary goal of the Campaign
and PB, and in stark contrast to the technocratic view embraced by the ANC in
South Africa, planning becomes "an instrument of social mobilization" and specifically a means of reengaging citizens in the process of public decision-making.

A close examination of the institutional design of the Campaign reveals a
striking isomorphism with the generic features of PB. Indeed, the four design
principles that we identified in the Introduction as defining PB are also present in Kerala: (1) giving citizens a direct role in city governance by creating a

range of public fora (microregional councils, district councils, sectoral committees, plenary meetings, delegate councils) in which citizens and/or delegates can publicly articulate and debates their needs; (2) linking participatory inputs to the actual budgeting process through rule-bound procedures; (3) improving transparency in the budgeting process by increasing the range of actors involved and publicizing the process and by the same token reducing the possibility of elite-capture; and (4) incentivizing agency by providing tangible returns to grass-roots participation.

In Kerala, the Campaign is part of the annual plan exercise led by the Kerala State Planning Board, but supported by tens of thousands of volunteers trained by the KSSP. The process begins at the local level, where each of the states' 990 rural panchayats is granted "untied" funds (between 29–35 percent of total plan expenditures) and mandated to produce a local plan and to design and budget for specific projects across the full range of development sectors.[5] Panchayats are required to develop their plans through a series of nested participatory exercises in which citizens are given a direct role in shaping policies and projects. In a first stage, open, public gram sabhas are held to determine broad priorities and to elect delegates to task forces for each of ten development sectors.[6] The task forces—which also include one government official and one elected representative—then develop a shelf of projects to be presented to the panchayat. The panchayat finalizes a budget based on projects proposed by the task forces and presents the budget (which is distributed in advance) to a second gram sabha. All budgeted projects that involve targeted beneficiaries (for example, housing for the poor) are required to have a beneficiary committee and to publish lists of beneficiaries for gram sabha approval. The plans formulated at the panchayat level are submitted to the higher level (the block), which formulates its own plan by integrating panchayat plans. The cycle is then repeated at the district and finally the state level. Fully one-third of the final statewide plan is as such a direct product of this bottom-up planning exercise.

There is now a solid body of research on the impact of the Campaign. As one might anticipate, there has been significant variation in the degree to which local participatory governance structures have taken root in a state marked by enormous cultural and social heterogeneity. But there is little doubt that overall the Campaign has promoted more participatory forms of democracy and that the causal links parallel what we have found for PB in Brazil.

First, the Campaign has enabled a very significant devolution of authoritative decision-making powers. Survey research conducted in 2002 has found that in almost all panchayats gram sabhas were held on a regular basis, task forces were constituted, development plans were created, and beneficiaries committees were set up (Heller, Harilal, and Chaudhuri 2007). The quality of local plans varied significantly, and the process of integrating panchayat plans into higher-level plans was ad hoc at best. But given that local government development had long been the preserve of top-down line-department bureaucracies implementing schemes hatched in Trivandrum (Kerala's capital) or even New Delhi, the very fact that budgets and plans were being formulated at the village-level marks a dramatic departure from the past.

Second, the most decisive impact of the Campaign has been on the level and composition of participation. Data collected from all 990 panchayats for the first two years of the campaign shows that 10.3 percent of the electorate participated in the first annual gram sabhas in 1996 and 10.6 percent in 1997 (Chaudhuri and Heller 2003). The social composition of the Campaign, moreover, improved drastically in the second year. In the first year of the Campaign, Scheduled Caste and Scheduled Tribe (SC/ST) participation was well below the average rate, but by the second year SC/STs were participating in greater proportions than non-SC/STs.[7] Similarly, women's relative participation increased dramatically after the first year, rising to 40 percent of all participants in 1997–98. Data collected from the sample of seventy-two panchayats found that representation of women and SCs in task forces (the bodies charged with designing projects) was lower than in gram sabhas, but still impressive.

Third, the Campaign's elaborate set of nested institutions have secured the chain of sovereignty and made citizen participation meaningful. In a large-scale survey of key respondents, 64 percent reported that priorities expressed in the gram sabhas were "always reflected" in the final plan. Similarly, task forces were also very effective: 80 percent of respondents said that task force projects were "almost always" or "always" included in the final panchayat plan. To use the terminology developed in our analysis of PB, there is clear evidence in most panchayats that the annual cycle of planning and budgeting falls squarely into the category of *binding participation.*

Fourth, an important effect of the Campaign was to draw civil society in. A whole new generation of younger activists and politicians came alive with the introduction of the Campaign. More than one hundred thousand volunteers participated in the original launch of the Campaign, and more than fourteen thousand local elected officials who before were limited to largely ceremonial roles were given meaningful functions. Local civil society organizations that had no local state to engage with found a new partner in panchayats. A number of local studies have explicitly tied the rapid rise in "self-help groups" (generally formed by lower-caste women) to the matching funds made available by the campaign (John and Chathukulam 2002; Manjula 2000; Seema and Mukherjee 2000), and registration data collected from seventy-two sample panchayats show a three-fold increase in the number of self-help groups during the campaign (Heller, Harilal, and Chaudhuri 2007). Whether we would classify this overall pattern of bringing civil society in as one that conforms to our typology of *affirmative* or *mobilized* democracy is difficult to say. There have been complaints, including some aired by KSSP leaders, that once the early and highly mobilized stage of the Campaign ended, the process become overly bureaucratic and increasingly dominated by local politicians. However, the marked increase in civil society activity, especially among women's groups, suggests that the Campaign has created new spaces for civil society.

Evaluating the developmental impact of participatory reforms is clearly an area that calls for more research and better methodologies. Having said this, the near-consensus view among researchers is that the Campaign and PB have had significant positive effects on developmental outcomes. In both cases, the mechanisms at work have been the increased accountability of officials and elected representative and the greater transparency—or, more accurately, the increased publicness—of the budgeting process. Stated somewhat differently, participatory structures have reduced the transaction costs of influence for traditionally marginalized groups and increased the transactions costs of influence (and capture) for traditional elites. Many of the officials and CSO leaders we interviewed in PB cities were able to provide clear, detailed, and precise information about the budgeting process in PB cities, in sharp contrast to their counterparts in the non-PB cities. In the case of Kerala, there is also excellent qualitative evidence that decentralization and participation resulted in the much better use of local information and also triggered significant innovation and horizontal diffusion of new, grass-roots "best practices" (Thomas Isaac and Franke 2002).

THE MALLEABILITY OF PARTICIPATION

One of the most important lessons that we can draw from these cases is that not only is it possible to create institutions that allow for meaningful forms of citizen engagement, but also the conditions for successful participation are not rigidly determined. When offered genuine opportunities for participation, local actors will get involved. Participation is not a function of stock variables such as human and social capital, which can only be accumulated slowly over time. It is a function of much more malleable factors, such as institutional design, openings in the opportunity structure, alliances, and new incentives. When subordinate groups do not participate, it is not because they don't have the skills or the determination, but because the obstacles to participation are too high. There are "transaction costs" to participation, and careful design and political action can go a long way in changing those costs.

A related point is that participation can have dramatic knock-on effects. This is true not only in the sense of demonstration effects (more groups and communities join as the returns become clear) but also in the sense of expanding the possibilities and meanings of citizenship. Of the many obstacles the poor face, none is more debilitating than the cultural constraints of limited cognitive horizons and limited experience of working the system. The "performance of competence and innovation" that even the most modest forms of participation offer confronts these constraints by nurturing what Appadurai calls the "capacity to aspire" (2004). In sum, participatory institutions that are carefully designed and properly scaled can significantly expand opportunities for the poor and the most marginalized groups to practice citizenship.

The case of South Africa is a sober reminder that even when civil society is highly mobilized and highly motivated it nonetheless remains highly dependent on the institutional and political environments for finding effective modes of engagement with the state. Brazil and Kerala do, however, point toward some qualified claims about the conditions for successful participation. There has been enormous variation within each case. In Kerala, the Campaign had a much greater impact in rural areas than in municipalities, in part because political efforts were focused on panchayats. Even across Kerala's 990 panchayats, the level of participation varies enormously and in statistical tests does not correlate with regional factors (which might act as a proxy for social capital) or any of a large number of stock variables (such as population, population density, economic measures, and so forth) (Chaudhuri and Heller 2003). There is, however, a strong correlation between proxy measures of rural union organization, suggesting a link with existing mobilizational capacity. A similar picture emerges in Brazil. As we have seen, the preexisting strength of civil society has a direct bearing on the degree to which PB reforms deepen democracy. João Monlevade stands out as the only case in which reforms led to a *mobilized democracy*, one in which civil society has developed real powers to engage with the local state while maintaining its capacity for autonomous action.

Having said this, the equally important point is that in three of our four cases PB was successfully implemented in a context of relatively weak civil societies. Similarly, with their clientelistic pasts and oligarchical elites, Cambaragibe and Gravataí were not likely sites of broad-based participation, but this is precisely what PB achieved.

When this is coupled with the finding from Kerala that rates of participation of subordinate groups increased rapidly after the first year of the Campaign, it becomes clear that participation is highly plastic and is very much an artifact of politics, both in the sense of formal political opportunities that result from institutional changes (that, in turn, can follow from changes in ruling party) and social movement politics that can strengthen civil society capacities.[8]

LOCAL CAPACITY AND PREFERENCE FORMATION

One of most common policy-world objections to decentralized participation is that poor communities do not have the capacity to engage directly in decision-making and that too much participation can be disruptive, time-consuming, and even lead to conflict. It is interesting to note that this is the same logic that informs the Schumpeterian argument for representative democracy in complex societies.[9] Governance problems are far too complex for ordinary citizens, hence the need to delegate decision-making to representatives, or in the high modernist (Scott 1998) version of this argument exemplified by the African National Congress, to technocrats and experts. The normative premise of participatory democracy directly rejects this view on the simple grounds that democracy is fundamentally about preference formation, and that claims about lack of capacity are often little more than polite ways of legitimizing the transfer of decision-making powers from citizens to elites. Of course, it is critical not to confuse a normative ideal with a practical set of processes. But the cases we have examined leave little doubt that even citizens with little more capacity than their own commitment to democratic engagement can effectively participate in local government.

Before PB was introduced in our four cases, local citizens had few if any channels through which to influence public action and no prior experience of planning or local development. Under PB, ordinary citizens have proven more than capable of forming their preferences, making city budgets, and negotiating with department officials. Kerala does enjoy high literacy rates and a history of social mobilization. But Keralites had virtually no experience with local government and had never been afforded an opportunity to shape local development.

Opposition to the Campaign centered almost exclusively on claims that local actors did not have the required expertise to formulate plans. Yet when offered the opportunity, that is precisely what local citizens did. Participatory reforms have also taken hold among communities that have long suffered from the effects of social exclusion, most notably in the case of Ecuador (Van Cott 2008), or have long been subordinated to highly authoritarian forms of control as in the case of Indonesia (Gibson and Woolcock 2008). In all these cases, the creation of institutional spaces for deliberation unleashed new forms of claim-making.

Having said this, creating spaces for local preference formation does pose enormous challenges. Preference formation without a secure chain of sovereignty will inevitably lead to dashed expectations and delegitimation. There is arguably nothing more dangerous to the prospects of participatory democracy than participatory processes that are hollow. Local preference formation can unleash parochialism, elevating local demands over broader demands, and can also make coordination of multiple inputs difficult, if not impossible. But this is precisely what the challenge of institution building is all about. What our case studies revealed, more than anything else, was the degree to which PB architects were preoccupied with addressing these challenges. As we have seen, activists and administrators spent a tremendous amount of time and energy fine-tuning the process in order to preserve the chain of sovereignty. Bootstrapping democracy also called for devising a range of innovative institutions, such as citywide thematic and sectoral councils and delegates' caravans, to specifically address problems of coordination.

POLITICAL AGENCY AND NEW ALLIANCES

Even as we recognize that participation has been possible and consequential in some Brazilian municípios, and that it has in large part emerged from civil society and social movements, we must not slip into the voluntarism of the a-political treatments of civil society. As Michael Watts has noted, "The danger of conceiving of development as dialogue and negotiation—even if the powers of rights driven social movements are upheld and enforced—is that development's primary reality remains struggle, strife and conflict" (2000, 82). To make full sense of PB and other cases such as Kerala and Ecuador, one has to acknowledge the historical and political configuration that made it possible and specifically that created a balance of power that was amenable to reform from below. Three key elements of a favorable "ecology of actors" (Evans 2002; Heller 2001) for participatory democracy can be identified: reformist elements within the state that recognize the limits of traditional elite-driven developmentalism, civil societies that enjoy sufficient organizational capacity and operational autonomy to align with, but not be co-opted, by the local state, and a programmatic left-of-center political party that can orchestrate the necessary political conditions for reform.[10] Of course, such fortuitous alignments are not easy to come by. It is particularly important to bear in mind the power equations that often pit technocrats against activists, bureaucrats and politicians against civil society, and institutional logics against mobilizational logics, all of which come into sharp focus in cases like South Africa. But we must also recognize that local government is often an arena where alliances across the state-society boundary can develop and produce synergistic outcomes (Evans 2002). Many of the government officials we interviewed in our study supported PB as a way to develop ties to partners in civil society. The architects of the Campaign in Kerala were very open about using civil society to break the hold of the rent-seeking "bureaucrat-politician" nexus. These observations fit neatly with Chalmers, Martin, and Piester's (1997) argument that the decline of corporatism and populism in Latin America has opened up room for "associative networks" that cut across traditional state-society boundaries. In contrast to the assumption in much of the democracy literature (as well as neoliberal views of governance) that participation and representation do not sit well together, instituted participatory democracy can produce cooperative arrangements between officials and civil society actors that strengthen both governance and democracy.

BOOTSTRAPS AND PROJECTS

In the development literature it has now become fashionable to reject blueprints, or as Evans (2004) has put it so colorfully, "institutional monocropping." The failure of the one-size-fits all approach of the Washington consensus, and the increasing recognition that there is no single model of democracy, has made ideas of bootstrapping and context sensitivity more intellectually appealing. Yet we want to argue that when it comes to thinking about participatory democracy, we need both bootstraps and blueprints, or better yet, projects. The idea of a project underscores the notion that democracy is always unfinished and that democratic deepening must remain a central preoccupation of governance and politics. The idea of participatory democracy has received wide attention, even to the point of becoming vacuous and inviting sharp critiques of the "tyranny of participation." We are not concerned with these critiques in so much as the object of their ire is generally the international donor community (and its funded NGOs), which has pushed participation as a recipe rather than as a project. Our concern instead has been with national and local political processes, in which the demand for participation has been directly linked to political struggles. When one examines real-world experiments in participatory democracy, what is striking is just how isomorphic they are in terms of their basic normative orientations and core design features. In all the well-documented cases, the discursive frames have presented a critique of representative democracy as perverted by power and social exclusion, emphasized generative projects predicated on notions of expanding citizenship in which political and civil rights are explicitly tied to the social and economic rights, and emphasized the value of deliberation over bargaining.[11] Common design features have included increasing direct involvement by citizens and CSOs in governance; the centrality of inclusive assemblies and various fora; mechanisms for linking fora to decision-making bodies; a range of direct accountability measures, such as limiting the powers of delegates; procedures for increasing access to information; and a range of incentives and facilitations that increase the probability of participation by subordinate groups.

There is hardly any room in the sociology of Bourdieu for projects. These would constitute little more than the grand rules of a game in which only privileged groups have the symbolic resources (including communicative prowess) to reinforce their domination.[12] Habermas is more comfortable with the idea of a democratic project and readily identifies social movements as its central protagonists. But Habermas's vision of reclaiming the emancipatory potential of a modernized civil society, based as it is on his grounding in Western democracies, rests on assumptions about the ability of the "parliamentary complex" to be fully sensitized and accessible to the influence of a pluralistic civil society, conditions that are hardly satisfied in most democracies in the global South. Our emphasis on bootstrapping then captures a middle position. It captures the idea that projects carry dangers, because either they do not fit, or they end up reproducing the old (the more things change, the more they stay the same) and that we should in particular reject the various high modernisms that would substitute blueprints for political projects. But bootstrapping also restores the possibility that (a) institutional design matters and can make a sustainable difference in how power is organized and legitimated (contrary to Bourdieu and the view that institutions always reproduce the existing balance of power), and (b) that agents matter and that for all the constraints they face they can be inventive, even ingenious, in making history of conditions not of their choosing.

This notion of bootstrapping a democratic project is fully supported by the cases we have reviewed. Much as has been the case in Kerala (Heller 2001, 2005) democratic decentralization was made possible by openings from above but was born of experiments that were developed and elaborated through a continuous process of learning by doing. When the PT first came to power in Porto Alegre, it had only vague notions about how to govern in a participatory way and turned to social movements for ideas about how to "reverse the priorities." It eventually drew on a combination of local inspiration, lessons from other cities, and iterated experiments about what worked and what didn't. Similarly, the architects of PB in all of our cases drew directly from Porto Alegre and other cases, but they also jerry-rigged local practices and institutions to fit local contexts. The parallel with Kerala here is quite striking. It was the CPI(M)'s electoral victory that opened a space for democratic decentralization. But it was a close alliance between the reformist faction of the party and civil society actors that made is possible to push through the reforms as part of a larger project of mobilizing participation. Indeed, if the Planning Board (the lead agency of the reforms) had not been able to tap into the mobilizational capacity, local experience, and creativity of civil society organizations, especially the KSSP, the Campaign would never have taken off. In the first two years of the Campaign, the interaction of the Planning Board and KSSP activists, resulted in an almost constant process of institutional fine-tuning that most notably included new strategies for increasing subordinate group participation, on-the-fly responses to coordination problems and a constant preoccupation with protecting the participatory cycle from political interference. These observations from Brazil and Kerala are further reinforced by Van Cott's (2008) detailed comparison of decentralization reforms in Bolivia and Ecuador. In Bolivia, decentralization was politically initiated from above with no input from civil society, and the reforms were implemented with relative uniformity across the country. While this did secure a considerable degree of fiscal devolution, it also limited the capacity of local actors to improvise local processes. Van Cott argues that this, in turn, undermined the participatory potential of the reforms. In contrast, decentralization in Ecuador was more piecemeal and less prescriptive, leaving local actors more room and incentive to innovate. In her case studies, Van Cott finds that where local mayors were highly committed and had strong ties to civil society organizations, institutional reforms were far more likely to emphasize participatory and deliberative processes. Finally, the case of South Africa emphatically drives home the dangers of promoting blueprints from above. Because it views itself as the only legitimate heir of the anti-apartheid movement, the ANC has, for all intents and purposes, become hostile to the idea of an independent civil society. This, in turn, has opened the path to a very high modernist and top-down vision of transformation, one that has shifted power from nonstate actors to technocrats, patronage politicians, and consultants.

BRINGING IN CIVIL SOCIETY

Participatory budgeting reforms have provided fodder for new, critical thinking on the nature of alternatives to representative democracy. Drawing on the lessons from our study we consider the question of representation of demands in participatory processes and the role played by civil society organizations. In making the case for PB, proponents have argued—and our study has confirmed—that PB represents a pointed and self-conscious break from clientelism, bossism, and similar forms of patrimonial intermediation that have long shaped both political and civic forms of representation in Brazil. It seeks to bypass traditional forms of mediation and create a parallel chain of sovereignty by creating new spaces and channels of citizen engagement with the local state.

But PB represents something else as well. By carefully specifying the rules and processes of participation and linking civil society inputs to specific forms of governance, it also represents a break from a more simplistic notion of dialoguing with social movements. Early attempts at participation in Brazil were guided by the vision that it would be enough to "open the doors of government" and that civil society organizations would then "enter" (Filho 1993). Though civil society organizations do, of course, find representation in PB, by design participation is *not* organized along civil society lines, and key moments, such as opening assemblies, are always open to all residents, whether they belong to an organization or not. Civil society demands are processed through formally organized public spaces, which in effect means they are held to the higher standards of deliberative reasoning; rather than just *exercising* influence (through whatever highly uneven sources of leverage different CSOs might have) they have to *make* their case.

But as we also demonstrated in Chapters 4 and 5, PB reforms were instituted in widely differing contexts, and the actual architecture of PB that was adopted put varying degrees of emphasis on civil society mediation. Each of our four PB cities represents a slightly different configuration of forms of civil society mediation, which in turn corresponds to different regimes of participatory democracy and specifically what we have respectively labeled as affirmative and mobilizational democracy. Below we discuss each of these regimes, their potential to address democratic deficits across contexts, as well as their limits.

João Monlevade was an example of *mobilized democracy*; Gravataí and Camaragibe were examples of *affirmative democracy*, Camaragibe with mediation, and Gravataí without. Reframing it in terms of the role of civil society as a mediator, we have an example where civil society plays an important autonomous role (João Monlevade), an example where civil society activists are assisted in this mediating role (the delegates in Camaragibe), and one example where civil society plays no role (Gravataí). Each illustrates the possibilities and limits of each type of participatory democracy and a comparison shows the trade-offs.

Relying on civil society for mediation, as was the case in João Monlevade, leaves civil society in the most autonomous position and can potentially be the most innovative, if least inclusive process. Innovative because civil society plays a propositional role and is able to intervene into government designs; potentially least inclusive because voluntary organizations, by definition, seldom have the resources to attract participants and run participatory processes in the same capacity as state institutions. At the other end of the spectrum is the case of Gravataí, where the state played the central role in creating and managing participatory spaces. This means that while this is potentially the most inclusive model, since the state can in principle promote participation independently of the existing distribution of associational capacities, we have the least room for societal innovation in the process since civil society plays no role. Finally, the case of Camaragibe occupies an in-between position, with the privileged role of delegates who mediate between government and participants. The potential downside to this model is the possible discrediting of voluntary associations by virtue of their dependence on the state, or, as was the case in Camaragibe, the blurring of identities between civil society and the state.

This fine balancing act emerged out of political crafting and trial and error by administrators who drew on previous experience, which we discussed in Chapter 4. It also goes to the heart of a vexing issue for participatory democracy, the relationship between participatory fora and civil society. Autonomous institutions of civil society are generally positively valued as being the repositories of democratic practices and impulses in society; organizations in civil society might also have the best information and access to certain problems that the participatory scheme is designed to address. But relying on organized civil society in an institutional design might, for example, inadvertently favor citizens who are represented by formal and established organizations against citizens who do not have such representation. It might also inadvertently reproduce and harden "movement oligarchies" by giving leaders of such organizations—that may not always meet our normative standards of democratic functioning—additional legitimacy and political capital. And what happens to civil society when participatory democracy is instituted? If participatory fora are parallel to—that is, they coexist with—civil society, then it is not unreasonable to expect they may in certain settings empty out fora of civil society, as they may provide more efficient (and state-backed) ways of addressing certain problems. If participatory fora interface directly with civil society, might they co-opt movements?

The architects of Participatory Budgeting in Brazil envisioned another form of engagement altogether. In clear contrast to visions of democracy that imagine the spontaneous representation of civil society within the state, the state-sponsored participatory institutions of PB promoted forms of association that were distinct from and often in conflict with those of civil society. By design, these institutions addressed some of the representational failings of associational networks by broadening the base of participants and introducing clear criteria of accountability. In some cases, notably Gravataí, this led to tension with traditional neighborhood associations accustomed to clientelistic practices. Insofar as the associational networks that PB nurtured were distinct from those already existing in civil society, they had two distinct effects. First, the extralocal networks created through PB fora have created new ties *across* communities, movements, and sectors, generating precisely the kind of bridging ties that many analysts have argued promote development (Storper 2004), rather than unleashing parochialisms in a society marked by social authoritarianism (Dagnino 1998). Second, PB associationalism had an affirmative character, facilitating participation by groups with historically weak associational capacities. Thus, participation in PB in general has been far more pronounced in working-class and poor communities (Avrtizer 2009; Baiocchi 2005; Goldfrank forthcoming; Wampler 2009), has often provided citizens with no previous experience of engagement new opportunities to participate, and, as we found in the case of Camaragibe, has opened doors to traditionally excluded groups such as Afro-Brazilians. The democratizing effect here is clear. To borrow from Hirschman's famous formulation, promoting the politics of voice (binding participation) can act as a counter to the politics of loyalty (clientelism, communalism) or the politics of exit (apathy, crime, flight). Given the involutionary dynamics of so many poor urban communities in the global

South (for example, the rise of sectarian politics) and increased concern with social disintegration, this may be an especially important lesson.

It is also important to emphasize that the form of representation of the PB is unique in two respects. First, the delegates are a form of representation that is parallel to, but independent of, the elected legislative council. Following Pitkin's well-known conceptualization, authorization takes a very direct form of a closed and substantive mandate. Delegates in PB are elected specifically to represent the bundle of demands that emerge from the neighbourhood assemblies to the Municipal Council of the Budget. Second, the PB process is not legally binding. The municipal legislature is not legally held to approve the budget presented by the Municipal Council of the Budget, but in all the cases that we labeled *binding participation* it did just that. Authorization, in other words, is not secured through a formal representative chain of popular sovereignty, but rather through an instituted—that is, rule-bound—process that is effective only to the extent it produces a set of demands that enjoy a high degree of public legitimacy. In this respect, PB is the archetype of Habermasian public sphere: its authorization and capacity to influence the political sphere is grounded not in legal sanction (which it does not have), but rather in its procedurally rational and substantively deliberative mode of legitimacy-producing reason (Habermas 1996).

The identification of these different forms of participatory democracy underscores a central theoretical premise of this book. As we have argued, serious engagement with the question of democratic deepening requires that we examine state-society relations in their full complexity. States can be affirmative, promoting forms of association that are deeper and more inclusive, much as they can be colonizing, reducing citizens and civil society organizations to dependent clients. Civil societies can be innovative and can mobilize a range of counterpowers to entrenched political interests (the Habermasian view), but they can also amplify the voices of the more organized at the expense of the least organized (the Bourdieuian view). How the relations between local states and civil society congeal into a particular configuration is a function of the historical balance of power between state and civil society, but it is also, as we have seen, very much open to organized agency. As the broader reforms that Brazil's democracy has experienced in the past two decades and our own local cases underscore, agency can come in both the form of innovative civil society organizations and proactive state reformers.

APPENDIX

APPENDIX A
The Research

The central piece of our research was fieldwork. The fieldwork supplemented the sometimes substantial information available about each city's finances, politics, and participatory processes (if any), as well as official data about the municipality itself. Researchers were tasked with filling out a "municipal-level factsheet" using informal interviews, archival research, and interviews with experts, and then carrying out semistructured interviews with key respondents in each municipality.

The field research in each municipality was organized into the following sequence:

1. A first attempt to fill out the municipality-level fact sheet using information from secondary sources. This was done at the outset, prior to the field visit.

2. A first visit of roughly ten days that was used to complete the municipality-level fact sheet, establish contacts, identify potential key respondents, and perhaps to even carry out some of the semistructured (key respondent) interviews or open-ended interviews with significant actors.

3. Following the first visit, a thorough review was conducted of the information obtained from the first visit. Areas where more information was needed to complete the municipality fact sheets were identified, appointments for further interviews were made, and so forth.

4. A second visit, again of roughly ten days, for completion of all interviews (key respondents and significant actors).

Our research objective was to carry out semistructured interviews with at least a dozen key informants in each municipality who occupied different positions in social space for the period in question (1997–2000). In each municipality, we spoke with several key informants: this included members of the mayor's office, heads of finance and planning departments, public works officials, city council members from the mayor's party and from largest opposition party, activists from the PT and from opposition parties, leaders of neighborhood associations, unions, NGOs, church groups, and participants (delegates and councilors) in the PB process. The instrument itself underwent several revisions. Based on feedback from a pilot study of the first matched pair (Sapucaia and Gravataí), we adapted our questionnaire and held a workshop with field researchers.

They were organized into teams of two—that is, two field researchers who were present at all interviews. Interviews sometimes lasted several hours and were recorded and transcribed. The almost two-thousand pages of text made up the bulk of the evidence that we worked with for this book.

Drawing on insights from collaborative ethnography, as described by May and Patillo-McCoy (2000; see also Butcher and Nutch 1999), we relied on an interactive process in which we aggregated and offered preliminary summary results for each of the cases and circulated this back to the field researchers in a workshop. We created categories for each of the variables based on how responses were clustered, in effect attempting to identify "natural" breaks in the data. The final results reported here are the result of this iterative process between field researchers and the principals.

We do not reproduce the questionnaire here but will make it available electronically to anyone interested.

APPENDIX B

Selected Indicators for the Case Municipalities

Table A.1 Selected Human Development Indicators, 2000

Município	State	Life Expectancy	Adult Literacy (%)	School Attendance (%)	Per-Capita Income (in 2000R$)**	Human Development Index (IDH-M)	National Ranking (IDH)	Population Below Poverty Line (2000)
Camaragibe*	PE	70.66	84.26	85.48	173.44	0.747	1963	44.97
Quixadá	CE	69.59	68.41	83.18	101.00	0.673	3406	56.52
João Monlevade*	MG	74.64	94.14	83.66	240.90	0.807	423	39.47
Timóteo	MG	75.71	93.41	90.22	297.93	0.831	127	41.00
Mauá*	SP	68.50	93.36	85.93	274.82	0.781	1025	50.60
Diadema	SP	69.93	93.20	83.90	292.40	0.790	801	50.09
Gravataí*	RS	73.60	94.87	81.93	288.59	0.811	356	43.74
Sapucaia do Sul	RS	73.60	94.49	81.12	271.38	0.806	449	42.73

* PB municipality 1997–2000
** 1.93 Brazilian R$ = 1 US$ in December 2000
(Source: PNUD 2003)

NOTES

Preface

1. See the definition at *http://searchcio-midmarket.techtarget.com/sDefinition/0,,sid 183_gci214479,00.html.* Accessed on August 1, 2010.

2. See Mangabeira Unger (2004).

Introduction

1. There are various literatures that we view as part of the normative turn in democratic theory: the participatory democracy literature in which Carole Patemen's classic (1970) remains a key theoretical statement; the Empowered Participatory Governance approach associated with Fung and Wright (2003); the vast literature on social capital, most famously represented by Putnam, Leonardi, and Nanetti's *Making Democracy Work* (1993); the associational democracy literature best represented in Warren (2001) and Cohen and Rogers (1995); a vast and quite diverse literature on deliberative democracy that includes political theorists such as Amy Gutmann, Joshua Cohen, and John Elster; the paradigmatic work on discourse theory and communicative action by Habermas (1996); variants of radical democratic theory exemplified by Mouffe (2000), Laclau (2006), and Raciere (1995); and civil society literature that is also centrally preoccupied with the notion of democratic practices and best represented by Somers's (2008) work, a magisterial theoretical overview by Cohen and Arato (1992), and the recent contribution by Alexander (2006).

2. Among some of the few theoretically influential empirical cases on participatory democracy are Mansbridge (1980); Somers (1993, 1995); Rueschemeyer, Stephens, and Stephens (1992); and Fung (2004). The outpouring of recent empirical work has come mostly from Latin America and includes Baiocchi (2003b, 2005); Avritzer (2002, 2009); Nylen (2003); Wampler (2009); Van Cott (2008); Silva (2003); Rodgers (2010); Hernández-Medina (2010); Houtzager, Lavalle, and Harris (forthcoming); and Goldfrank (forthcoming). The participatory literature has had less traction in the case of India, but does include Heller (2000, 2001); Drèze and Sen (2002); and Rao and Sanyal (2010). Edited volumes that draw together a range of cases include Cornwall and Coelho (2007); Coelho and von Lieres (forthcoming); and Stokke, Tornqüist, and Webster (2009). Fung

and Wright's (2003) edited volume has been particularly influential. There are few carefully structured comparative studies ranging outside of Latin America on participatory democracy. Among the exceptions are Houtzager and Lavalle's (2010) careful survey-based examination of participatory practices in Latin America and India, and Williams's (2008) study of participatory democracy in Kerala and South Africa.

3. This reflects the broader post-Fordist transformation of the global economy characterized by what Brenner and Theodore describe "as the dynamic transformation of capitalist territorial organization from the nationally configured frameworks that prevailed during the Fordist-Keynesian period to an increasingly 'glocalized' configuration of global-national-local interactions in which no single scale serves as the primary pivot for accumulation, regulation, or sociopolitical struggle" (2002, 363).

4. Noted Brazilian scholar of informality Edésio Fernandes estimates that 50 percent of urban residents "have had access to land and housing through informal processes" (2007, 203).

5. For an extended discussion of the concept of the chain of sovereignty (originally developed by Pipkin), see Stokke, Tornqüist, and Webster (2009).

6. In economics, the concept of transaction costs refers to the fact that all exchanges carry certain costs, as for example the cost of writing up and enforcing contracts. We use the term "transaction costs of participation" to emphasize that involvement in democratic politics is not just a matter of rights, but also carries with it costs of time, money, and influence, and that such costs are unevenly distributed across groups.

Chapter 1

1. Linguistic competence is not a simple technical ability, but certain interlocutors are not allowed certain speech acts. Bourdieu gives the example of the farmer who did not run for mayor of his township, "But I don't know how to speak!" (1991, 146).

2. Burawoy summarizes the distinction between Bourdieu's notion of misrecognition and Gramsci's notion of hegemony: "Symbolic domination rests on the bodily inculcation of social structure, and the formation of a deep unconscious habitus whereas hegemony . . . rests on individuals being inserted into specific institutions that organize consent to domination. . . . Symbolic domination is seared into the individual psyche whereas hegemony is an effect of social relations on the individuals who carry them" (2008, 15).

3. In the case of Brazil, democracy has often been labeled by scholars working in this tradition as ineffective, deadlocked, and incapable of delivering positive results (see Ames 2001; Mainwaring 1999; and Weyland 1999).

4. In fairness, many civil society theorists such as Habermas and Fraser recognize this problem, but they generally deal with it at a very high level of abstraction.

5. This argument has recently been extended to explaining how subordinate-group mobilization in Chile, Costa Rica, Mauritius, and the Indian state of Kerala contributed to building and sustaining redistributive regimes (Sandbrook et al. 2007).

6. This closely follows Habermas's definition: "Civil society is composed of those more or less spontaneously emergent associations, organizations, and movements that, attuned to how societal problems resonate in the private life spheres, distill and transmit such reactions in amplified form to the public sphere. The core of civil society comprises a network of associations that institutionalizes problem-solving discourses on questions of general interest inside the framework of organized public spheres" (1996, 367).

7. Civil society associations can thus be distinguished from business associations (lobbies) or political associations (parties). The latter may be internally constituted by associational relations and, in this sense, rely on social resources of language, norms, and even identities and as such be *of* civil society, but they are not *in* civil society because the very logic or telos of their association is governed by money or power.

8. Alexander specifically defines civil society "as a solidarity sphere, in which a certain kind of universalizing community comes to be culturally defined and to some degree institutionally enforced" (2006, 13).

9. This section draws on Heller and Evans (2010).

10. We borrow the term and slightly alter its usage from Mamdani 1996.

Chapter 2

1. The term is borrowed from Mamdani (1996), who used it to describe the legacy of indirect rule in colonial Africa where local chiefs were elevated to the position of local despots by the colonial state.

2. See, among others, Evers (1985); Moises et al. (1982); Boschi (1987).

3. See the *Jornal de Santa Catarina,* September 28, 1980.

4. See the *Rio Grande Semanal,* July 26, 1979.

5. This section draws from Baiocchi (2003).

6. The literature is very diverse both in the cases it draws on and its conclusions. But see, for example, Araujo (1997); Arretche (2000); N. Costa (1996); R. Costa (2002); and Graham (1997).

7. These and the other calculations are discussed in Baiocchi (2008).

8. Although a city with high indicators to begin with, when compared to previous administrations and to changes in Brazil as a whole, the PT administration in Porto Alegre has brought significant improvements in service delivery through Participatory Budgeting, notably in the areas of basic sewage and water, primary public schooling, and public transportation. There is also evidence of increased civic mobilization around the PB meetings and a decrease in protests and petitions (Baiocchi 2005).

9. See the discussion in Ribeiro (2005).

10. Of the one hundred and four, twenty-five were carried out by leftist parties traditionally tied to social movements (the PDT, the PPS, the PSB, and the PV); twenty-two were carried out by left-of-center political parties originating in the country's pro-

democracy movement of the 1980s (the PMDB and the PSDB); and four were carried out by right-wing parties (the PTB and the PFL).

11. FNPP (2003); Cartilha do OP, 2.

Chapter 3

1. There are three notable, recent exceptions: Wampler's (2009) comparison of eight cities in Brazil; Goldfrank's (forthcoming) comparison of Caracas, Montevideo, and Porto Alegre; and Avritzer's (2008) comparison of four major cities in Brazil.

2. The distinction between generalization and extension comes from Burawoy's (1998) classic essay on the Extended Case Method.

3. We were inspired by Alford's insight that different "paradigms of inquiry" may come to the foreground in a research project. What he describes as a "paradigm of inquiry" refers to "the combination of theoretical assumptions, methodological procedures, and standards of evidence that are taken for granted in particular works" (1998, 2). We were also inspired by his assertion that different paradigms need not be treated as philosophical positions, but as part of a "pragmatic research strategy" to help develop effective research practice (1998, 2).

4. We owe a special debt of gratitude to our research collaborator—Shubham Chaudhuri—for this design.

5. This was the only pair that matched for the North, but both are somewhat outliers in terms of their size (less than ten thousand). Our analysis of these two cases did produce some interesting results. Both municípios have similar sociopolitical structures characterized by a strong, independent class of smallholders, but weakly organized civil society structures. The introduction of PB had a very marked impact on the quality of governance and local activism in São Miguel do Guaporé, in large part because it capitalized on the political independence of smallholders. Both cases are, however, difficult to compare to the other pairs and don't add much to the overall argument developed in the book. For a full discussion, see Baiocchi et al. (2006).

6. In his study of Rio De Janeiro, Gay provides an extensive discussion of the differences in style but similarities in substance between personalistic forms of clientelism associated with traditional parties of the right (for example, the PMDB), and the more organized forms of clientelism associated with parties of the Left, in his case the PDT. Gay notes that if both parties were interested in establishing "a captive and docile clientele in the favelas by milking the association between politics and public works," then the only difference was that the PDT was "committed to the idea of improving conditions in the favelas" (1994, 31), a difference that one might argue is not so insignificant. If the PT, as any other political party that has an instrumental interest in mobilizing support, is not beyond patronage, then it represents an even further departure from traditional clientelism in that rejecting clientelistic practices was at the heart of its ideological formation.

7. Cornwall and Coelho remark, "Claims to promoting popular participation appear on many a municipal government logo" (2007, 19).

Chapter 4

1. As we have discussed in Chapter 3, there were twelve in 1989–92, and thirty-six in 1993–96.

2. See the discussion in Baiocchi (2005) and Abers (2000). The claims, however, that cities or towns "need" certain preexisting levels of organization to make participatory democracy work are not borne out by the evidence, as the case of Gravataí shows. There is a long-standing friendly debate between Avritzer and Baiocchi about how to interpret Porto Alegre's case in this light. See Baiocchi (2003b, especially the chapter titled "Left in the City") and Avrtizer (2002), but especially the analysis of that city's districts in Baiocchi (2005) and Avritzer (2009) for a rebuttal.

3. In Wampler's (2009) study of eight PB cities, for example, there is a much greater adherence to this basic blueprint than in our study. This is probably partially due to the fact that he examined larger cities where PB had been working for some years.

4. Comparisons with cities in other countries are inherently difficult because of different budgeting practices, varied resource bases, and different levels of devolution. The case of South Africa does make for a good rough comparison because its overall level of economic development puts it in the same bracket as Brazil, and because it has roughly the same level of fiscal devolution as Brazil (both of which are high by middle-income country standards). As such, it is notable that South Africa's nine largest cities had capital expenditures that accounted for on average 17 percent of the total city budget, and that per-capita expenditures were roughly US$20 in smaller cities that are comparable in size to ours (Boraine et al. 2006).

5. By 2000, the administration received the following prizes, among others: the Prefeito Criança Prize of the ABrinq Foundation/UNICEF; the Prêmio Prefeito Criança 1999, Programa Saúde da Comunidade, pelo Projeto Meninas de Camaragibe; the Prêmio Saúde Brasil 1999, do Ministério da Saúde, Concurso de Experiências em Saúde da Família; the Prêmio Prefeito Criança 2000, Programa Saúde da Comunidade; the Prêmio FGV/FORD 2000, Programa de Administração Participativa; and the Prêmio FGV/FORD 2000, Programa de Atendimento à Mulher.

6. In late 1999, for example, almost *three thousand* adults (out of a population of seventy-seven thousand adults) participated in professional courses in areas like computing, sewing, and car repair. Another notable idea that emerged from Camaragibe's Participatory Administration was a municipal law approved in late 1997 that allowed the municipality to accept in-kind payments for those behind in city taxes.

7. In many ways, this echoes some of the ambitious ideas of the very first PT administrations to institute participation in all areas of administration in the form of popular

councils (such as in Diadema 1986–89), or to create a fourth, "popular" branch of government (such as in São Paulo 1989–92).

8. Its per-capita budget (that is, its total municipal budget divided by its population) was $124 Reais in 1997, or US$62, roughly one-fourth of Mauá's, for example. Between 1997 and 2000, the municipal administration was only able to raise 21 percent of its own budget, being dependent on transfers from the national Fund for Municipalities (FPM) to make up the shortfall for the rest.

9. In addition to the Josué de Castro Center, administrators developed partnerships with several other institutions, including the Brazilian Development Bank, the State Planning Department, and even once with UNDP (Pessoa 1997).

10. In the 1997–2000 period new councils were established in the areas of children and adolescents, social services, public safety, culture, and economic development.

11. While the municipality's total overall budget for 1997 was relatively high compared to the rest of municipalities under discussion here, coming to roughly R$500, or US$250, per capita, its yearly deficit was a staggering 29 percent of the total budget for the year. Unlike other cities under discussion here, the proportion of the budget available for capital expenditures never exceeded 6 percent during the four years.

Chapter 5

1. Literally, the SABs, or the *sociedades de amigos de bairro*.

2. The one umbrella organization that operated in Camaragibe—the Federation of Neighborhood Associations of Camaragibe (FAMOCA)—was much more a meeting place than an effective collective actor, according to our interviews.

3. This identity conflict is clearly illustrated by the case of actors mobilized by the Family Health Program. As noted above, this government program fostered significant mobilization in the city, which ended up impacting election results of 1997. As an interviewee stated, the Movement for Family Health was "the strongest movement involved in the campaign and in the government." However, this mobilization was not clearly a "social movement" in the sense that it neither resulted from nor was constituted by civil society; rather, it was mainly a product of the induction of governmental actors (members of the Secretariat of Health and community health agents).

4. Respondents singled out the municipal nucleus of the Union of State Teachers, the Metalworkers Union, the Chemical Workers Union, the Rubber Workers Union, and the Union of Municipal Teachers.

5. The limited reach of the more "combative segment" of civil society was generally judged as "very isolated." Though there was "an organized movement, it was one that was very scattered" and separate from the community movement.

6. The STMJM was, in this respect, a classic example of the form of the *social movement unionism* that Seidman (1994) has argued was critical to Brazil's democratic transition. In the 1990s, the STMJM, together with other unions in Brazil, attempted to

develop a more comprehensive and focused intervention in order to propose public policies responding to the period's "crisis of the union movement" (this reorientation of trade union action was called "citizen unionism").

7. Literally, *orçamento escutativo*, a play on *orçamento participativo*.

Conclusion

1. This is a vast debate that we do not directly engage in this book because much of it is focused on the politics of development agencies. For some useful references, see Cooke and Kothari's evocatively titled *Participation, the New Tyranny* (2001), and also see the response by Hickey and Mohan (2004).

2. For an extended discussion of this point for India and South Africa, see Heller (2009).

3. The following discussion of Kerala and South Africa draws heavily from Heller (2008).

4. The RDP promised that "Social Movements and Community-Based Organisations are a major asset in the effort to democratise and develop our society. Attention must be given to enhancing the capacity of such formations to adapt to practically changed roles. Attention must also be given to extending social-movement and CBO structures into areas and sectors where they are weak or non-existent" (quoted in Bond 2000, 95).

5. A World Bank report found that Kerala has the greatest degree of local expenditure autonomy and is the most fiscally decentralized state in India, second only to Colombia in the developing world (2000, I:28–29).

6. We focus on rural gram sabhas because the research summarized here only covers rural areas. Each panchayat has an average population of twenty-seven thousand. Gram sabhas are held at the ward level (10–12 per panchayat). The panchayat council has one elected representative from each ward. In comparative terms, each panchayat would be roughly equivalent to a district in our municípios or a ward of the population size of the subdistricts in Gravataí. Elections to the gram sabhas are held every four years and are fiercely competitive.

7. Schedule Caste is the bureaucratic designation for "untouchables," now referred to as *dalits*. Scheduled Tribe is the bureaucratic designation for "tribals," now referred to as *adivassis*.

8. The concept of the plasticity of participation is more fully developed in Chaudhuri and Heller (2003).

9. For a classic critique of elite theories of democracy, see Pateman (1970). For a more recent critique that also takes up the question of publics more directly, see Avritzer (2002).

10. Both Van Cott (2008) and Williams (2008) emphasize the role of political parties in promoting participatory democracy.

11. In the context of Andean countries, Van Cott notes, "Andean indigenous movements over the past 25 years have developed a common ideology of intercultural, participatory, deliberative, and transparent government that infuses indigenous parties' vision of governance" (2008, 13).

12. In his scholarly work, Bourdieu was quite skeptical about the possibilities of democratic politics, but toward the end of his life he openly defended and supported social movements opposing neoliberalism.

BIBLIOGRAPHY

Abers, Rebecca. 2000. *Inventing local democracy: Grassroots politics in Brazil.* Boulder, CO: Lynne Rienner Publishers.

———. 1996. From ideas to practice: The Partido dos Trabalhadores and participatory governance in Brazil. *Latin American Perspectives* 23 (4): 35–53.

Abrucio, Fernando. 1998. *Os barões da federação.* São Paulo: Hucitec/ Edusp.

Adler, Glenn, and Jonny Steinberg. 2000. *From comrades to citizens: The South African civics movement and the transition to democracy.* New York: St. Martin's Press.

Afonso, José Roberto Rodrigues, and Luiz de Melo. 2000. Brazil: An evolving federation. In *IMF/FAD Seminar on Decentralization.* Washington, DC.

Alexander, Jeffrey. 2006. *The civil sphere.* Oxford: Oxford University Press.

Alexander, Jeffrey, and Phillip Smith. 1993. The discourse of civil society: A new proposal for cultural studies. *Theory and Society* 2: 151–207.

Alford, Robert. 1998. *The craft of inquiry: Theories, methods, evidence.* New York: Oxford University Press.

Alsop, Ruth J., and Nina Heinsohn. 2005. Measuring empowerment in practice: Structuring analysis and framing indicators. *World Bank Policy Research Working Paper 3510.* Washington, DC: World Bank.

Alvarez, Sonia E. 1997. Reweaving the fabric of collective action: Social movements and challenges to 'actually existing democracy' in Brazil. In *Between resistance and revolution: Cultural politics and social protest,* ed. Richard G. Fox and Orin Starn, 83–117. New Brunswick, NJ: Rutgers University Press.

———. 1993. Deepening democracy: Popular movement networks, constitutional reform, and radical urban regimes in contemporary Brazil. In *Mobilizing the community: Local politics in the era of the global city,* ed. Robert Fisher and Joseph Kling. Newbury Park, CA: Sage Publications.

Alves, Maria Helena Moreira. 1985. *State and opposition in military Brazil.* Austin: University of Texas Press.

Ames, Barry. 2001. *The deadlock of democracy in Brazil.* Ann Arbor: University of Michigan Press.

Angrist, Joshua, and Victor Lavy. 1999. New Evidence on Classroom Computers and

Pupil Learning. NBER Working Papers 7424. National Bureau of Economic Research, Inc.

Appadurai, Arjun. 2004. The capacity to aspire: Culture and the terms of recognition. In *Culture and public action*, ed. Michael Walton and Vijayendra Rao, 59–84. Stanford: Stanford Social Sciences.

Araujo, José. 1997. Attempts to decentralize in recent Brazilian health policy. *International Journal of Health Services* 27: 109–24.

Armony, Ariel C. 2004. *The dubious link: Civic engagement and democratization.* Stanford: Stanford University Press.

Arretche, Marta. 2000. *Estado federativo e politicas sociais.* Rio de Janeiro: Editora Revan.

Assies, Willem. 1992. *To get out of the mud: Neighbourhood associativism in Recife 1964–1988.* Amsterdam: Center on Latin American Research and Documentation.

Atkinson, Doreen. 2007. Taking to the streets: Has developmental local government failed in South Africa? In *State of the nation: South Africa 2007*, ed. Sakhela Buhlungu, John Daniel, Roger Southall, and Jessica Lutchman, 53–77. Cape Town: Human Social Science Research Council.

Auyero, Javier. 2001. *Poor people's politics: Peronist survival networks and the legacy of Evita.* Durham, NC: Duke University Press.

———. 1999. From the client's point(s) of view: How poor people perceive and evaluated political clientelism. *Theory and Society* 28 (2): 297–334.

Avritzer, Leonardo. 2009. *Participatory institutions in democratic Brazil.* Baltimore, MD: Johns Hopkins University Press.

———. 2008. Democratization and citizenship in Latin America: The emergence of institutional forms of participation. *Latin American Research Review* 43 (2): 282–89.

———. 2002. *Democracy and the public space in Latin America.* Princeton, NJ: Princeton University Press.

Avritzer, Leonardo, and Brian Wampler. The spread of participatory budgeting in Brazil: From radical democracy to participatory good government. *Journal Of Latin American Urban Studies*: 37–52.

Azevedo, Sérgio de. 1997. Políticas públicas e governança em Belo Horizonte. *Cadernos IPPUR XI* 1: 63–74.

Azevedo, Sérgio de, and Antônio Augusto Prates. 1991. *Planejamento participativo, movimentos sociais e ação coletiva.* São Paulo: Anpocs-Vértice.

Baiocchi, Gianpaolo. 2005. *Militants and citizens: The politics of participatory democracy in Porto Alegre.* Stanford: Stanford University Press.

———. 2003a. Participation, activism, and politics: The Porto Alegre experiment. In *Deepening democracy: Institutional innovations in empowered participatory governance*, ed. Archon Fung and Erik Olin Wright, 45–76. London: Verso.

———. 2003b. *Radicals in power: The workers' party (PT) and experiments in urban democracy in Brazil.* London and New York: Zed Books.

Baiocchi, Gianpaolo, Shubham Chaudhuri, Patrick Heller, and Marcelo Kunrath Silva. 2006. Evaluating empowerment: Participatory budgeting in Brazilian municipalities. In *Empowerment in practice: From analysis to implementation*, ed. Ruth Alsop, Mette Bertelsen, and Jeremy Holland, 95–128. Washington, DC: World Bank.

Baiocchi, Gianpaolo, Patrick Heller, and Marcelo Kunrath Silva. 2008. Making space for civil society: Institutional reforms and local democracy in Brazil. *Social Forces* 86 (3): 911–36.

Banck, Geert A. 1986. Poverty, politics, and the shaping of urban space: A Brazilian example. *International Journal of Urban and Regional Research* 10: 522–40.

Bardhan, Pranab. 2002. Decentralization of governance and development. *Journal of Economic Perspectives* 16 (4): 185–206.

Beall, Jo, Owen Crankshaw, and Susan Parnell. 2002. *Uniting a divided city: Governance and social exclusion in Johannesburg*. London: Earthscan Publications, Ltd.

Beozzo, José Oscar, and Apolo Heringer Lisboa. 1983. PT: Avaliação eleitoral. *Vozes* 77: 18–36.

Berman, Sheri. 1997. Civil society and the collapse of the Weimar Republic. *World Politics* 49: 401–29.

Bond, Patrick. 2000. *Elite transition: From apartheid to neoliberalism in South Africa*. London: Pluto Press.

Boraine, Andrew, Owen Crankshaw, Carien Engelbrecht, Graeme Gotz, Sithole Mbanga, Monty Narsoo, and Susan Parnell. 2006. The state of South African cities a decade after democracy. *Urban Studies* 43 (2): 259–84.

Boschi, Renato Raul. 1999. Descentralização, clientelismo e capital social na governança urbana: comparando Belo Horizonte e Salvador. *Dados* 42: 655–90.

———. 1987. *A arte da associacao: Politica de base e democracia no Brasil*. São Paulo: Vertice.

Bourdieu, Pierre. 1991. *Language and symbolic power*. Cambridge: Polity Press.

———. 1984. *Distinction: A social critique of the judgment of taste*. Cambridge, MA: Harvard University Press.

———. 1977. *Outline of a theory of practice*. New York: Cambridge University Press.

Branford, Sue, and Bernardo Kucinski. 1995. *Brazil: Carnival of the oppressed*. London: Latin American Bureau.

Brazil. 1988. *Constituição da República Federativa do Brasil*. Brasília: Senado.

Brenner, Neil, and Nik Theodore. 2002. Cities and the geographies of "actually existing neoliberalism." *Antipode* 34 (3): 349–79.

Buechler, Steven M. 1997. New social movement theories. In *Social movements: Perspectives and issues*, ed. Steven M. Buechler, 295–319. Mountain View, CA: Mayfield Publishing Company.

Burawoy, Michael. 2008. Does the working class exist? Burawoy meets Bourdieu. Lecture given at Havens Center, University of Wisconsin, Madison, Wisconsin. http://burawoy.berkeley.edu/Bourdieu/Lecture%203.pdf. Accessed on August 6, 2010.

———. 1998. The extended case method. *Sociological Theory* 16 (1): 4–33.

———. 1991. *Ethnography unbound: Power and resistance in the modern metropolis.* Berkeley: University of California Press.

Butcher, Dick, and Frank Nutch. 1999. Reflections on doing interactive ethnography. *The Discourses of Sociological Practice* 2 (1): 10–14.

Caldeira, Teresa Pires do Rio. 1984. *A política dos outros: O cotidiano dos moradores da periferia e o que pensam do poder e dos poderosos.* São Paulo: Brasiliense.

Calderón, Adolfo Ignacio, Vera Lúcia Michalany Chaia, Aldaíza de Oliveira Sposati, and Luiz Eduardo W. Wanderley. 2002. *Gestão municipal: Descentralização e participação popular.* São Paulo: Cortez Editora.

Calhoun, Craig. 2002. Imagining solidarity, cosmopolitanism, constitutional patriotism, and the public sphere. *Public Culture* 14 (1): 147–71.

Camaragibe. 2000. *Conselho de Delegados da Administração participativa.*

Campbell, Donald. 1969. Reforms as experiments. *American Psychologist* 24: 409–29.

Campbell, Tim. 1997. *Innovations and risk-taking: The engine of reform in Latin American countries.* Washington, DC: World Bank.

Carvalho, José Murilo de. 1987. *Os bestializados: O Rio de Janeiro e a república que não foi.* São Paulo: Companhia das Letras.

Carvalho, Inaia. 1997. Decentralization and social policies in Bahia. *Caderno CRH* 26–27: 75–105.

Carvalho, Maria. 2002. *Orcamento participativo nos municípios paulistas.* São Paulo: Polis.

Castro, Maria H. de. 1988. Equipamentos sociais e poli_tica local no po_s-64: dois estudos de caso. *Espaço e Debates* 24: 67–74.

Chalmers, Doug, Scott Martin, and Kerianne Piester. 1997. Associative networks: New structures of representation for the popular sectors? In *The new politics of inequality in Latin America,* ed. Douglas A. Chalmers, C. M. Vilas, K. Hite, S. B. Martin, K. Piester, and M. Segarra, 543–82. New York: Oxford University Press.

Chaudhuri, Shubham, and Patrick Heller. 2003. The plasticity of participation: Evidence from a participatory governance experiment. New York: Columbia University ISERP Working Paper.

Chavez, Daniel, and Benjamin Goldfrank, eds. 2004. *The left in the city: Participatory local government in Latin America.* London: Latin American Bureau.

Coelho, Vera Schatten P., and Bettina von Lieres, eds. Forthcoming. *Mobilizing for democracy: Citizen engagement and the politics of public participation.* London: Zed.

Cohen, Jean L., and Andrew Arato. 1992. *Civil society and political theory.* Cambridge, MA: MIT Press.

Cohen, Joshua, and Joel Rogers. 1995. Secondary associations and democratic governance. In *Associations and democracy,* ed. Erik Olin Wright. London: Verso.

———. 1983. *On democracy.* New York: Penguin Books.

Comaroff, Jean, and John Comaroff. *Millennial capitalism and the culture of neoliberalism*. Durham, NC: Duke University Press.

Cooke, Bill, and Uma Kothari. 2001. *Participation, the New Tyranny*. London: Zed Books

Cornwall, Andrea, and Vera Schattan Coelho. 2007. Spaces for change? The politics of citizen participation in new democratic arenas. In *Spaces for change? The politics of citizen participation in new democratic arenas*, ed. A. Cornwall and V. S. Coelho, 1–29. London: Zed Books.

Costa, Nilson. 1996. Policy innovation, distributivism, and crisis: Health care policy in the 1980's and 1990's. *Dados* 39: 479–511.

Costa, Ricardo. 2002. Decentralization, financing and regulation reform of the public health system in Brazil during the 1990's. *Revista de Sociologia e Politica* 18: 49–71.

Couto, Claudio Goncalves. 1995. *O desafio de ser governo: O PT na prefeitura de Sao Paulo*. São Paulo: Paz e Terra.

Dagnino, Evelina. 2005a. Meanings of citizenship in Latin America. IDS Working Paper 258, Institute of Development Studies, Brighton, UK.

———. 2005b. ¿Sociedade civil, participação e cidadania: De que estamos falando? In *Políticas de ciudadanía y sociedad civil en tiempos de globalización*, ed. Daniel Mato, 95–110. Caracas: FACES, Universidad Central de Venezuela.

———. 1998. Culture, citizenship, and democracy: Changing discourses and practices of the Latin American left. In *Cultures of politics, politics of cultures: Re-visioning Latin American social movements*, ed. Sonia E. Alvarez, Evelina Dagnino, and Arturo Escobar, 33–63. Boulder, CO: Westview Press.

———. 1994. Os movimentos sociais e a emergência de uma nova noção de cidadania. In *Os anos 90: Política e sociedade no Brasil*, ed. Evelina Dagnino, 103–18. São Paulo: Editora Brasiliense.

de Tocqueville, Alexis. 1839; 1840. *Democracy in America*. New York: G. Adlard.

Dorf, Michael, and Charles Sabel. 2006. *A constitution of democratic experimentalism*. Cambridge, MA: Harvard University Press.

Drèze, Jean, and Amartya Kumar Sen. 2002. Democratic practice and social inequality in India. *Journal of Asian and African Studies* 37 (2): 6.

———. 1995. *India: Economic development and social opportunity*. Delhi and New York: Oxford University Press.

Emirbayer, Mustafa, and Mimi Sheller. 1999. Publics in history. *Theory and Society* 28: 145–97.

Evans, Peter. 2004. Development as institutional monocropping: The pitfalls of monocropping and the potentials of deliberation. *Studies in Comparative and International Development* 38 (4): 30–52.

———. 2002. *Livable cities?: Urban struggles for livelihood and sustainability*. Berkeley: University of California Press.

Evers, Tilman. 1985. Identity: The hidden side of new social movements in Latin America. In *New social movements and the state in Latin America*, ed. David Slater, 50–65. Amsterdam: CEDLA.

Fernandes, Edésio. 2007. Constructing the 'right to the city' in Brazil. *Social & Legal Studies* 16 (2) (06): 201–19.

Fernandes, Leela, and Patrick Heller. 2006. Hegemonic aspirations. *Critical Asian Studies* 38 (4) (12): 495–522.

Ferreira, Ana L. S. 1991. *Lages: Um jeito de governar*. São Paulo: Instituto Pólis.

Figueiredo Júnior, José Rubens de Lima, and Bolivar Lamounier. 1997. *As cidades que dão certo: experiências inovadoras na administração pública brasileira*. Brasília: MH Comunicação.

Filho, Arno Augustin. 1993. A experiência do Orçamento Participativo na administração popular da Prefeitura Municipal de Porto Alegre'. In *Porto Alegre: O desafio da mudança*, ed. Carlos H. Horn, 49–68. Porto Alegre: Editora Ortiz.

Filho, David Capistrano. 1991. *Mil dias de governo popular*. Santos: Prefeitura Municipal de Santos.

Fontes, Breno. 1995. Gestion local en el nordeste de Brasil. *Revista Brasileiro De Ciencias Socias*: 123–42.

Fox, Jonathan. 1994. The difficult transition from clientalism to citizenship. *World Politics* 46 (2): 151–84.

Fraser, Nancy. 1992. Rethinking the public sphere: A contribution to the critique of actually existing democracy. In *Habermas and the public sphere*, ed. Craig Calhoun, 109–43. Cambridge, MA: MIT Press.

Fung, Archon. 2004. *Empowered participation: Reinventing urban democracy*. Princeton, NJ: Princeton University Press.

Fung, Archon, and Erik O. Wright. 2003. *Deepening democracy: Institutional innovations in empowered participatory governance*. London: Verso.

Gay, Robert. 1995. Democracy, clientelism, and civil society. *Contemporary Sociology* 24: 769.

———. 1994. *Popular organization and democracy in Rio de Janeiro: A tale of two favelas*. Philadelphia, PA: Temple University Press.

———. 1990. Community organization and clientelist politics in contemporary Brazil: A case study from suburban Rio de Janeiro. *International Journal of Urban and Regional Research* 14 (4): 648–66.

Gibson, Christopher, and Michael Woolcock. 2008. Empowerment, deliberative development, and local-level politics in Indonesia: Participatory projects as a source of countervailing power. *Studies in Comparative International Development* 43 (2): 151–80.

Gohn, Maria da Gloria. 1982. *Reinvidicações populares urbanas*. São Paulo: Cortez.

Goldfrank, Benjamin. Forthcoming. *Deepening local democracy in Latin America: Participation, decentralization, and the left*. Pittsburg: Pennsylvania State University Press.

Gomes, Angela Maria de Castro. 1991. *O Brasil de JK*. Rio de Janeiro: Fundação Getúlio Vargas.

Graham, Lawrence. 1997. *Social policy dilemmas under decentralization and federalism*. Seoul, Korea. Korea Institute for International Economic Policy, Seminar Paper Series (Taeoe Kyongje Chongch'aek Yon'guwon, Korea).

Grazia, Grazia de, and Ana Clara de Torres Ribeiro. 2002. *Orçamento participativo no Brasil*. São Paulo: Editora Vozes.

Habermas, Jürgen. 1996. *Between facts and norms: Contributions to a discourse theory of law and democracy*. Cambridge, MA: MIT Press.

———. 1989. *The structural transformation of the public sphere: An inquiry into a category of bourgeois society*. Cambridge, MA: MIT Press.

———. 1984.

Hagopian, Frances. 1994. Traditional politics against state transformation in Brazil. In *State power and social forces: Domination and transformation in the third world*, ed. Joel Migdal, Atul Kohli, and Vivienne Shue, 37–63. Cambridge: Cambridge University Press.

Hansen, Thomas Blom. 1999. *The saffron wave: Democracy and Hindu nationalism in modern India*. Princeton, NJ: Princeton University Press.

He, Baogang. 2006. Participatory and deliberative institutions in China. In *The search for deliberative democracy in China*, ed. E. Leib and Baogang He, 176–96. New York: Palgrave.

Hernádez-Medina, Esther. 2010. Social inclusion through participation: The case of the participatory budget in Sao Paulo. *International Journal of Urban and Regional Research* 34(3): 512–32.

Heller, Patrick G. 2009. Democratic deepening in India and South Africa. *Journal of Asian and African Studies* 44 (1): 97–122.

———. 2008. Local democracy and development in comparative perspective. In *Consolidating developmental local government: Lessons from the South African experience*, ed. Mirjam van Donk, Mark Swilling, Edgar Pieterse, and Susan Parnell, 153–74. Cape Town: University of Cape Town Press.

———. 2005. Reinventing public power in the age of globalization: Decentralization and the transformation of movement politics in Kerala. In *Social movements in India: Poverty, power, and politics*, ed. Raka Ray and Mary Katzenstein, 79–106. New York: Rowman and Littlefield.

———. 2003. Reclaiming democratic spaces: Civics and politics in posttransition Johannesburg. In *Emerging Johannesburg: Perspectives on the post-apartheid state*, ed. Richard Tomlinson, Robert Beauregard, Lindsay Bremner, and Xolela Mangcu, 155–84. New York: Routledge.

———. 2001. Moving the state: The politics of democratic decentralization in Kerala, South Africa, and Porto Alegre. *Politics & Society* 29 (1): 131–63.

————. 2000. Degrees of democracy: Some comparative lessons from India. *World Politics* 52 (4): 484–519.

————. 1999. *The labor of development: Workers and the transformation of capitalism in Kerala, India.* Ithaca, NY: Cornell University Press.

Heller, Patrick G., and Peter Evans. 2010. Taking Tilly south: Durable inequalities, democratic contestation, and citizenship in the southern metropolis. *Theory and Society* 39 (3–4): 433–50.

Heller, Patrick G., K. N. Harilal, and Shubham Chaudhuri. 2007. Building local democracy: Evaluating the impact of decentralization in Kerala, India. *World Development* 35 (4): 626–48.

Hickey, Samuel, and Giles Mohan. 2004. *Participation: From tyranny to transformation? Exploring new approaches to participation in development.* London: Zed Books.

Holston, James. 2008. *Insurgent citizenship: Disjunctions of democracy and modernity in Brazil.* Princeton, NJ: Princeton University Press.

Houtzager, Peter P., and Adrian Gurza Lavalle. 2010. Civil society's claims to political representation in Brazil. *Studies in Comparative International Development* 45 (1): 1–29.

Houtzager, Peter P., Adrian Gurza Lavalle, and Graziela Castello. 2005. Citizens and states in the post-reform period: Direct, contentious, and detached relations in São Paulo and Mexico.

Houtzager, Peter P., Adrian Gurza Lavalle, and John Harris. Forthcoming. Citizen-state relations after the double transition: A comparative study of citizenship practices and associational representation in São Paulo, Mexico City, and Delhi.

IBGE. 2002. *Sistema de contas nacionais.* Rio de Janeiro: Government of Brazil.

Instituto Pólis. 2001. *125 dicas do Instituto Pólis.* São Paulo: Instituto Pólis.

Jacobi, Pedro. 2000. *Politicas Socias e ampliação da cidadania.* Rio de Janeiro: FGV Editora.

————. 1987. Movimentos sociais: Teoria e pratica em auestao. In *Uma revolucao no cotidiano? Os novos movimentos sociais na America Latina,* ed. Paulo Krische. São Paulo: Brasiliense.

Jaffrelot, Christophe. 1996. *The Hindu nationalist movement in India.* New York: Columbia University Press.

Jessop, Bob. 1994. Post-Fordism and the state. In *Post-Fordism: A reader,* ed. Ash Amin, 251–79. Oxford: Blackwell.

John, M. S., and Jos Chathukulam. 2002. Building social capital through state initiative: Participatory planning in Kerala. *Economic and Political Weekly* (May 18): 1939–48.

Kaldor, Mary. 2004. Global civil society: An answer to war. *Journal of International Relations and Development* 7: 444–47.

Keck, Margaret E. 1992. *The workers' party and democratization in Brazil.* New Haven, CT: Yale University Press.

Keil, Roger. 1998. Globalization makes states: Perspectives of local governance in the age of the world city. *Review of International Political Economy* 5 (4): 616–40.

Kowarick, Lúcio, and André Singer. 1994. The Workers' Party in São Paulo. In *Social struggles and the city: The case of São Paulo*, ed. Lúcio Kowarick, 225–56. New York: Monthly Review Press.

Kugelmas, Eduardo, and Lourdes Sola. 1999. Recentralization/decentralization dynamics of the federative regime in 1990's Brazil. *Tempo Social* 11: 63–81.

Laclau, Ernesto. 2006. *On populist reason*. London: Verso.

———. 2000. Constructing universality. In *Contingency, hegemony, universality: Contemporary dialogues on the left*, ed. Judith Butler, Ernesto Laclau, and Slavoj Žižek, 281–308. London: Verso.

———. 1996. *Emancipation(s)*. London: Verso.

Latour, Bruno. 2005. *Reassembling the social, an introduction to actor-network-theory*. Oxford: Oxford University Press.

Lebauspin, Ivo. 2000. *Poder local x exclusao social*. Petropolis, Brazil: Vozes.

Mahajan, Gurpreet. 1999. Civil society and its avatars: What happened to freedom and democracy? *Economic and Political Weekly* 34: 1188–96.

Mainwaring, Scott. 1999. *Rethinking party systems in the third wave of democratization: The case of Brazil*. Stanford: Stanford University Press.

Mamdani, Mahmood. 1996. *Citizen and subject: Decentralized despotism and the legacy of late colonialism*. Princeton, NJ: Princeton University Press.

Mangabeira Unger, Roberto. 2004. *False necessity: Anti-necessitarian social theory in the service of radical democracy*. London: Verso.

Manjula, B. 2000. Voices from the spiral of silence: A caste study of samantha self-help groups of uloor. Paper presented at International Conference on Democratic Decentralisation, Thiruvananthapuram, India.

Manor, James. 1999. *The political economy of democratic decentralization*. Washington, DC: World Bank.

Mansbridge, Jane J. 1980. *Beyond adversary democracy*. New York: Basic Books.

Marquetti, Adalmir. 2002. Participação e redistribuição. *Inovação democrática no Brasil*, ed. Zander Navarro, 129–56. São Paulo: Cortez.

Matta, Roberto da. ed. 1992. *Brasileiro, cidadão?* São Paulo: Cultura Editores Associados.

———. 1991. *A casa e a rua: Espaço, cidadania, mulher e morte no Brasil*. Rio de Janeiro: Guanabara Koogan.

———. 1979. *Carnavais, malandros e heróis: Para uma sociologia do dilema Brasileiro*. Rio de Janeiro: Zahar Editores.

May, Reuben, and Mary Pattillo-McCoy. 2000. Do you see what I see? Examining a collaborative ethnography. *Qualitative Inquiry* 6 (1): 65–87.

McAdam, Doug, Sidney Tarrow, and Charles Tilly. 2001. *Dynamics of contention*. New York: Cambridge University Press.

McCarney, Patricia. 1996. New considerations on the notion of governance. In *Cities and governance: New directions in Latin America, Asia, and Africa*, ed. Patricia Mc-Carney. Toronto: Centre for Urban & Community Studies, University of Toronto.

Medeiros, Antonio Carlos. 1994. The politics of decentralization in Brazil. *Review of Latin American and Caribbean Studies* 57: 7–27.

Meneguello, Rachel. 1989. *PT: A formação de um partido 1979–1982*. Rio de Janeiro: Editora Paz e Terra.

Migdal, Joel S., Atul Kohli, and Vivienne Shue. 1994. *State power and social forces: Domination and transformation in the third world*. Cambridge Studies in Comparative Politics. New York: Cambridge University Press.

Misao, Jean Pierre, Tamlyn Monson, Tara Polzer, and Loren Landau. 2010. *May 2008 violence against foreign nationals in South Africa: Understanding causes and evaluating responses*. Forced Migration Studies Programme (FMSP), University of the Witwatersrand. *http://www.cormsa.org.za/wp-content/uploads/2009/05/may-2008-violence-against-foreign-nationals-in-south-africa.pdf* Accessed on August 6, 2010.

Mische, Ann. 2006. *Partisan publics, communication and contention across Brazilian youth networks*. Princeton, NJ: Princeton University Press.

Moises, José Alvaro, Luiz Gonzaga de Souza Lima, Tilman Evers, Herbert José de Souza, and Ximena Bazzarra. 1982. *Alternativas populares da democracia: Brasil anos 80*. São Paulo: Vozes.

Montero, Alfred P. 2001. Decentralizing democracy in Spain and Brazil in comparative perspective. *Health Policy* 52: 113–27.

———. 1998. *Shifting states in uneven markets: Political decentralization and subnational industrial policy in contemporary Brazil and Spain*. Rights versus Efficiency Paper Series, Paper No. 1. New York: The Institute of Latin American and Iberian Studies, Columbia University.

Moreira Alves, Marcio. 1980. *A força do povo: Democracia participativa em lages*.

Mouffe, Chantal. 2000. *The democratic paradox*. London and New York: Verso.

Negt, Oskar, and Alexander Kluge. 1993. *Public sphere and experience: Toward an analysis of the bourgeois and proletarian public sphere*. Minneapolis: University of Minnesota Press.

Nickson, Andrew. 1995. *Local governments in Latin America*. Boulder, CO: Lynne Rienner Publishers.

Nylen, William. 2003. *Participatory democracy versus elitist democracy: Lessons from Brazil*. New York: Palgrave McMillan.

———. 1998. Popular participation in Brazil's Worker's Party: Democratizing democracy in municipal politics. *The Political Chronicle* 8: 1–9.

O'Donnell, Guillermo. 1999. *Counterpoints: Selected essays on authoritarianism and democratization*. Notre Dame, IN: University of Notre Dame.

———. 1993. On the state, democratization and some conceptual problems: A Latin

American view with glances at some postcommunist countries. *World Development* 21 (8): 1355–59.

———. 1988. Challenges to democratization in Brazil. *World Policy Journal* 5 (2): 281–300.

O'Donnell, Guillermo, Philippe C. Schmitter, and Laurence Whitehead. 1986. *Transitions from authoritarian rule: Prospects for democracy.* Baltimore, MD: Johns Hopkins University Press.

Oliveira, Francisco Mesquita de. 2003. Cidadania e cultura política no poder local: O conselho da administração participativa de Camaragibe. Master's thesis, Universidade Federal de Pernambuco, Brazil.

———. 1986. E agora PT? In *E agora PT? Caráter e identidade,* ed. Emir Sader, 9–35. São Paulo: Brazilense.

Oxhorn, Philip. 1995. *Organizing civil society: The popular sectors and the struggle for democracy in Chile.* University Park: Pennsylvania State University Press.

Pateman, Carol. 1970. *Participation and democratic theory.* Cambridge: Cambridge University Press.

Pichardo, Nelson. 1997. New social movements: A critical review. *Annual Review of Sociology* 23: 411–30.

Pinheiro, Paulo Sérgio. 1991. Police and political crisis: The case of the military police. In *Vigilantism and the state in modern Latin America: Essays on extralegal violence,* ed. M. K. Huggins, 167–88. New York: Praeger.

PNUD. Programa das Nações Unidas para o Desenvolvimento. 2003. Atlas do Índice do Desenvolvimento Humano (IDH) no Brasil (Database). Brasilia, Brazil.

Pont, Raul. 2001. Porto Alegre, e a luta pela democracia, igualdade e qualidade de vida. In *Porto Alegre: Uma cidade que conquista,* ed. Raul Pont, 1–11. Porto Alegre: Artes e Oficios.

Pontual, Pedro. 1997. *Orcamento parcipativo em Sao Paulo na gestao luiza erundina.* São Paulo: FASE.

Pozzobon, Regina. 1998. *Porto Alegre: Os desafios da gestao democratica.* São Paulo: Instituto Polis.

Putnam, Robert D., Robert Leonardi, and Raffaella Y. Nanetti. 1993. *Making democracy work: Civic traditions in modern Italy.* Princeton, NJ: Princeton University Press.

Rancière, Jacques. 1999. Disagreement: Politics and philosophy. Trans. J. Rose. Minneapolis: University of Minnesota Press.

Rao, Vijayendra, and Paromita Sanyal. 2010. Dignity through discourse: Poverty and culture of deliberation in Indian village democracies. *The Annals of the American Academy of Political and Social Science* 629 (1): 146–72.

Reilly, Charles. 1995. Public policy and citizenship. In *New paths to democratic development in Latin America: The rise of NGO-municipal collaboration,* ed. Charles A. Reilly, 1–28. Boulder, CO: Lynne Rienner Publishers.

Riley, Dylan. 2005. Civic associations and authoritarian regimes in interwar Europe. *American Sociological Review* 70 (2): 288–310.

Rodgers, Dennis. 2010. Contingent democratisation? The rise and fall of participatory budgeting in Buenos Aires. *Journal of Latin American Studies* 42 (1): 1–27.

Roniger, Luis. 1994. The comparative study of clientelism and the changing nature of civil society in the contemporary world. In *Democracy, clientelism, and civil society*, ed. Luis Roniger and Ayes Gunes-Ayata, 1–18. Boulder, CO: Lynne Rienner Publishers.

Rueschemeyer, Dietrich, Evelyne Huber Stephens, and John D. Stephens. 1992. *Capitalist development and democracy.* Chicago: University of Chicago Press.

Sabel, Charles. 2004. Bootstrapping Development: Rethinking the Role of Public Intervention in Promoting Growth. Paper presented at the Protestant Ethic and Spirit of Capitalism Conference, Cornell University, Ithaca, New York.

Sabel, Charles, and William H. Simon. 2009. Minimalism and experimentalism in American public law. Unpublished manuscript. Available at: *http://www2.law.columbia .edu/sabel/papers.htm.* Accessed on July 1, 2010.

Sales, Teresa. 1994. Raizes da desigualdade social na cultura política Brasileira. *Revista Brasileira de Ciencias Sociais* 9 (25): 26–37.

Samuels, David, and Fernando Abrucio. 2000. Federalism and democratic transitions. *Publius* 30: 43–61.

Samuels, David, and Richard Snyder. 2001. The value of a vote: Malapportionment in comparative perspective. *British Journal of Political Science* 31 (4): 651–71.

Sandbrook, Richard, Marc Edelman, Patrick Heller, and Judith Teichman. 2007. *Social democracy in the global periphery: Origins, challenges, prospects.* Cambridge: Cambridge University Press.

Santos, Guilherme Wanderley dos. 1979. *Cidadania e justiça: A política social na ordem Brasileira.* Rio de Janeiro: Editora Campus.

———. 1993. *As razoes da desordem.* Rio de Janeiro: Rocca.

Schneider, Sérgio, Marcelo Kunrath Silva, and Paulo Eduardo Moruzzi, eds. 2004. *Políticas públicas e participação social no Brasil rural.* Porto Alegre: Editora da UFRGS.

Scott, James C. 1998. *Seeing like a state: How certain schemes to improve the human condition have failed.* New Haven, CT: Yale University Press.

Seema, T. N., and Vanitha Mukherjee. 2000. Gender governance and citizenship in decentralised planning. Paper presented at International Conference on Democratic Decentralisation, Thiruvananthapuram, India.

Seidman, Gay. 1994. *Manufacturing militance: Workers' movements in Brazil and South Africa, 1970–1985.* Berkeley: University of California Press.

Sen, Amartya Kumar. 1999. *Development as freedom.* New York: Alfred A. Knopf.

Shapiro, Ian. 2003. *The state of democratic theory.* Princeton, NJ: Princeton University Press.

Silva, Marcelo Kunrath. 2003. Participation by design: The experiences of Alvorada and Gravataí, Rio Grande do Sul, Brazil. In *Radicals in power: The workers' party (PT) and experiments in urban democracy in Brazil,* ed. Gianpaolo Baiocchi. London: Zed.

Singer, André. 2001. *O PT.* São Paulo: Publifolha.

Skocpol, Theda. 1985. Bringing the state back in: Current research. In *Bringing the state back in,* ed. Peter Evans, Dietrich Rueschemeyer, and Theda Skocpol, 3–43. New York: Cambridge University Press.

Snyder, Richard. 2001. Scaling down: The subnational comparative method. *Studies in Comparative International Development* 36 (1): 93.

Somarriba, Mescês, and Otavio Dulci. 1997. A democratização do poder local e seus dilemas: A dinâmica atual da participação popular em Belo Horizonte. In *Reforma do estado e democracia no Brasil,* ed. S. Azevedo. Brasília: Editora UnB.

Somers, Margaret R. 2008. *Genealogies of citizenship: Markets, statelessness, and the right to have rights.* Cambridge: Cambridge University Press.

———. 1995. Narrating and naturalizing civil society and citizenship theory: The place of political culture and the public sphere. *Sociological Theory* 13: 229–73.

———. 1994. Rights, relationality, and membership: Rethinking the making and meaning of citizenship. *Law and Social Inquiry* 19 (1): 63–112.

———. 1993. Citizenship and the place of the public sphere: Law, community, and political culture in the transition to democracy. *American Sociological Review* 58 (5): 587–620.

Souza, Celina de. 2001. Participatory budgeting in Brazilian cities: Limits and possibilities in building democratic institutions. *Environment and Urbanization* 13 (1): 159–84.

———. 1996. Redemocratization and decentralization in Brazil: The strength of the member states. *Development and Change* 27 (3): 529–55.

———.. 1997. *Constitutional engineering in Brazil: The politics of federalism and decentralization.* New York: St. Martin's Press.

Stepan, Alfred. 2000. Brazil's decentralized federalism. *Daedalus* 129 (2): 145–69.

Stokke, Christian, Olle Tornqüist, and Neil Webster. 2009. *Rethinking popular representation.* New York: Palgrave McMillan.

Storper, Michael. 2004. Society, community and economic development. *Studies in Comparative and International Development* 39 (4): 30–57.

Swilling, Mark, and Laurence Boya. 1997. Local governance in transition. In *Managing sustainable development in South Africa,* ed. Patrick Fitzgerald, Anne McLennan, and Barry Munslow, 165–91. Cape Town: Oxford University Press.

Tauk Santos, Maria Salett 2002. Desenvolvimento local e cidadania: desafios e estratégias de comunicação da gestão participativa popular da Prefeitura de Camaragibe/PE. VI Congress of the Latin American Communications Association (ALAIC), Santa Cruz de La Sierra, Bolivia, June 5–7.

Teixeira, Ana Claudia Chaves. 2002. O OP em pequenos municípios rurais: contextos, condições, e formatos de experiência. In *A inovação democrática no Brasil*, ed. Zander Navarro. São Paulo: Cortez.

Teixeira, Ana Cláudia Chaves, and Maria do Carmo Albuquerque. (2005). *Orçamentos participativos: Projetos politicos, partilha de poder e alcance democrático*. São Paulo: Instituto Pólis.

Telles, V. S. 1987. Movimentos sociais: Reflexões sobre a experiência dos anos 70. In *Uma revolução no cotidiano? Os novos movimentos sociais na América Latina*, ed. I. Scherer-Warren and P. Krische, 54–85. São Paulo: Brasiliense.

Tendler, Judith. 1998. *Good governance in the tropics*. Baltimore, MD: Johns Hopkins University Press.

Tenório, Fernando G., and Filho. 2006. Cidadania Deliberativa: Um estudo de caso. In *Inovação no campo da ges_ão pública local: Novos desafios, novos patamares*, ed. P. R. Jacobi and J. A. Pinho, 99–119.

Therborn, Göran. 1977. The rule of capital and the rise of democracy. *New Left Review* 103: 3–41.

Thomas Isaac, T. M., and Richard W. Franke. 2002. *Local democracy and development: The Kerala people's campaign for decentralized planning*. World Social Change. Lanham, MD: Rowman & Littlefield.

Tilly, Charles. 2004. *Social movements, 1768–2004*. Boulder, CO: Paradigm Publishers.

TSE. 1997. Tribunal Superior Eleitoral. Resultados das Eleições (Database). Brasilia, Brazil.

Van Cott, Donna. 2008. *Radical democracy in the Andes*. Cambridge: Cambridge University Press.

Van Donk, Mirjam, Mark Swilling, Edgar Pieterse, and Susan Parnell, eds. 2008. *Consolidating developmental local government: Lessons from the South African experience*. Cape Town: University of Cape Town Press.

Walzer, Michael. 1992. The civil society argument. In *Dimensions of radical democracy: Pluralism, citizenship, community*, ed. Chantal Mouffe, 89–107. New York: Verso.

Wampler, Brian. 2009. Participatory budgeting in Brazil: Constestation, cooperation, and accountability. College Park: Pennsylvania State University Press.

———. 2007a. Can participatory institutions promote pluralism? Mobilizing low-income citizens in Brazil. *Studies in Comparative and International Development* 41 (4): 57–58.

———. 2007b. A guide to participatory budgeting. In *Participatory budgeting*, ed. Shan Anwar. Washington, DC: World Bank.

Warren, Mark. 2001. *Democracy and associations*. Princeton, NJ: Princeton University Press.

Watts, Michael. 2000. Development at the millennium: Malthus, Marx and the politics of alternatives. *Geographische Zeitschrift* 88 (2): 67–93.

Weffort, Francisco. 1984. *Por que democracia?* São Paulo: Brasiliense.

Weyland, Kurt Gerhard. 1999. Constitutional engineering in Brazil. *American Political Science Review* 93: 1006.

———. 1996. *Democracy without equity: Failures of reform in Brazil.* Pittsburgh, PA: University of Pittsburgh Press.

———. 1995. Social movements and the state: The politics of health reform in Brazil. *World Development* 23 (10): 1699–712.

Williams, Michelle. 2008. *The roots of participatory democracy: Democratic communists in South Africa and Kerala, India.* New York: Palgrave Macmillan.

World Bank. 2006. *World development report: Equity and development.* Washington DC: The World Bank and Oxford University Press.

———. 2000. *Overview of rural decentralization in India: Approaches to rural decentralization in seven states,* volume I. Washington, DC: World Bank.

Yashar, Deborah J. 2005. *Contesting citizenship in Latin America: The rise of indigenous movements and the postliberal challenge.* Cambridge: Cambridge University Press.

INDEX